Nicaragua—A New Kind of Revolution

Nicaragua—
A New Kind of Revolution

Philip Zwerling & Connie Martin

LAWRENCE HILL & COMPANY
Westport, Connecticut

Copyright 1985 by Phillip Zwerling and Connie Martin

All Rights Reserved

Published in the United States of America
by Lawrence Hill and Company, Publishers, Inc.
520 Riverside Avenue, Westport, Connecticut 06880

Library of Congress Cataloging in Publication Data
Zwerling, Philip.
  Nicaragua : a new kind of revolution.

  1. Nicaragua—History—1979–   . 2. Interviews—
Nicaragua. 3. Revolutions—Religious aspects—
Christianity. 4. Nicaragua—Church history. I. Title.
F1528.Z9   1985   972.85'053   85-5422
ISBN 0-88208-181-0
ISBN 0-88208-182-9 (pbk.)

1 2 3 4 5 6 7 8 9

Printed in the United States of America

To Jesse, Rena, and Seth

Contents

Introduction ix

1. From Guerrilla Commander to
   Top Cop   WALTER FERRETY   3

2. The Divided Church   FATHER BISMARK CARBALLO   12
   FATHER FRANCISCO SOLANO

3. Christians in the Revolution   FATHER EDGARD PARRALES   29
   RAFAEL SOLÍS

4. A New Culture   ROSARIO MURILLO   38
   FATHER ERNESTO CARDENAL

5. An Economy in Transition   ROGELIO RAMÍREZ   47
   RAMIRO GURDIAN

6. Educating the People   CARLOS TUNNERMANN   64
   LUCÍA CASCO
   FATHER FERNANDO CARDENAL

7. Rebuilding the Country   SAMUEL SANTOS   82

8. Women in the Revolution   GLENDA MONTERREY   90
   AMANDA PINEDA
   DR. MAYRA LOURDES BOLAÑOS

9. Health Care for the Nation   DR. FERNANDO SILVA   106
   DR. MAYRA PASOS

10. Working the Land   TOMÁS CRUZ DÍAZ   118
    SANTO PEDRO MARTÍNEZ
    GREGORIO VÁEZ
    FATHER PETER MARCHETTI

11.	Organizing Labor	EDGARDO GARCÍA	133
12.	Human Rights	SISTER MARY HARTMAN FRANCISCO LEÓN MIGUEL MORALES	140
13.	The Atlantic Coast	RAY HOOKER REVEREND NORMAN BENT	153
14.	A Free Press or Censorship?	XAVIER CHAMORRO PEDRO JOAQUÍN CHAMORRO AUGUSTÍN CÓRDOVA NELBA BLANDON	180
15.	The Comandante	TOMÁS BORGE	206
16.	The Contras	SALVADOR ICAZA RODRIGO GURDIAN	214
17.	The Wounded Fighters	NOEL RICARDO LAGUNA SANTO DOMINGO LOPEZ ALGUITES FLORES GREGORIO CANTAREJO ZAMORA MARTÍN SÁNCHEZ DELU PÍNEDA	223
18.	Life in The Barrio: Ciudad Sandino	JUANA ROMERO NUBIA ROMERO MAURA OTERA SISTER PEGGY HEALY	232

Introduction

The United States is on the verge of fighting a land war in Central America that includes all the elements of our failed intervention in Indochina. With U.S. trainers and advisors in El Salvador, thousands of regular U.S. Army troops engaged in on-going maneuvers in Honduras, CIA-supported guerrillas operating against Nicaragua from its northern (Honduran) and southern (Costa Rican) borders, and U.S. Navy flotillas on permanent station off both the Atlantic and Pacific coasts, the fuse is burning down on a full-blown military confrontation.

I've just returned from six months in Nicaragua, a country already at war. I traveled the length and breadth of this country, no bigger in size than Iowa, and made side trips to all of its neighbors. I met young Nicaraguan soldiers recovering from wounds who showed me military equipment they had captured from the (CIA-backed) contras stamped with the familiar initials "U.S." I saw tens of thousands of ordinary Nicaraguans armed with obsolete rifles and machine guns on weekend military training and night-time vigilance patrols in their own barrios. I saw rural schools surrounded by bomb shelters and watched grade-school children practice air-raid drills. I traveled to Nicaraguan ports and watched divers and patrol boats hunt for mines laid by the CIA. And I suffered the shortages of food and medicine that people under siege there face every day. I want other people in our country to share this reality as well.

Sandinista Interior Minister Comandante Tomás Borge has said that the battle for Nicaragua will be won or lost in the United States. We've all been reading the U.S. press reports and official government pronouncements that consistently malign every aspect of the Nicaraguan Revolution. These are all designed to create a climate of public opinion at home that would support the Reagan administration plans for direct intervention in Central America.

I'm neither a politician nor a journalist. I'm a minister committed to religious ideals and human values. So, for six months in 1984, I talked to people—people in the government, in the churches, in the barrios, in the fields, in prisons, and on the front lines. I talked to people who had taken up arms against the Revolution from exile in Honduras and listened to critics of the Sandinistas within the church and business communities. These interviews are their truths. The reader can judge the facts and make his own interpretation.

This book is designed to show people at home another face of the Revolution in Nicaragua through the words and the voices of the people in it. I believe people in the U.S. will respond to the very human stories, fears and hopes of these Nicaraguans. The Nicaraguans are not faceless, subversive hordes about to storm our southern borders. They are simply people trying their best to rebuild their country after a terribly destructive war—which is exactly what we did 200 years ago.

Here are the stories, and ideas and feelings of 45 different people. Their viewpoints often differ. But I felt no need to alter their words to embroider the tremendously positive reality I found in Nicaragua.

I think I saw a revolution that works. Little Nicaragua, with fewer than three million people, on July 19, 1979, ended 45 years of dictatorship by three Somozas (a father and his two sons). It was a dictatorship established, paid for and embraced by every U.S. president since Calvin Coolidge. The wealth was drained out of the country by the Somozas and the multinationals. It left behind a Nicaragua where 46% of the children died before their fifth birthday and 50% of those who survived suffered from malnutrition; a country where the annual per capita income was below $600 a year; where life expectancy was 52 years, and where more than 50% of the adults were illiterate.

It was a country to which we had sent armed mercenaries: William Walker in 1854, U.S. Marines in 1912, and 5,000 Marines again (from 1927 to 1933) to fight and lose a guerrilla war against a Nicaraguan army led by Augusto César Sandino. This national hero was later murdered (in 1934) by Anastasio Somoza, the first Somoza, with the aid of the U.S. ambassador. Then the very memory of Sandino was erased from official histories.

Poor, their true culture stolen and replaced by the alien *Yanquis*, and facing the violent repression of our surrogate National Guard, these people fought a bloody revolution in 1978–1979 that left 50,000 dead. Then they began to rebuild with a Literacy Crusade, a Health Crusade, and industrial and agricultural development.

Today they are paying for their success with the enmity of the United States government and a war that has already claimed 7,000 casualties. If the Nicaraguan Revolution poses any danger to us or its neighbors, it is the danger of being a good example. In Honduras, I saw children of 14 and 15 at dusk covering themselves with cardboard to sleep on the sidewalks of Tegucigalpa, the capital, in a country thoroughly dominated by an overwhelming U.S. military presence. In the streets of Guatemala City, I heard the shots as police, armed to the teeth by yet another military dictatorship, "accidentally" shot a young musician to death. In Peru, I saw children—descendants of the Inca Empire—barefoot and dressed in rags in the high Andes.

Latin America is searching today for an alternative to the poverty, dictatorship and foreign domination which have been its history. The Nicaraguan example offers a model of independent national development outside the competing orbits of the United States and the Soviet Union.

In Nicaragua, I saw a revolution that is Christian, not Communist. You can see it in the words and lives of the priests and nuns who serve this government at every level. You can see it in the lay people who explain their participation in terms of their religious faith. And you can see it in the political priorities drawn from an agenda shaped by today's liberation theology. On November 4, 1984, 75 percent of the eligible voters went to the polls in Nicaragua's first free and fair elections. Of seven political parties contesting for votes for the offices of President and Vice-President and ninety seats in the new National Assembly, the Sandinista Party, the FSLN, garnered 67 percent of the votes cast.

The Reagan administration understands this reality even if our people don't. In May 1980, Reagan advisors at the Heritage Foundation prepared the so-called Santa Fe Document, which targets religion and the church as the new East-West battlefield in Latin America. This simplistic analysis of a new moral movement has led our government into new alliances with a conservative Catholic hierarchy and insurgent Protestant evangelicals who preach resignation in this world in return for salvation later.

In fact, liberation theology—while it may use Marxism as a tool to understand, analyze and condemn patterns of economic and political oppression—takes its imperative from Jesus, not Marx. It simply asks, "Where would Jesus be born and live today?" And when the answer is the slums of Nicaragua or the shanty towns of Lima rather than the palaces of the rulers and the rich, the only moral response is to stand with the poor and to share their oppression and their struggle, even as God chose to manifest Her presence with them two thousand years ago.

Christian clergy and laypeople today are leading protest marches, forming cooperatives, publishing opposition papers, and occasionally taking up arms in the underdeveloped countries of Latin America, Africa and Asia. This identification of social justice with a Gospel ministry is reshaping churches and nations. This—the role of the church in Nicaragua—is the story of the Revolution which we ought to learn. It has its applications here at home.

Several years ago, in my first interview with Father Ernesto Cardenal, I asked him if Christians in Nicaragua were, in fact, creating the Kingdom of God on earth. "No, not creating the Kingdom," he said, "but getting closer." That distance can be measured not only in material accomplishment but also in personal spiritual growth. Religion is alive and well in Nicaragua, both in the churches and in the people's hearts.

My sabbatical is over now and I'm back at work as Senior Minister of The First Unitarian Church of Los Angeles, but I will never forget the people I met and interviewed in Nicaragua. I had only to get them talking and out would come the most amazing stories of struggle and courage told matter-of-factly, as a given of life, first under the Somoza dictatorship and now in the Sandinistas' revolutionary society.

My only prayer is that our country will allow the people of Nicaragua to build their own dream in peace.

Acknowledgments

This book is the outgrowth of a six-month sabbatical granted by the congregation of the First Unitarian Church of Los Angeles. Without their support and aid this book would not have been possible.

Connie Martin, my wife and co-worker, conducted several of the interviews and transcribed many more. Her enthusiasm and help kept me going.

Michael Baumann and a "Perspectiva Mundial" tour conducted the interview with Ray Hooker, which I have edited and included.

Nicaraguan friends Neftalí Cortés, Margarita Gurdian, Orlando Pérez and Lucilla Santos came to our rescue each time we encountered roadblocks.

Government Press Office personnel Myrna Torres, Mary Fran Doyle, and Leonor made the arrangements for many of the interviews.

Larry Boyd, Ruth Margolis, Peter Kelley and Connie and I took the pictures.

Amy Shahinian and John Schaffer typed and typed.

And Lawrence Hill matched his enthusiasm with financial help when it counted.

Philip Zwerling

Nicaragua—A New Kind of Revolution

1. From Guerrilla Commander to Top Cop
Walter Ferrety

Police stations make me nervous. It's the uniforms, the guns, and the overwhelming sense of power and authority housed there that get to me. Usually I'm present as a supplicant: to visit a prisoner, to be booked into a cell myself following civil disobedience at a peace demonstration, or waiting to see an officer to ask politely for whatever dispensation he may offer.

But here I am in police headquarters in Managua—in Nicaragua Libre—surrounded by different uniforms but similar guns, waiting for an interview with the chief of police. In six years in Los Angeles. I never got a meeting with Chief Daryl Gates, even after I wrote asking him to explain to me why his Public Disorder Intelligence Division was spying on my church.

I'm more at home in churches than in police stations, but the chief, a friend of a friend in the States, had met me at the airport upon my arrival to help me get 25 wheelchairs and a few dozen soccer balls through customs and into the hands of needy Nicaraguan civilian organizations. This police chief, who doubles as director of the national soccer league, took me to a soccer game to present the balls—desperately needed for teams across the country. Afterwards, he took me to a shelter for juvenile delinquents where the police guards bring their own children to play with the young inmates. For me it was the humanization of my conception of a policeman and the beginning of a curiosity to learn more.

The police station in Managua is the headquarters of the national Policia Sandinista, a division of the Ministry of the Interior, where Tomás Borge Martínez—the sole surviving founder of the Frente Sandinista de Liberación Nacional (FSLN) that triumphed over Anastasio Somoza Debayle after 17 years of guerrilla war—heads the department and is a member of the nine-person National Directorate. The Directorate is balanced by a three-member Junta of National Reconstruction, a 51-member Council of State and a seven-member Supreme Court.

Walter Ferrety, Photo by Ruth Margolis

My appointment is with Walter Ferrety, the chief of police, who is a former guerrilla commander, and the man Tomás Borge calls "my son." Without any police training, or much formal education, Ferrety directs a national police force, 6,000 unpaid auxiliary volunteers, and 150,000 Nicaraguans formed into committees of Revolutionary Vigilance to fight common street crime and to protect the Revolution from subversion, sabotage, and destabilization.

It's one thing to make a revolution and another to protect it, as the people have learned in Guatemala, Cuba and Grenada. Chief Ferrety has been on both sides of that process. Once in the streets fighting Somoza, he now faces President Reagan and the *contras* from his post in Managua.

As we sit in his office, decorated with photos of Nicaraguan revolutionary leaders like Augusto César Sandino and Carlos Fonseca, a founder of the FSLN killed fighting Somoza in 1977, and the Argentinian "Che" Guevara, I'm struck again by the youth and inexperience of Nicaragua's new leaders. Ferrety, born in the Managua barrio of Altagracia in 1950, was not yet thirty-four when we spoke. His father was a heavy equipment operator and his mother worked in the home. She died when Walter was six. After the fifth grade Ferrety dropped out of school because his family could not afford to buy him clothes and books. "Our father," he told me, "was very dedicated to the family, but there was simply no money." So Ferrety, at 14, went to work as an office boy and spent his free time in the city's libraries educating himself. "I learned," he said, "everything I could. And when I went to the U.S. in 1970 I studied in the libraries again, at night."

Ferrety spent six years in San Francisco. "I went to the States with my father. We were economic immigrants looking for work to survive. I was 19. I began work, like all Latinos in the States, as a dishwasher. My father was too old to work. Later I worked as a janitor, a cook's helper and a handyman. I learned English from friends. I attended Pacific High School but I never graduated because I had to work and never finished my courses.

"And then I got involved in political work and had even less time to spend in school. Political work really became important in 1972 when an earthquake devastated Managua, killing 10,000 people and leaving tens of thousands more destitute and homeless. We Nicaraguans worked to send international aid back home. Millions of dollars were sent down and almost all of it went directly into Somoza's pockets. The complete corruption of the dictatorship became very clear. Somoza wanted everything for himself."

* * *

PHILIP ZWERLING: But surely you were an anti-Somocista before this?

FERRETY: Yes, but let me go back a little. When I was 14, a representative of the Socialist Party came to my home to talk to my brother and I listened to what he had to say. I began to attend secret meetings, and then I became an organizer for the party. I worked to organize two or three barrios for the party, to raise issues of health and safety—for the tenants and against the landlords. But all of this had to be done clandestinely. And so I began at the age of 14 in this struggle for my Nicaragua.

Z: And how did Somoza and the Guardia respond to this work?

FERRETY: It was very dangerous. I helped organize the first union in a local plywood factory and directed the first strike there. Once the Guardia caught me selling papers supporting the strike and beat me up. But we knew the dangers of the Guardia. I learned that when I was four years old. There was a woman who lived near our family in the barrio. She would often visit in our home. And then she disappeared. We children asked our mother where she had gone and what had happened to her. Our mother told us that the Guardia had killed her.

But even that doesn't go back far enough. I had a grandfather who fought against the Yanquis even before Sandino. He fought at Masaya in 1912 with General Benjamin Zeledón, who was killed there by the U.S. Marines. In Nicaragua we have always been fighting for our freedom. And that was a part of my life. If you lived in Nicaragua and thought about things, you had to act and become part of the struggle.

Z: And what form did that fight take for the six years you were in San Francisco?

FERRETY: Well, the FSLN could operate in the U.S., could make demonstrations, and could publicly expose the cruelties of the Somoza dictatorship. We had an office and made propaganda against the regime. Of course, the office was vandalized, the printing press broken, and the files stolen. To this day we don't know if this was done by Somoza's agents or by the FBI. And, of course, those of us who worked there were stopped in the street or in our cars by the police. They would ask us where we were going and what we were doing. They would call us "communists" and tell us to go back to Nicaragua. We got to know the police methods there.

Z: And you returned to Nicaragua in 1977?

FERRETY: I returned in the middle of 1977. I was called back by the FSLN to join the military struggle. In a safe house in Managua they taught me how to use an old rifle and a .45 caliber pistol. That was all my military training. I knew the city of Managua and so I was assigned to clandestine work in the capital. I worked to organize the people in the poor barrios of Altagracia, Lezcano and Tipitapa, to find safe houses and to gather arms and vehicles.

Z: Here in the capital, with Somoza and the National Guard nearby, it must have been dangerous work?

FERRETY: Of course we had to hide from the Guardia, but we were able to move within the city and even out into the countryside. You see, the people supported us. This is a peaceful people, but a rebellious people to the dictatorship. The people, at the risk of arrest and torture, hid us and protected us. The people worked with us because they had been waiting for the FSLN to come to their barrios. Little by little we gathered support in every section of Managua. And with such support our armed groups could act. I myself led attacks against Somoza's police stations. In one attack, Comandante Camilo Ortega [brother of President Daniel Ortega Saavedra] was killed. We made commando attacks as well in other cities, like Granada. And we made the assault on the National Palace.

Z: Please describe the raid on the Palace, because this action made international headlines and gave the world its first glimpse of the popular support for the anti-Somoza struggle.

FERRETY: We received orders to prepare to kidnap a cousin of Somoza to trade him for our *compañeros* who were in prison. Then we received instructions to drop these plans for a new action, an attack on the National Palace, which was the seat of the Somoza government and where the Chamber of Deputies held its meetings. For this we needed a base camp to prepare for the assault. One campesino, an illiterate peasant named Domingo who had been working with us, told me that he knew of a place, a beautiful farm on the outskirts of Managua. And this peasant recruited his patron, a lawyer who owned the farm, to give us shelter there.

Once we had a place, we could gather men and arms and vehicles. We had another safe house in the city. In all, we had 25 soldiers divided into two groups. One was under the command of Dora María Tellez and the traitor Edén Pastora and the other under the command of Comandante Hugo Torres and myself.

The plan was to approach the Palace disguised as members of the Guardia. For this we got trucks. We wanted them painted olive green. But the *compañero* who painted them used a brilliant green color, which didn't look like any military color at all. But by then we had no choice, and so that's what we used.

We had Guardia uniforms for our fighters. And we smuggled arms out to the farm hidden in trucks filled with caramel from a candy factory. We spent one night cleaning the caramel off the guns.

Somoza had recruited very young boys right off the street into a special squadron of his army. They had special training and special privileges. They were his personal guard and they were feared even by other members of the Guardia. So we recruited some young boys to impersonate these troops. Out at the farm we gave them special haircuts that were distinctive of this Guardia unit. There was one boy whose hair we cut in this way, but then we found that he was too small and too young to handle a weapon. We couldn't let him come with us. I remember he cried, "I can't go home looking like this, the people will kill me on the street as a Guardia."

We all took turns giving each other haircuts to look like the Guardia. Then we dressed and armed ourselves and drove to the Palace, in the very center of Managua, in two trucks. It was 12:30 in the afternoon, August 22, 1978.

The Palace has four entrances. Our two groups approached at the opposite east and west entrances. On the west, my group got out of our truck and walked to the door in military formation. We were 12. There were Guardia at the door. They challenged us and asked us what we were doing. Our young imposters shouted, "*El Jefe viene*," meaning that Somoza himself was coming. The Guardia stepped out of the way and in a moment we were on top of them and disarmed them.

I had been given the special assignment of capturing José Mora, the minister of the interior, who controlled the police and the prisons where many of my *compañeros* had been tortured.

When I was told by Comandante Torres that it was my job to capture this minister, I said that I would kill him when I found him. But Torres said he was an important person for the negotiations and that I had to make sure he didn't die. I said I would try to take him alive. But I didn't really care.

Once inside the Palace we ran upstairs and banged on every door, looking for Mora's office. And when we found it the door was locked and we had to kick a hole in it. We ordered those inside to come out through the hole. And this fat Minister Mora said to me, "How can I pass through that?" And I told him, "Pass through or die," and he crawled through on his hands and knees.

We captured him and his staff. The other column captured all of those present in the council, 59 deputies in all. After months of planning we had seized the Palace in less than five minutes. We, the 25 of us, now held 2,400 office workers there as well.

Somoza reacted quickly and sent his helicopters to attack the Palace, firing their guns. We put the prisoners in the windows so they could see who they were shooting at and that ended the attack.

We gathered the prisoners together and began negotiations with Somoza. We had a direct line to Somoza in his bunker over a red phone in the Chamber of Deputies.

At our command, the Archbishop of Managua, Monsignor Miguel Obando y Bravo, was allowed to negotiate and to carry demands and responses back and forth between us and Somoza.

But Somoza was stalling for time and we had little time or food or water and few people to guard all of the prisoners and defend the Palace. We had to keep the Guardia from knowing how few we were. So when we were talking on the phone one of us would yell in the background, "Comandante 43, bring me something to drink," even though we were only 25 and had nothing to drink. We didn't have enough people to change the guard, so no one slept.

In the negotiations we demanded freedom for 100 political prisoners, $10,000,000 for the FSLN, the reading of our manifesto over national T.V. and radio, and safe passage out of the country. And, after 45 hours, all of this was arranged.

Somoza released 60 prisoners, including Comandantes Tomás Borge and René Núñez. Many came out ill, tortured or mistreated. Many prisoners who we asked for Somoza simply announced had died. We got the money. And Panama sent a plane to take us out of the country.

To get to the airport we needed one bus. But to keep up the pretense of being a large force we demanded three buses. And we took with us four of the most important prisoners, including Somoza's relatives and Minister Mora.

We had ordered the Guardia not to show their faces along the route to the airport. But all of the people came and lined the streets and cheered. It's difficult to describe because in that moment the people lost their fear of the Guardia and they clapped and cheered as we drove by. The airport was packed with more people. Emotions were very high and it was like a great celebration of the entire people.

Z: Did you believe it was going to be a successful mission or did you accept it as a suicide mission?

FERRETY: Look, I always had confidence because the FSLN had developed the capacity to fight and to win. The danger was at the beginning, in being discovered before we had reached our objective. But once we were in the Palace with so many prisoners, we knew we would have international attention and that Somoza could not kill everyone even as he wanted to.

Z: And you continued as a guerrilla commander following the victory at the Palace?

FERRETY: Yes. In the last two years of the Insurrection, in 1978 and 1979, it was our job to try to tie down the Guardia in fighting here in Managua while other columns were advancing out in the countryside. We fought the Guardia here in the barrios, in the neighborhoods. I led a group of 35 guerrillas as a mobile unit and we moved from barrio to barrio to confront the Guardia whenever it appeared they might be able to pacify an area. We fought superior forces in almost every case, but we kept the Guardia pinned down. The roads were in our hands. The people supported us. We knew where the Guardia were and what they planned. We fought all over the city and *compañeros* died in every barrio. You can see the memorials to the dead that now stand on every street corner where some young fighter fell in combat.

Z: And you were one of the commanders of the final insurrection in Managua in 1979?

FERRETY: Yes. It was very hard to be a commander because you wanted to save your force for the victory, but you also needed to risk losing your young people to win that victory.

Z: After the Triumph of the Revolution on July 19, 1979, you—who had been a guerrilla commander—were appointed by Borge, the new interior minister, to be the chief of police. Why? What preparation did you have for the job?

FERRETY: I had no preparation. Since 1980 I've been chief of police. As revolutionaries we have to respond to new situations. We try to do our duties. In the past we were soldiers, and before that journalists, doctors or workers, and now we are trying to complete a revolution. That isn't something that you study for. Each day I'm learning in this job.

Z: You know that in the U.S. and other countries a person would study police work and criminology and earn degrees and serve 20 years on the force before getting the job of chief?

FERRETY: Of course. But the situation here is different. Some day, in the future, we'll have a police academy and train people professionally, but it has been very difficult. With the situation in which we live in Nicaragua today, with an economy and a country to be rebuilt and with external aggression directed against us and people being killed, we can only do the best we can and prepare to defend our people and our Revolution.

People have not yet been trained in specialties of administration, etc. It's very hard. But we learn as we do it. And all of our policemen and women, the whole force, have been hired and trained in the last four and a half years.

Z: You know the police in the U.S., and you run the police here. How would you compare the roles of the police in our two countries?

FERRETY: Well, the only police I knew in the States I had trouble with because I was political and because I was Latino. They never knew me. They only treated me as a difficulty for them. And I saw them mistreat other Latinos and blacks whose social conditions brought them into conflict with the police. The police in the U.S. enforce or protect an economic system that serves some people and not others. And the police must act as a force of fear against those who are outside the system.

The police under Somoza functioned much the same way here. The people feared the police then. In those days you never called the police for help because the police might kill you. Now people here don't fear the police.

Z: What kinds of crimes do the police have to deal with here?

FERRETY: In the time of Somoza there was a system of corruption; of gambling, prostitution, drugs, graft and extortion. These were not crimes because the Guardia enriched themselves in this way. The Revolution has ended that culture of crime.

Today we deal with crimes of individuals, crimes like theft and assault. But in spite of difficult economic times, crime has decreased. In 1980, 38,320 crimes were reported, 21,400 in 1981, 10,538 in 1982, and 8,312 in 1983.

Crime is decreasing because of the revolutionary fervor of the people, because of vigilance in the neighborhoods, and because of the feeling of solidarity in building a new and equitable society together. We take rehabilitation seriously. We work with juveniles at the Evaluation Center in cooperation with the Ministry of Social Welfare, to strengthen the whole family when a kid gets in trouble. I just wish we would be left in peace to build up our country.

Z: You mean intervention by the U.S. and the contras?

FERRETY: Yes. In this country we have seen death and killing for a long time. We fought and many people died to win our sovereignty. My cousin was murdered by the National Guard. When I drive through Managua on official business as police chief, I pass places where friends died in the struggle. I knew these people and now I drive past the places where they died.

The men in the White House don't know death like we do. Perhaps if they knew this reality they would leave us alone. If they don't, then we will fight and die again, but we will never give up our Revolution.

When I was a guerrilla I carried a gun and I killed people. As a policeman I carry a gun, but now I know that I save lives. That has been the beauty and the power of this Revolution.

2. The Divided Church

Father Bismark Carballo
Father Francisco Solano

The Catholic Church in Nicaragua claims the allegiance of 85% of the country's 2.9 million people. Mistreatment of the church by the Sandinista government has been a charge used to rally international opposition to the Revolution. Religious persecution has become one of President Reagan's justifications for continued covert financial support to the contras.

On the other hand, the presence of Catholics, clergy and laypeople within the highest echelons of the government, within the mass organizations, and within the Frente Sandinista itself, has given some the idea that a new, revolutionary church has sprung forth in Nicaragua.

The actual situation is quite complex and has divided the institutional church at the highest levels.

Here two members of this same hierarchy describe their very different reactions to the Nicaraguan reality.

FATHER BISMARK CARBALLO, 33 and 10 years a priest, is the director of the national Radio Católica and press secretary and official spokesman for Managua's Archbishop Monsignor Obando y Bravo. FATHER FRANCISCO SOLANO, 43 years old and born in Indiana, a Capuchin priest for 15 years, has served all of that time on Nicaragua's Atlantic Coast. In 1982, Bishop Schlaefer named him Pro-Vicar Delegate of Southern Zelaya, and he performs the functions of a bishop in southern and central Zelaya, which encompasses one-quarter of Nicaragua's territory.

Though interviewed separately, they speak to the same issues and concerns of Nicaragua's Catholics today.

* * *

PHILIP ZWERLING: Father Carballo, how would you characterize church-state relations in Nicaragua now?

FATHER BISMARK CARBALLO: Relations between church and state are not too cordial. We have had a dialogue but relations are at a very low point and quite tense. In 1979, the Catholic Church supported the armed struggle against Somoza but the FSLN moved to monopolize this movement after the Triumph even though it had been made by many sectors, including the church. We worked with the new government until 1980 when their Marxism and materialism became apparent. And, of course, there were events during this time that hurt relations.

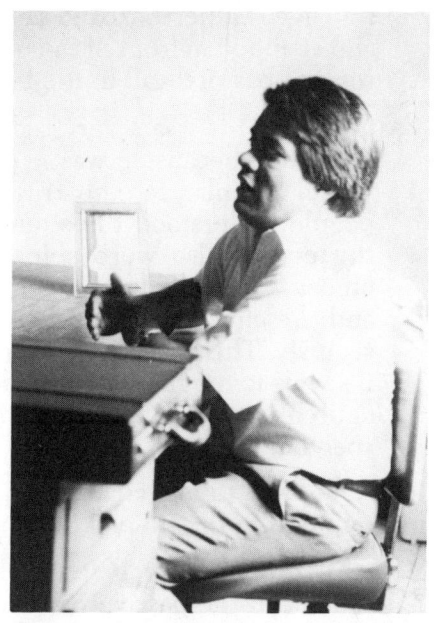
Father Bismark Carballo, Photo by Martin

For example, in July 1981, the Sandinista government stopped the television transmissions of the archbishop's masses; in 1982, they expelled six or seven foreign priests; in August 1982, I myself was a victim of Sandinista attack, and in 1983 there was the incident with the Pope, who was treated disrespectfully by the government during his visit here in Managua, and the government continues to interfere with my work at Catholic Radio.

In November 1983, the church and government met in a dialogue. We are not able to say much about this except that there was an exchange of ideas and there were supposed to be follow-up meetings after, but these are not being held at present.

Z: Would you care to say more about your own difficulties with the Sandinista Police?

(The facts are that photos of a naked Father Carballo appeared in all three daily newspapers and on Sandinista television in August 1982. How they got there is a matter of debate. The government says the police and a television crew were covering a demonstration at the Venezuelan Embassy in the Las Colinas suburb of Managua when they suddenly saw a naked man running down the street pursued by an armed assailant. Both men were filmed and taken into custody. The naked man turned out to be Father Carballo. His pursuer told police that he had returned home and found the priest in bed with his wife and was seeking revenge. Father Carballo said he was seized by the police, beaten and stripped in front of the news cameras after he emerged from a routine pastoral call to the home of a female parishioner.)

CARBALLO: This was a very sad situation for me and I don't like to speak of it because it was so painful. It seems to me that I was the victim of a plan to embarrass the church. Thanks be to God, the people understood the situation and thanks be to God, as well, the people also were able to hear later, from a state security officer who had fled the country, that this had been a trap for me and the church and had been planned in the offices of the state security. This was a very sad, very personal experience, although it seems to me that it has made the church stronger. For when the church is most persecuted, that is when Christianity is most respected.

Z: How have things changed in Nicaragua since the Revolution as opposed to the time of Somoza?

CARBALLO: I believe that it's difficult to compare the Sandinistas today and the past with Somoza because Somoza had 45 years in power and the Sandinistas have only had five. I can say that the church has suffered more in the five years of the Sandinistas than in the 45 years of the Somozas. The FSLN has a Machiavellian attitude toward the church.

Somoza weighed on the churches and Christians, but at least he always maintained a public image of respect for the church, and he respected the office of the archbishop as the legitimate pastor of the church. And whenever there was a problem they would have a dialogue.

The situation with the Sandinistas is different. They don't recognize the archbishop and his authority in the church. The government named four priests to government positions without a single consultation with the archbishop. They make personal attacks against the bishops, especially against the archbishop of Managua and his authority.

And here in Nicaragua now we have the creation of the "Popular Church," a phenomenon of people with Marxist orientation who act as a religious mask for the Sandinistas. The Popular Church is not a Nicaraguan phenomenon. It was born in Chile during the time of Allende, out of a movement called "Christians for Socialism." Basically their program was to try to make a breach for the entrance of Marxism into Latin America through the churches. The Popular Church in Nicaragua tries to justify this project as well. Marxism in Nicaragua tries to show people that Christianity doesn't have answers to their needs and that the only solution for Christians is to follow the path of Marxism. The Popular Church is a political movement with a Christian face. That's true in El Salvador as well, and it's international as a political force.

So, we have many problems and things have never been good, but I can say that the church has suffered more in the past five years than in the previous 45.

Z: How does the hierarchy view the presence of priests and prominent Catholic laypeople in the Sandinista government?

CARBALLO: The four priests in government were appointed by the government without even the respect of a consultation. The church attempted dialogue with these priests. In 1981, the Church said the priests had to leave the government and return to their former posts because it is church teaching that priests are not to take a public political role in government. This is possible in times of emergency, but by 1981 this emergency had passed in Nicaragua. But the priests agreed to a compromise to give up their priestly duties to remain in the government. They promised to refrain from celebrating mass, publicly or privately, hearing confession, or using the title "father" or "priest." And this is the situation today. They are in government and they aren't there as priests or as representatives of the church and supposedly they are not celebrating mass. But the priests have not lived up to their promise. We hear that sometimes they do celebrate mass and sometimes the Sandinista papers refer to them by the title of "father," so they have not respected this agreement.

As to the Catholic laypeople in government, the Church doesn't say anything because they ought to play their role in politics. We are asked, though, how these Christians can serve an ideology that is an enemy of the Church. In these cases it seems that these lay Catholics demonstrate more faithfulness to this ideology than they do to the Church.

Z: Will what is happening in Nicaragua be, in any way, a model for development in Latin America?

CARBALLO: In 1979 the majority of Nicaraguans in the church thought this Revolution could be a model for Latin America in the sense that a change had been made according to Christian values and that now there would be respect for human rights—both social and individual—a mixed economy, and an open political system. All of that seemed possible. But now, no. This is no longer a model. Because now it's a dictatorship of a Marxist party. People who speak against the dictatorship are called counter-revolutionaries; even people like Edén Pastora, who was a military leader, or Alfonso Robelo, a former member of the Sandinista Junta. Many people have been labeled contras for asking for civilian rule.

It's a very difficult moment for this country. Will there be a civil or violent answer to this situation? In this sense world public opinion has an influence on this internal situation. Because now there is no liberty here.

I'm the director of Catholic Radio but I can't even broadcast the mass live as it occurs. We have to tape the mass for the censors first. We can't use some of the Pope's words or some messages from the archbishop. It's curious because the censor has no theological preparation and sometimes acts stupidly. For example, one Sunday the message was on the Exodus of the Old Testament and this theme was prohibited because today many Nicaraguans have gone into exile. And so we can't talk about the Exodus, which is the word of God in the Old Testament.

We have an old program here on tape that we use of Bishop Fulton Sheen from New York. In one show he talked about "courtesy" and this program was prohibited because the censor said that "courtesy" was a bourgeois value.

This is a basic denial of liberty to the church. For example, the Jews lost their synagogue. We have a situation of denial of basic human rights and this can't be a model for the rest of Latin America.

Z: What happened when Pope John Paul II visited Nicaragua on March 4, 1983?

CARBALLO: We had news that the Pope wished to visit here as early as July 1982. But the government censored this news and didn't let us speak of it until January 1983. And this was because of a July 1982 letter from the Pope to the archbishop of Managua condemning the Popular Church.

The Pope could make only one visit to Central America, so it was arranged for him to visit several countries and to speak on a different theme in each country, so that at the end we would have one papal vision of doctrinal orientation in Central America. In Nicaragua, he chose to speak on "Catholic education" and the "unity of the Church." In El Salvador, he talked about violence.

The night before the Pope came to Nicaragua there was an act of violence against a group of Catholics who had come to the plaza to hear the Pope. The Junta wanted only people from the Sandinista Defense Committees to be in the plaza because these are the political organizations of the FSLN.

So the situation was very clear. We didn't have the power to overcome these tactics. The Pope came as a pastor to be received by Christians, but the Frente Sandinista wanted only their organization to fill the plaza. With attacks and blows, the Catholics were kept away.

The following day the Frente Sandinista tried to manipulate what was meant to be the talk of a pastor to his flock and to force the Pope to condemn the violence and the counterrevolution. But, as I explained, the Pope had decided on different themes for his talks in different countries and he planned to speak against violence in El Salvador. When the Pope spoke here without mentioning violence, people interrupted the Pope and began to yell and provoke the crowd. At the same time government officials raised their fists to urge these disruptions. Some in the crowd had amplification equipment to disrupt the Pope's talk.

The government said that the mothers of those who had been killed by the contras the week before asked the Pope to say a word for their dead sons and daughters, but the Pope had already written them a letter and there is a place in the mass to publicly remember all of the dead. They wanted a public statement in the plaza against the contras.

There was a total lack of respect for the Pope and this was stage managed by the Popular Church to make a political statement.

Z: Let's speak about the church's position on some immediate issues facing Nicaragua. First, the new election law and national elections planned for November 4, 1984.

(The elections were held as planned, with the governing Sandinista National Liberation Front taking 67 percent of the vote with the rest split among candidates of six smaller parties. The FSLN president-elect was Daniel Ortega Saavedra and the vice-president Sergio Ramírez Mercado. But the major opposition, three parties backing former Sandinista Junta member Arturo José Cruz, boycotted the election [Cruz himself refused to register] charging the Sandinistas with not allowing fair and free campaigning. Of the 96 seats in the National Assembly, the Sandinistas controlled 61. Of the approximately 1.5 million registered voters, 82 percent were reported to have cast ballots. Eleven of 3,892 polling places were closed because of attacks by U.S.-backed rebels on the Honduran border.)

CARBALLO: There will be a pastoral letter on the elections and we are waiting for this. But we can say now that it is important to have free and fair elections. Without freedom of expression, which we believe is basic, there can be no free elections. All parties must have equal access to the voters through the communications media.

Z: And the Law of Military Service, which establishes a registration for a draft?

CARBALLO: The Episcopal Conference has made a public statement. There are several levels to it: first, the church affirms that every state has the legitimate right to form a defensive military force for the nation; second, that there is no moral reason to oppose such military service; and third, that according to the declaration, Nicaragua is a special case because here the army is at the service of a single political party, the FSLN. The army is at the service of an ideology. And therefore, the archbishop said that no one is obligated to support an ideology they do not believe. In fact, they then have the obligation of conscientious objection because no one need be at the service of Sandinista ideology. If the army was national there would be no objection to military service, but in the case of Nicaragua, where the army operates on behalf of the FSLN, no one is obligated to serve.

The government never consulted the church on the Law of Military Service, and our position on this has put us into direct conflict. Fifteen young men have been imprisoned and forced to serve in contradiction to the teachings of their church. There is no respect for rights. Two foreign priests were expelled from the country for writing in favor of conscientious objection.

Z: And masses for the militia dead?

CARBALLO: An accusation has been made against the church that we will not celebrate mass for those who have voluntarily joined the militia and been killed. This is not true. It's a misinterpretation of church policy. For two or three years after the Triumph of the Revolution, the church permitted masses to be held wherever the soldiers had fallen and died. But after that time, the church said that the church building itself was the place to hold masses for the dead. And since that date this has been done. The malicious interpretation is that priests will only celebrate mass in the church and not, say, on the street corner. But the problem was that many times these masses in the streets became political acts of the government. Our principle now is that we celebrate such masses only in the church for whoever has died.

Z: What about the dissolution by the bishops of ACLEN, the organization founded and run by the priests of Nicaragua which had an elected, clergy representative on the Council of State, the Nicaraguan parliament?

CARBALLO: This matter was open to much manipulation to the detriment of the church. ACLEN was an organization strictly of Nicaraguan priests. The group that controlled ACLEN favored the government and embarrassed the church. And so the bishops dissolved ACLEN. It operated against the church authority, and the Pope has stressed the need for obedience to the bishops in the Catholic Church.

Z: Why hasn't the church hierarchy attacked the contras who have taken up arms against the Nicaraguan government?

CARBALLO: For us this question of condemning the contras is a serious problem, for the counterrevolutionaries are Nicaraguans too. This is a struggle between Nicaraguans and Nicaraguans. It is hard for the church to maintain its neutrality in view of the East-West struggle now taking place in Nicaragua, and the very real possibility of foreign intervention.

There is a saying among North Americans that "When the elephants fight, the ants get stepped on." Now Nicaragua is a pawn in this battle between superpowers of the East and West and we have to use our political savvy to assure the rights of Nicaraguans in our country.

The church condemns violence wherever it comes from. But we are not free today in Nicaragua to do this because the Frente Sandinista wants us to condemn only the violence of the contras. But there is also violence and death directed against Nicaraguans by the government here.

The problem is very difficult. One bishop, Monsignor Vega, has said, "The Church is like a man with two pistols held at his head, one demanding he condemn the contras, the other demanding he condemn the Sandinistas." This is a very difficult situation.

Z: Is the Nicaraguan church today a focus of internal political opposition to the government?

CARBALLO: I don't believe that the role of the church is a political role. It seems to me that here we have a materialist philosophy and government trying to indoctrinate a Christian people. And we are defending Western and Christian values here.

Z: Could an analogy be made between the situation of the church here and the church in Poland?

CARBALLO: If the FSLN doesn't change its policies they will make us a silent church as they have tried in Poland. But this will not be permitted here.

Z: The charge has been made that the hierarchy has transferred and moved priests who worked closely with the people in the poor barrios and spoke for the projects of the government. Is this true?

CARBALLO: What happened is that lies are repeated not by the people but by the Sandinistas. I can assure you that transfers of priests are carried out only for ecclesiastical reasons and with respect for the rights of the clergy. Transfers are never made for revenge but for the good of the community, the church and the priest. The Sandinistas present this as a political problem as a persecution of the priests by the hierarchy.

This interpretation depends on the priest. If the priest has a good identification with his bishop, he understands the change and there's no problem and the people understand. But many times the priest, when he has a problem with his bishop or his church, protests a transfer and the people join the protest out of ignorance.

Z: What do you see for Nicaragua and the church in the future?

CARBALLO: The history of Nicaragua is a curious one. Things, we have seen, can change from day to day. What will happen tomorrow will happen. There are armed men fighting in the north and in the south. There is a Sandinista government in power that has chosen a military and violent road. U.S. forces are positioned now on ships off both of our coasts. So it is difficult to say what will happen. But as Christians we live in hope.

* * *

PHILIP ZWERLING: Father, how would you characterize church-state relations in Nicaragua now?

FATHER FRANCISCO SOLANO: On the hierarchial level, on the level of the bishops, relations between the Catholic Church and the Nicaraguan government are quite strained. On the popular level, on the level of common, ordinary, Christian people, Catholic people, relationships are—for the most part—quite amenable.

I've seen no religious persecution on the part of this government. I am aware of cases in which religious persons have been harassed because of public political positions—at times mistakenly, at times in a gross way. In ordinary circumstances these positions might be nothing more than manifestations of the right to dissent. However, in the context of war, constant aggression, destabilization by the CIA and the real possibility of invasion, together with manipulation by international news media to increase aggression and justify invasion—such positions by influential people mean more death and destruction, primarily to innocent people, and increased suffering by the poor.

On the other hand, in November 1983, I was met in one of the communities I was visiting in southern Zelaya, in the chapel, by counterrevolutionaries who expressed their discontent with me, tried to "mentalize" me according to their position, tried to oblige me to take up arms with them, and finally threatened my life. There were very real possibilities I would be eliminated by them.

Father Francisco Solano, Photo by Zwerling

They insisted that Archbishop Obando was in prison in Managua. I knew that at that time he was in Venezuela. They told me that Father Carballo was in prison. I knew he was not. They told me they were defenders of the faith, religion and the ministry. So, their principal arguments were religious. But they were not sincere. They were manipulating religion and religious people. They had to know that they were telling lies for propaganda purposes, lies which in that isolated area of the country the peasant people would not be able to see through.

Z: When you reported this incident to your Church superiors were there any Church protests?

SOLANO: No, there were not.

Z: Wouldn't you say that's unusual? If Sandinista officials had detained and threatened a priest, wouldn't this have become an international incident?

SOLANO: Quite possibly so. But it is a pattern that anomalies on the part of the Sandinista authorities are readily denounced, whereas actions from the other side are not mentioned.

Z: One example given to me of Sandinista persecution of the Church has been the cancelling of the archibishop's televised masses. Do you feel this was religious persecution?

SOLANO: The mass that the archbishop previously televised every Sunday was discontinued. It was not because of his religious personality, and for that reason it was not religious persecution. The archibishop has been identified as being in opposition to the government. The television channel is a government channel. It would be odd in any country for a religious figure to be given time on a government TV channel. That this was discontinued is not surprising. For example, I can't imagine that a church figure who opposes the government in the U.S. would be tolerated for very long on a government channel.

Z: Has the Church hierarchy made the decision to oppose this government?

SOLANO: I don't think it's a decision on the part of the bishops as a whole, but some of the bishops—the more influential bishops.

Z: From where does this opposition come?

SOLANO: These are complex matters with many explanations. One is personal experience and perceptions of certain incidents. For example, for Monsignor Obando, a very strong experience for him at the very beginning of the Revolution was his visit to Nicaraguan students on the Isle of Youth in Cuba. Here he was not allowed to celebrate mass. This was an extremely powerful—and negative—experience for him, and it has influenced all of his subsequent perceptions of the Revolution.

Z: How have your personal experiences here influenced your perceptions of the Revolution?

SOLANO: My experience has been almost a totally happy and positive experience of the Revolution. Relations on a grass-roots level, on an intermediary level, and on the highest levels of the Sandinista government have been good experiences. I've found an immense amount of sincerity, openness, a will to collaborate, to change, to modify, to correct anomalies or abuses. A very sincere will.

Z: How would you contrast your five years here since the triumph with your 10 years under the Somoza dictatorship?

SOLANO: There's no comparison. Somoza's regime was unreformable, the corruption was so extensive that—except for Divine intervention—it was unchangeable. From almost the beginning of the time that I have been in Nicaragua—and I had very little political consciousness then—I realized that sooner or later there would have to be a revolution in Nicaragua. There was no other way to rectify the corruption of the government.

There were numerous cases of religious persecution then. Religous people were suspected of being subversives. Certain priests were labeled Communists who were in no way Communists but had claimed abuses of human rights and justice. Reprisals were taken through bureaucratic rules to make religious work difficult. Some lay Delegates of the Word were murdered. A Church-supported cooperative in the Suina area was dissolved. Some meetings were controlled. This was in Zelaya, and the persecution was worse on the Pacific Coast.

Z: And what changes have you seen since the Triumph?

SOLANO: There are so many areas to speak of: education, financial support for poor people, medical care, government technical aid to peasants, building projects of new homes, the promotion of the dignity of women. It's all over; the difference is like night and day. Any effort made on behalf of the poor is supported by the resources of the government now. The change is simply day and night.

Z: How should people understand the role of Catholic priests and laypeople in this government?

SOLANO: On the basis of official Church positions expressed at Vatican II, it is not only permissive but expected of Christians to participate in the construction of the world we live in. It's an obligation of Christians to take on concrete commitments in all areas of human society, including the political.

The work of Catholic clergy in this government at this time is a response to a great need for people with special talents. I think that all of the church ministers in government recognize they are responding to a temporary need for the good of the people.

Z: Is there a problem when Catholics share power in a government with Communists and Socialists?

SOLANO: I've experienced no difficulty in that way. Christian people should collaborate and share in all possible aspects of life with other people: believers and unbelievers. It is a manipulation of the Sandinista Revolution to attach to it the adjective "Marxist." If a true accurate description is to be given, it would be necessary to say, each time the Marxist label was used, that this is also a Christian revolution. For the Sandinista Revolution, in its fundamental principles, is far more Christian than Marxist.

The values of justice, fraternity, sharing, cooperation, each one using their spiritual and material goods for the welfare of society rather than for their own egotistical interests, aspirations for peace, equality among people, and numerous others, are all evangelical Christian values and fundamental values of the Sandinista Revolution.

Z: Will the Church's reaction to the Nicaraguan Revolution determine the future of the church here? Will there be conflicts within the church over its orientation to the Revolution?

SOLANO: Divisions exist today. But I don't expect the church to be split asunder. Theologically there is much freedom for disagreement and individuality among Catholics. The Church has traditionally claimed authority in the fields of faith and morals. Politics does not enter into the competency or authority of the Church. So there is room for diversity in personal commitment.

Z: Has the Catholic Church, once defender of the status quo, now become a catalyst for change in Latin America?

SOLANO: If the Church is not a catalyst for change she can certainly not be faithful to her Gospel commitment. Gospel signifies, in its fundamental sense, change, "metanoia," conversion, change of attitude, change of life. This is why the Gospel is preached: to effect concrete change. So if the Gospel values are being promulgated somewhere by a paticular group, it would be the most natural thing for Christians to support that movement.

Z: Many have labeled the so-called Popular Church a Marxist invention for infiltrating the Church. How do you see the Popular Church working in Nicaragua, in your vicarate?

SOLANO: Popular Church has many meanings. The pejorative sense that has been attached to it in Nicaragua refers to a parallel church that supposedly exists outside of unity with the bishops of Nicaragua. I have not experienced this. It certainly does not exist in Zelaya. No concrete case of such a phenomenon in Nicaragua has been found by the bishops, to my knowledge.

If Popular Church is defined as a church with lay initiative, this is encouraged by the hierarchical Church in Vatican II, Medellín and Puebla. The church in the base communities is the model chosen for Latin America on an institutional level. The result of such lay initiative has been changes and renovation of the church into a Living Church. It's had great impact on people's lives.

There is the danger for the hierarchy, for the bishops, or even priests, that ecclesial base communities can appear threatening as if something is happening apart from their control. But those of us who have been involved concretely in these communities have experienced entirely the contrary. The base communities tend to fortify and strengthen the unity of the church.

Z: You were in Managua during the visit of the Pope in 1983, although you were ill and watched the proceedings on television. What were your reactions to that visit and the controversy that surrounded it?

SOLANO: On a feeling level, my reaction was great sadness that somehow there was not a meeting of feelings and that the event was publicized from the political posture of those reporting the event. I feel that if the Holy Father was aware of how that visit was used and reported he would also be very disappointed. The themes the Pope chose to speak on did not address the felt concerns of people on a popular level. Perhaps the information he received that led him to address these areas as priorities was not an accurate expression of the priorities felt by the people. People were experiencing a very difficult human situation: a lot of suffering, attack, death. People were not prepared to deal on a more theoretical level with principles of Catholic education and Church unity. Those are concepts I don't think anyone would challenge, but they were concepts that did not speak to the most felt need at that time.

Except for the possibility of a few people—a few people who you might expect anywhere in the world to oppose the authority of the Church or of the Pope—apart from these people, Nicarguans did not mean to be disrespectful. Perhaps there were errors made, but this must be interpreted in light of the living reality of this situation. For example, some in the crowd had microphones to lead popular acclamations. I personally feel that the way they were used was a grave mistake. However, their use was symbolic of the conviction of many in Nicaragua that popular power should have equal possibilities with the expression of other types of power.

The Holy Father's personal experience is probably very different from what is being lived in Nicaragua. The Polish Church and Polish Catholics are different. The attitude there might be one of awe, silence and expectation. The Nicaraguan people are culturally different—they're noisy and expressive, which should not be interpreted negatively. And the Revolution gives little people more channels to express themselves.

In regard to the incident in the plaza, it's important to realize that the response that was given was provoked and planned by a certain sector of the Catholic Church. No one was supposed to be in the plaza before a certain hour on the morning of the day of the Pope's visit, for reasons of order and security. However, a group had been organized by a certain sector of the church to march at 10 p.m. the previous night and to take their places in the plaza before the hour designated by the government. This was a provocation. That group was organized in a vocal and aggressive way, and in an antirevolutionary attitude. It was the slogans they were shouting that the Sandinista groups responded to. This problem would probably not have happened if that group had not provoked it. I understand that members of religious orders and congregations of the Catholic Church lost their reserved places at the very front of the crowd because they were aggressively occupied by the group I mentioned.

Z: What Catholic Church organization are you referring to?

SOLANO: It was an organization centered around a particular ecclesiastical personage.

Z: Who?

SOLANO: I'd rather not say.

Z: In Nicaragua there is a popular slogan that says, "Between Christianity and the Revolution there is no contradiction." How do you react to that slogan?

SOLANO: In the Nicaraguan Revolution as I have experienced it, I can embrace that slogan. Many of the fundamental principles of the Revolution coincide with Gospel principles. Others not only coincide, but have been inspired by Christian principles. Those which are cited as contradictory—for example, hate and class struggle—I perceive as being social and historical facts to be evangelized rather than premises of the Nicaraguan Revolution.

Z: Do you expect the first elections to be free and democratic?

SOLANO: I, and the majority of the Nicaraguan people, welcome the coming elections. The amount of liberty is conditional, of course. In the U.S., for example, certain parties of Communist or Socialist tendencies are not given the same opportunity to compete for power as the other, capitalist parties are given. Those parties are controlled, limited and censored. There will be freedom of elections here as there is in the U.S., also within a definite reference (with a socialistic-revolutionary context). I expect these will be the first truly free elections in the history of Nicaragua.

Z: What about military service? Father Carballo and the bishops have denounced this as mere service to an ideology?

SOLANO: Well, the reality of military service in any country is in service to a particular ideology. That's the way it is in the U.S. or any other country. There's nothing different about Nicaragua.

Z: Why do you think the bishops dissolved the association of Nicaraguan priests (ACLEN)?

SOLANO: Somehow or other some people were afraid that this was something not completely under their control and that it was necessary to do away with it.

Z: The charge has been made that the Nicaraguan Catholic hierarchy has become a witting or unwitting tool of the conservative parties, the U.S. government and the CIA to oppose the Sandinista government. What's your reaction to that charge?

SOLANO: Well, I agree with that, but I do think it has been unwitting. There's a type of political naiveté within the church. The church has been used, and is being used, for political motives and ends which she really does not want. There is naiveté and lack of political consciousness on a large scale. I maintain the hope that none of it is intentional.

Z: Is there room within the church for discussion and a change of attitude?

SOLANO: It's almost nonexistent now.

Z: Do you think that the church should take a more forceful stand in condemning the contras or should it condemn only the violence in general?

SOLANO: Say that the church is against violence, certainly. The vast majority of the violence comes from the counterrevolutionaries. So, if the church's response were proportionate, she'd certainly have to have denounced 1,000 times more the violence of the contras to the violence of the Sandinistas.

Z: Has the church hierarchy moved, or transferred, priests out of certain barrios and parishes because they supported the Revolution? Were these political decisions?

SOLANO: Of course, effectively, if not intentionally. Political agreement could be a criterion for whether or not a priest has a good identification with his bishop.

Z: What is the future of the church and the Revolution in Nicaragua?

SOLANO: The church will always have a place in the Revolution because of those who are participating in the development of the country and the Revolution. Motivated by their faith, they've earned the right to be recognized within the Revolution.

The counterrevolutionary activity and the possibility of intervention are fearsome things, but they do not paralyze the people who continue to respond to the Revolution with extreme commitment. The attacks against the Revolution have served to strengthen, not weaken, the Revolution. It is not having the effect hoped for by Reagan and his administration. It's provoking opposite effects. I would hope that the U.S. could be inspired in its relationships with other countries by its own revolution—to let other countries determine their own destiny and national life on the basis of their own principles, and without outside intervention.

Z: Is Nicaragua a totalitarian state or a free country today?

SOLANO: It's as free as other countries. It's certainly more free than the U.S., in the sense of opportunity for people who formerly had no voice, who now have a voice; the poor, marginated and dispossessed. In that sense, it's an outstanding example of democracy.

Z: You were born in Indiana and became a Nicaraguan citizen in December 1979. Why?

SOLANO: Fifteen years ago (although such is no longer the case) there was a Capuchin commitment to remain permanently in the country to which you were originally assigned as a missioner. I came to Nicaragua with that commitment. As I came into contact with the Nicaraguan church on the peasant level, I realized I identified my life aspirations within that context. I contemplate dying here and being buried here. This is my life in a definitive way. So I sealed that commitment and identification by taking on Nicaraguan nationality.

One Capuchin value is the vow of poverty. Here was a way to live my vow of poverty by giving up the security that my North American citizenship assured me. It was a form of "giving up" something dear on the human level in order to acquire something better on the spiritual level. It was part of my conversion. I had long contemplated this move, but with the coming of the Triumph it was an opportune moment to identify with these people at a time when the future was open for good or ill. So it was a way of sealing my fate with theirs.

3. Christians in the Revolution
Father Edgard Parrales
Rafael Solís

One of the most unusual aspects of the Nicaraguan Revolution has been the large number of Christians at all levels of government. These include Catholic clergy and laypeople who first helped organize the opposition to Somoza and who now help shape and administer the revolutionary process. In separate interviews I spoke with two leaders about their personal religious journeys of faith and of their perceptions of Christians in this Revolution.

FATHER EDGARD PARRALES, 42, is one of four Catholic priests in active service to the government. Father Parrales, who has earned degrees in theology and law, was appointed minister of social welfare in 1980, and became Nicaragua's ambassador to the Organization of American States in 1982. The other three priests in the government are: Father Ernesto Cardenal, the minister of culture; Father Miguel D'Escoto, the foreign minister, and Father Fernando Cardenal, the former director of the Literacy Crusade and present vice-minister of the Sandinista Youth. In January 1985 Father Parrales publicly announced his resignation from the priesthood.

RAFAEL SOLÍS, 30, is a subcomandante of the People's Sandinista Army. Previously Nicaragua's first ambassador to the U.S., he is currently the Army's representative to the Council of State, Nicaragua's interim parliament, and serves as the council's secretary. Solís grew up in Father Parrales's church youth group.

*   *   *

FATHER EDGARD PARRALES: I am the only priest in the government who was previously a parish priest. The others were artists, professors and intellectuals. I served as a priest for 13 years in three different parishes of Managua.

Father Edgard Parrales, Photo by Margolis

My last parish was at Santa Marta. As part of the service there we would have a dialogue in church. I'd come down from the pulpit and walk in the aisle between the pews with my wireless microphone to talk with the people. We discussed the Gospel and its implications. Even if people didn't agree with my interpretations, they respected me while making up their own minds. They were wealthy people and, in the end, I didn't have a majority support there. So I left that parish in 1980. When I resigned, the bishop appointed a conservative priest, a sycophant. Now it's a parish of contras.

I am a lawyer, too, and before the Revolution I was involved in the student movement at the university. I defended some of them on political charges. The majority of the Catholic University youth supported the FSLN after leaving the Christian Democrats. In fact, many of today's government leaders came from the Catholic youth movements.

Many people don't realize how bad things were under Somoza. I'm 40 years old, but I have never voted, because elections under Somoza meant nothing. In those days I would speak against Somoza in my sermons, not in a political way but in an ethical way. And I participated in demonstrations to free political prisoners, including a sit-in at the cathedral. I gave press interviews. Sometimes I was put in jail. Sometimes I was threatened by phone, and sometimes I was followed on the street.

After the Triumph of the Revolution, the conservative wing of the church took a position against the Revolution; the progressive wing supported the Revolution. The two groups are very defined now against and in favor of the Revolution. And the bishops have grown more distant from the people.

This is a struggle in which the Catholic Church is hardening its opposition to the Revolution and they are provoking an abyss between the Catholic, established, Church and the Revolution. For me, they are acting as an authority and not as servants of the Gospel.

Who is going to lose in this battle? Not the conservatives or the progressives, but the faith that is stagnant because the bishops worry more about their authority than about outreach and preaching the faith.

The hierarchy cannot turn the people against the Revolution. Our people are religious, but they are religious with or without the bishops. They will always be religious but at the same time they support and enter into their Revolution.

The institutional Church can slow the development of a new way of being Christian but it cannot finally stop it. It's inevitable, because it is an expression of human and Christian hope. If the hierarchy doesn't understand this, they will be overtaken by history.

Jesus broke down the structures of his day and placed human beings above the old rules. And today structures are being broken down again to serve people. We will see the changing of the Church.

There is no such thing as the so-called Popular Church. There is a movement to develop the consciousness of Christians and their faithfulness. The "base communities" are integrated into the parishes and have announced their obedience to the bishops and the church. But they also offer analysis and criticism, which is unusual. The bishops don't like to answer questions and they are not used to criticism. The people are not developing a parallel church outside of or opposed to the hierarchy. They offer obedience but not the obedience of a "doggie."

Archbishop Obando y Bravo was anti-Somocista but never pro-Sandinista. He supported the Revolution only when the Right, the industrialists and the old-line politicians, supported the Revolution to finally overthrow Somoza.

The Reagan administration knows that the Nicaraguan Revolution, of Christians and Marxists working together, could be a model for all of Latin America, and have tried to stop it. They have succeeded in creating a distance but they have not broken the union of the Christians and the Revolution.

The main points of Christianity are love, justice and peace, and these are not found in Church structures but in concrete, revolutionary work.

We suppose that the CIA tries to use the church in Nicaragua. We suspect it. There seem to be strong links between the business community, the church and the CIA. In the Santa Fe document, Reagan targeted the churches to use against the Revolution. But they can't really succeed in the end. Because the more people learn and grow intellectually, the more they really understand the Gospel message.

The Church will change. You know Bishop Romero (martyred in El Salvador) was a very conservative priest. But when he became bishop he saw what was happening. He saw friends, priests, being killed. And he changed.

There are two kinds of ideologies: the ideology of people and human needs, and the ideology of rules and structure. Human beings are above structures. They are the most important values. God became man in Jesus to show us just how important men and women are. Their welfare must be our greatest concern, not the welfare and structure of an institution, even the institution of the Church. The Church is simply an instrument to serve people. When it doesn't serve people it must be changed. But change threatens the bishops, the Pope and the entire Church hierarchy. We are not against "structure"—because every society needs a structure. We are against an inert structure. The structures must be at the order of the people, not vice versa.

When the Pope was in Nicaragua the people asked for prayers for the people who had been killed that week in fighting the contras, but he would not do it. He didn't have the intelligence to understand the moment and give the people what they needed. He could have acted to bring people together.

The Pope used the liturgy for a political message. That was disrespectful of the liturgical office. The people were not disrespectful. The Pope is blocked by the limits of his own mind and his experience in Poland to be so strongly anti-Communist.

We Christians in the Revolution are a kind of symbol to the population. People, when they see me, say "Father Parrales." I don't say, I am "Ambassador" Parrales or "Father" Parrales. I am Edgard Parrales. But when people recognize me as a priest they smile and in their faces I see a sense of satisfaction and identification with the Revolution.

I cannot say who in the government is religious and who is not. But what is important is that people trust us, that they know we have integrity, that we are true to our principles, and that we can be trusted.

I express my ideas as my ideas in the government, not as a priest. I speak out of who I am and what I believe and in that way I have influence in the government. I don't try to project an image of a priest but the broader image of an honest and thinking person.

The bishops gave me an initial permission to join the government. Later, they tried to say that there was a misunderstanding and attempted to revoke it. I told them I hadn't misunderstood anything and stayed in the government. I worked with the Revolution before the victory too, and the bishops never told me to stop. Vatican II opened the door to a new way of living and thinking. Now they are trying to close that door.

After a crisis in the Church there is now an agreement with the bishops that allows us priests to serve in the government as long as we do not carry out the functions of a priest. I accept these requirements by discipline, but I don't like it. I'd prefer to say, "I won't sign any agreement and you do as you like." I think of myself as a priest.

The "agreement" was a victory for the bishops to separate us as priests from the people. So now they can work on the people without any contradiction because only they can speak as priests. But everyone knows we are priests. If they had suspended us it would have worked against them because the people would have seen us as victims. The major part of the Nicaraguan population is at the same time revolutionary and Christian.

For me it is a specification of my personal vocation to serve in the government. To be fully a priest we don't serve only a liturgical function. The deeper ideal of the priesthood is to live the Gospel, live the Gospel in every moment and in every way, and I am doing that. There is no contradiction between my Christianity, my priesthood and my service in the government. You cannot say, "I will be a political man" or "I will be a religious man." You must live an integrated life.

For example, Junta Coordinator Daniel Ortega [elected President November 4, 1984, in the first election] had his children baptized privately. And Tomás Borge, minister of the interior and a founder of the FSLN in 1961, has a wall adorned with crucifixes outside his office. It's called the "room of the crosses."

I feel that Borge, supposedly the "old, red man of the FSLN," speaks the same language I do more than some bishops. Some bishops are more concerned about the structure of the church than about the spirit.

There are many Christians serving in this government: two of them, Luis Carrion, second in command at the Interior Ministry and the late Dr. Leonte Herdocia, director of the Human Rights Commission, came out of the University Christian movement. Then there's Rafael Solís, vice-president of the Council of State; Renaldo Teffel, at the Ministry of Social Welfare; Carlos Tünnerman, minister of education; Miguel Vijil, minister of housing, and Ricardo Chavaria, vice-minister of electricity, also a former priest.

In Nicaragua, we talk about the birth of the "new man" and the "new woman." For us this signifies a combination of religious and historical ideals. Some people in the Revolution say that they are atheists, but they really mean they are agnostics. But in general, deep in their souls they are believers. They were raised and educated as Christians but became agnostics because they saw the brotherhood of the Christian Church with the state power of Somoza and the wealthy class.

The institutional churches are guilty of driving these revolutionary leaders out of the church because of the poor choices the church has made.

The greatest accomplishments of this Revolution have been in education, health, social welfare, housing and agriculture—in serving the people.

I am a Sandinista. I am a Sandinista and a member of the FSLN. This is not a contradiction with my priesthood. And it has not been a contradiction for my conscience or my understanding of the Gospel. I find more contradictions with my standing within the hierarchical Church and my own conscience. Being a Sandinista is a way for me to give an answer to my life and my religious ideals.

I would like to say something that I haven't said to anyone. I ask you to treat it prudently. I'm in touch with my bishop and I've asked to leave the priesthood. I have for a long time been disappointed with the structure of the church. I tell you this to be completely honest with you. I have been in doubt. I have been in reflection. And I have consulted many people. I will leave the Church. I feel better having made this decision because I didn't feel fully free, individual or realized before. Instead of being full of liberation, I perceived the church as a jail.

I fought to change the Church, but it changes very slowly and a conservative spirit has been imposed. For me the Gospel is a message of liberation, but I do not find liberation in the Church today.

One of the things that disappoints me is that there is no room for dialogue. The Church hierarchy doesn't understand that in dialogue authority becomes stronger. But when you just tell people what to do, without dialogue or reason, people reject such authority. When someone tells me something, I want to know the reasons and not just be told he's the authority. The Church today is managed by decrepit old men.

Perhaps my decision to leave will be used against the Revolution, but it is actually a personal decision. Without the Revolution I might have acted earlier because the opportunities the Revolution gave me to discharge my priestly vocation sustained me for a long time. But finally I decided I couldn't stay. As a lay person I will work for a new conception of the Church with more liberty than I have now. In the Church now, as a priest, I am handcuffed.

At this point in my life I feel quieter, more at peace, more satisfied than ever before. What I believe and what I am doing today are the same. I have searched my conscience and know that I am doing the right thing. I am building my own model of my life.

U.S. policy is bound to fail against Nicaragua because when these outside attacks increase, internal support for the Revolution also increases. The Nicaraguan people have the Revolution as their own. They love it, support it and will defend it.

The guerrillas in El Salvador are having successes now. When they can't be held back, the U.S. may send the Navy and Marines into El Salvador and blockade Nicaragua and Cuba at the same time. New offensives by the contras in the north could lead to an invasion by Honduras. If the U.S. enters militarily into Central America we will ask for international support wherever we can get it. Even from the Soviet Union. Even if this leads to a superpower confrontation in Central America.

I am optimistic about the future of Nicaragua because I think we can beat the blockade. We are suffering from Reagan's policies. But I think we will overcome all of these obstacles and demonstrate a new society and new values to the whole world.

We will win. We will win here, in El Salvador and throughout Central America. The model of Christian involvement in this Revolution is a step forward in the experience of the Latin countries in the search for a new life and a new society. We are an example of the Christian movement's participation in social change. I am very hopeful for Nicaragua. We are going to build a new and stronger society—something new in the world.

* * *

SUBCOMANDANTE RAFAEL SOLÍS: I was born and raised in Managua. I attended the Colegio Central America, which was the high school for wealthy people here. When I was 13 or 14 there was a priest there, from Spain, very advanced in his ideas, who introduced us to some of the social realities in the country, including life in the poor barrios here in Managua and life on the Atlantic Coast, where the people were very poor. We read about this and found opportunities to work in the barrios as well.

For me, coming from a wealthy family and background, it was a new and awakening experience. In 1970, when I was 16, we sat in at the large downtown cathedral to protest the treatment of political prisoners by the Somoza dictatorship. We took over the church and stayed there. Priests were with us, Fernando Cardenal and Edgard Parrales. And we stayed in the cathedral until the government made some concessions.

In 1971, the Christian student movement went beyond simply expressing sentiments against Somoza and began concrete work in the poor neighborhoods of the capital. And we began contacts with the Sandinistas. The Christian movement was limited because we were mostly from the upper classes and because, although we wanted to help the people and were motivated to get involved, we didn't really have a political analysis of the situation or political strategies for change. These came later from the armed opposition, from the Sandinistas.

We began to work bit by bit with the Sandinistas. And by '73 or '74 we were integrated into the Frente Sandinista because Christians were accepted into the movement like everyone else. The Christian movement was our entry into the opposition. Many of us later became guerrillas and fighters. In all the protests and demonstrations of this period priests like Fernando Cardenal, Edgard Parrales and Uriel Molina were with us as leaders. And there are many leaders of the government today who came out of our Christian youth movement, including Comandante Luis Carrion, my superior [a member of the FSLN's National Directorate], Comandante Dora María Tellez, and 25 or 30 others.

For me the Christian movement, when I was 14 or 15, and for other students, was our first contact with the reality of life in Nicaragua for the poor, and this helped arouse and shape our revolutionary commitment. Because we were all from the middle and upper classes, we met workers and peasants for the first time and understood the repression of the Somoza dictatorship. We were changed personally and individually by these experiences.

There was one zone where we worked, in the northern part of the city, where they had been flooded by Lake Managua. They were very poor and conditions were miserable. They lived in houses of paper and cardboard, whatever they could scavenge. We helped in the construction of a health center and a latrine. We did this work, we helped, but we had no political understanding and could do no political work with these people. And so we couldn't really change things for them.

It was a personal awakening for us, and the development of our intellects. Out of these experiences we later became real revolutionaries. We developed ourselves in the Christian movement intellectually and socially and later politically.

When I became a guerrilla fighter I knew some of the priests who took up arms. I fought on the southern front with Father Gaspar García Lavianna, a Spanish priest who had served a parish in San Juan del Sur. He was a great man, a religious man and a real fighter. He was a good friend to me and to the other guerrillas. We were impressed with his sentiments and his love for the people, but he also lacked a political understanding, an ideology.

Rafael Solís, Photo by Connie Martin

Father Gaspar was killed fighting with us on the southern front.

We can say today that our Revolution is influenced by Christian values in the number of Christians in the government. And Christian themes of justice and equality are principles of this Revolution. The Frente Sandinista includes Christians and other revolutionaries, all kinds of people with all kinds of individual beliefs. These are coinciding points of view which advance the process of the development of the "new person" of the Revolution. The presence of Christians in this movement has been intense. And today, to defend this Revolution from attack, I know Christians who are fighting now on the northern front against the contras from Honduras.

Christians are active now in social welfare, in setting up cooperatives, etc. The Revolution and Christians have maintained good relations and Christians have been integrated into the Revolution whether or not they join the Frente Sandinista.

Practically speaking, I'm not a Christian today. I don't usually attend church. But I was married in the Catholic Church and all of my children have been baptized Catholic. I maintain relations and work with several Christian communities in my barrio. Catholicism is a part of my life and certainly was a major part of my development.

4. A New Culture

Rosario Murillo
Father Ernesto Cardenal

ROSARIO MURILLO, 32, is the author of four books of poetry. In 1981, she was elected director of the Writers' Union and a year later director of the Sandinista Association of Cultural Workers (ASTC), an organization including all seven artistic unions. She is married to President Daniel Ortega.

* * *

PHILIP ZWERLING: How did the ASTC, as a guild of cultural workers, develop and how does it function?

ROSARIO MURILLO: To understand this development you must look at the history of cultural work in the revolutionary struggle. And this work goes back to the time of Sandino [who fought against the occupying U.S. Marines, 1927–1933] when artists were involved as fighters, as solidarity workers, as intellectual supporters—publishing papers and magazines—here in Nicaragua and internationally. Also, we had the phenomenon of popular culture, especially music, which celebrated the values of the Sandinista struggle, in songs and even in novels and stories.

This involvement of intellectuals and artists in the Nicaraguan anti-imperialist struggle continued through time. In the 1960s, this could be seen in the poetry and prose of Sergio Ramírez [a member of the Junta of National Reconstruction; elected vice-president in November 1984] and Fernando Cordillo [who died in exile and for whom the home of the ASTC is named], who as intellectuals participated in the FSLN. Their art was a part of a militant revolutionary struggle. It spoke of that struggle, celebrated the struggle and so advanced the fight.

Artists were integrated into the Frente Sandinista and were a part of the movement through their artistic works and their personal lives. Their art helped to develop the ideological struggle as well.

In 1974, *Grupo Gradas* [Steps] was formed [by Murillo, among others], which broke with past schemes of cultural work because of its emphasis on mass work through dance, music and poetry in which all people, whether they thought of themselves as artists or not, became creators of culture.

During the armed struggle there was an explosion of popular culture, seen in popular theater performed in the streets, on the barricades and in the liberated zones, in songs sung about the insurrection, in dances and processions in the barrios, in the combative poems that were written, and in the graffiti that were drawn on the barrio walls.

Rosario Murillo, Photo by Connie Martin

And we must remember the experience of Padre Cardenal and his community at Solentiname, which was destroyed by the Guardia in 1977. The movement of primitivist painting was begun there among peasants who became outstanding artists and interpreted Biblical themes into contemporary events.

Peasants and workers were involved and moved in the revolutionary struggle through the art that was created in their communities. These are the roots out of which, at the Triumph of the Revolution, came the Association of Sandinista Cultural Workers. The ASTC was formed to continue the cultural struggle of our people. We constitute an ideologial front in the fight to create new values and a new society.

In this guild of artists we continue the historical struggle to develop culture, to supply the necessary material needs for artistic work: to start magazines to publish the work of writers; to obtain musical instruments; to recognize and support artists; to provide technical artistic assistance to peasant communities; to develop cultural expression in the armed forces; to professionalize the arts and guarantee salaries for artists so that they can spend their time writing or painting; to develop our own resources for artistic materials (as in obtaining paints from the volcanic material that is so prevalent here); to involve artists in the social struggles for health care and for more and better housing; to establish international contacts for cultural cooperation with other countries; and to establish libraries and exhibitions.

The seven guilds that comprise the ASTC are dance, music, theater, writing, plastic arts, photography and circus. The circus is particularly important to us because this is a new art that was founded with the Revolution and which never existed here before.

Our goals are at the same time to professionalize the artistic work and to make this work available to the mass of people. We have 9,000 members, of whom 100 are full-time artists. These are artists who are learning more, teaching others, producing works and building our culture. Nicaragua never before had this climate in which to create art. Without the Revolution we could not exist as artists. Our art goes all over the world—to Japan, Mexico, the Soviet Union, the United States—to show and explain the values of our Revolution.

And in all of this work we strive for excellence. You may have read a review in *Nuevo Diario* (one of the national daily newspapers) which criticized a new painting exhibition for its surrealistic style and said that only a realistic style suited a revolutionary society. The artist who was criticized is now drafting a reply explaining that here we work in all styles: realism, surrealism, primitivism and abstraction, and that our goal in art is to produce the best art regardless of style. This guild supports that diversity and commitment to excellence. The question is quality, not style. In this we work to defend artistic liberty in order to develop the best and broadest artistic work. Out of this absolute liberty for culture we are recognizing an explosion of work in the plastic arts, which didn't exist before, in dance, theater and painting.

Literature, for example, has lagged behind, not for lack of liberty but for lack of time. The writers have had to do other work to earn their living and had less time for their art. We are working to raise the money so that a writer can be supported for several months at a time while working on a novel or poetry. This is a form of liberty, of time to produce, that we support as well. And from this liberty comes new and exciting works of art.

Z: How does this present work compare to the cultural life of the country under the Somoza dictatorship?

MURILLO: In the past the economic domination of our country by other powers also meant the cultural domination of our people by foreign cultures—Spanish, British and North American. But all during this time Nicaraguans resisted the suppression of their own culture. This really heroic resistance can be seen in everything from the fact that our stores were always called *pulperias* by our people rather than "groceries," as such English words were used in other Latin American countries. This was a rejection of domination. It can be seen in the survival of native Nicaraguan food dishes, in folklore and community festivals. All are expressions of resistance and of victory over domination.

For example, theater was poorly developed here under the dictatorship. Only five or six Nicaraguan plays were ever performed because plays from Spain, England and the United States were preferred by the rich elite who could attend the theater. But the traditional Nicaraguan theater continued in street theater and church processions. This theater was never recognized or supported. The dictatorship never publicized indigenous theater and tried to impose another culture.

And, of course, under Somoza many artists contributed their lives to the struggle for independence rather than to their art. For example, Rigoberto López, a student, a poet, was obsessed with this struggle. At the age of 19, in 1956, he executed the first Somoza [Anastasio I], shooting him at a social reception in León, and was immediately shot dead by Somoza's guards. Other poets, like Ricardo Morales and Leonel Rugama, also died fighting Somoza even though they were able to write and travel and could have devoted their lives only to their poetry. They sacrificed their poetry for the Revolution. And the Revolution has given birth to poets and poetry. This is a Nicaraguan phenomenon.

Z: How is cultural work in Nicaragua affected by North American hostility to this Revolution?

MURILLO: North American politics affect the development of the arts in Nicaragua. The economic blockade limits the development of all of the social programs of the Revolution, including cultural development. The mining of the ports affects the importation of artistic as well as all other materials and devastates the economy of the country. This covert war impoverishes us in culture, in health, in education—in every field. A rigorous austerity must be imposed simply to survive. Machinery breaks down and ships can't enter our port with the parts we need to repair or maintain them.

For us, specifically, all sorts of artistic supplies are limited. The U.S. government is cutting us bit by bit in the whole country. But the cultural work goes on. For example, cultural brigades go out, under the protection of the army, into the war zones to work with the peasants and to develop the level of culture in the countryside.

Z: I find that everyone in Nicaragua seems to have played some part in the struggle against the Somoza dynasty. Did you, as a poet, also take part in this struggle?

MURILLO: I began work with the Frente Sandinista in 1970 [at age 18]. In 1973, my first book of poetry was published. In 1974, I helped to found Grupo Gradas. During this time I did clandestine work, propaganda work and maintained a safe house. In July 1976, I was arrested and imprisoned. When I was released I went into exile and did work abroad. I returned to Nicaragua and worked with Radio Sandino, which broadcast from areas of Nicaragua controlled by the rebels, and I edited a cultural magazine published clandestinely here in Nicaragua.

Z: What kind of a future do you hope for your children?

MURILLO: Well, I have seven children and the future I hope for them is the same future I hope for all Nicaraguans. I want to see them educated and growing in a new society.

The only fear I have is the effect of the CIA and North American terror here in Nicaragua. Our children ought to be able to live free of fear and trauma. But they see and read about the war; they see the bomb shelters and trenches we have had to dig. And all of this affects them. This is the effect of Ronald Reagan's politics in Nicaragua.

But, independently of this, I am hoping that our children will have the chance to be educated, to become technicians and workers, artists and intellectuals, and to reach a level of education that they never would have had before the Triumph of the Revolution. I hope they might be able to grow up as integrated human beings, as new men and new women. And this means as people without egotism, without economic exploitation, with a sense of working for the welfare of other people. This is my hope for the future.

* * *

ERNESTO CARDENAL has been Nicaragua's minister of culture since the Triumph of July 19, 1979. A Roman Catholic priest and a poet, Cardenal, 59, studied at the Trappist monastery in Kentucky where Thomas Merton was his novice master. The author of many books of poetry, he founded a religious community on the archipelago of Solentiname in Lake Nicaragua in 1966. When young people from this community joined the FSLN in the attack on the National Guard barracks in San Carlos in 1977, Somoza ordered the complete destruction of the Solentiname community. For the next two years, Cardenal represented the FSLN internationally. His office and the Ministry of Culture now occupy the mansion and estate where Anastasio (II) Somoza lived, near the center of Managua. For this interview, he was dressed—as always—in a white *cotona* (peasant shirt) which, as a symbol of indigenous culture, has become popular again following the Triumph.

Z: You've been minister of culture for four and a half years. What would you say have been the major accomplishments of those years?

ERNESTO CARDENAL: There are so many I would have to write a list, it seems to me. But the most important has been the development of a democratization of culture, building a culture that is open and accessible to the masses—in dance, music, theater, publications, libraries, movies. We have made all available to the people, as participants and as spectators.

Nicaragua had a literary tradition, painting and music, but these were for a small elite group and there was nothing for the rest. There was great literature, but it was available to very few people. Now we have great literature, great culture and it's available to everyone.

We're not seeking a low level of bad culture for everyone but rather an elevated culture that is really accessible to all of the people, rich or poor, in the city or in the countryside. We seek an integration of popular culture and high culture, of indigenous culture and international culture.

Certainly, before, we experienced cultural imperialism from Spain, Britain and the United States, as each had political influence in Nicaragua. But the struggle for liberation that culminated in the Triumph of the Revolution was a struggle against all forms of imperialism, including cultural imperialism.

All of culture was imported previously. But this is not dominant anymore because we are developing our own indigenous culture. We don't prohibit any type of cultural art here. We have music, records and dance from other countries, including the United States, but now we also have more, we have our own music and dance as well. We have national culture and international culture. Even though the U.S. is making war on us today, we still celebrate U.S. artists who made a contribution to peoples' culture

Father Ernesto Cardenal, Photo by Peter Kelly

internationally: artists like Walt Whitman, Robert Frost or Carl Sandburg. These poets are well known here even among our peasants. We're internationalists. We can't accept a chauvinism of culture. We want to develop all of our authentic Nicaraguan culture and international culture, both old and new.

We've rediscovered our folklore culture that was repressed under the dictatorship. And this includes dance, music in festivals and artisan crafts. We are traveling to preserve and spread the music and dance of our indigenous peoples on the Atlantic Coast: the Miskitos, Ramas and Sumos. And everything we do, we do in four languages: Spanish, Miskito, Sumo and English, for our Creole population that speaks English. The Atlantic Coast of Nicaragua is like another country and this is a culture we share with all Nicaraguans and preserve at the same time for the indigenous people. This rediscovery of indigenous culture causes a complete change of mentality for the people. Typical cooking, furniture, and dress of Nicaragua are rediscovered. And all Nicaraguans can see and talk about and enjoy their own culture with dignity and pride. For with the Triumph of the Revolution all Nicaraguans have the dignity of this cultural treasury, of a love of Nicaragua, of something to defend and to die for.

Z: How was culture repressed under the Somoza dictatorship?

CARDENAL: All of my books were prohibited here in Nicaragua. So many books were prohibited. Tolstoy's books were prohibited because he was a Russian. One time I went to Puerto Rico to a conference and returned to Nicaragua with books. All of these books were confiscated by customs. But I had bought them in Puerto Rico, a colony of the United States! Books that were permitted in the United States, books by or about Fidel Castro or "Che" Guevara, were prohibited in Nicaragua. When the books were taken away from me, I was assured that they were not stealing the books because they planned only to burn them. And in fact, every Thursday, before an attorney or notary public, books were burned in Managua. Today a Nicaraguan can buy any book. There is no censor and no book burnings. But we don't have enough books! Because we don't have enough dollars to buy and import books on the international market.

Z: In the past you've spoken of the Sandinista Revolution as a revolution of love. In what sense is that so?

CARDENAL: It's true because the Revolution was a triumph of *compañerismo* [brotherhood and sisterhood] and solidarity. Out of love so many Nicaraguans sacrificed their lives to bring freedom to Nicaragua. So many thousands of young people went into the mountains to teach the peasants how to read and write. This was out of love. And so many thousands of people were mobilized for the health campaigns to save the lives of the children who were without vaccinations before, who suffered from preventable diseases that were endemic here. There are so many who have worked to build homes or improve agriculture. All of this has been *compañerismo*, solidarity and love. For we understand "love" as love for others.

Z: What is happening now with the community at Solentiname?

CARDENAL: Somoza's Guardia destroyed everything, the buildings, the books in the library, the paintings and the archeological exhibits. Solentiname is being rebuilt now with many things we never had before: a school for the political education of peasant leaders, a dairy, a cheese factory and a factory for educational toys. All of these are new. The artisan work continues. And a great group of painters has gathered there. The primitivist paintings of Solentiname are now famous throughout the world.

Z: You are a Catholic priest, a government minister and a self-professed Marxist. How do you explain the strange mixture in a single person?

CARDENAL: I am a priest who is a servant of love. I am a poet whose poetry is at the service of love. I am a government minister in this Revolution as a servant of the people and as a servant of love. I am a Marxist because I discovered that Marxism offers a method for studying society and for changing it from a capitalist to a more just society. All of this relates to the reign of God on earth which Jesus Christ announced to humanity—a kingdom of God which includes justice and an end to class and oppression. For me there are no differences or contradictions in these things which I believe and which I am.

Z: Why do you think the United States sees Nicaragua as a danger to its interests?

CARDENAL: The U.S. is a capitalist country and an imperialist country. It looks for money, control and power. All of the actions of this Revolution have been for the people without regard to money, control or power.

It would be impossible to buy for a salary the work of a literacy teacher who left her home and went into the mountains to live for five months with the peasants, risking malaria and malnutrition, to work in the fields during the day and to teach them to read at night. Because once you began paying a salary commensurate with such work you would quickly run out of money. It would be impossible to buy for a salary the young people who defend this country with their lives on our northern and southern frontiers. You cannot buy their lives for dollars. The United States does not fear the Nicaraguan Army but rather the Nicaraguan example, which is an example for all of Latin America. And this is the great danger of Nicaragua, and nothing more.

Z: So many people were in the revolutionary struggle in Nicaragua for so many years. Were you, and others like you, always sure of victory over that long period of disappointment and setbacks?

CARDENAL: We always thought we would win. To struggle, we had to believe we would win. Because we believed in victory, we continued the struggle. But we never knew if we would live to see the victory. So many died. I was always sure we would win, but I never knew when.

5. An Economy in Transition

Rogelio Ramírez
Ramiro Gurdian

ROGELIO RAMÍREZ, 37, former professor of economics, municipal administrator and ambassador to Costa Rica, is presently vice director of INIES (Institute for Economic and Social Investigations) in Managua, a private agency of economic consultants which advises the Nicaraguan government. He is the brother of Sergio Ramírez, one of the three members of the Junta of National Reconstruction and newly elected vice-president.

* * *

PHILIP ZWERLING: Could you give us an idea of the Nicaraguan economy under Somoza?

ROGELIO RAMÍREZ: The economy, at least in the last years of the Somoza dictatorship, had two main aspects. The first was agricultural production for exportation used to import luxury goods for the elite. The other aspect was a thrust toward industrialization based upon the concept of a Common Market for Central America. However, that model of development never really got off the ground at all and the Common Market fell apart in a shambles.

These two thrusts of the economy sat on a concentrated social base in which property and capital were exclusively concentrated in very few hands. For example, in 1977, CEPAL [the Mexico-based Economic Commission for Latin America], after making an investigation, came to the conclusion that 5% of the population, represented by only 116,000 people, shared 28% of the national income. This elite earned an average of $5,500 per person per year. At the same time, at the other extreme, according to CEPAL, 50% of the population shared just 15% of the national income and received just $286 per person per year. This forms, in general terms, the basic characteristics of the Somocista economic

Rogelio Ramírez

model. Now, you add to this model a commitment to a policy of accumulation. Such a model never had the capacity for internal investment and development, or for satisfying the social necessities of most of the population. Instead, profits were invested in imported goods and luxuries, which only widened the gap between the haves and the have-nots. And such a growing economic disparity required ever-greater repression to maintain the whole system. In the end it was this disparity that generated the Sandinista Revolution.

You must remember that this model of domination—economic, political and social—always had the backing of the United States. This historical model, once alive in Nicaragua and supported by successive North American administrations, can be seen as general U.S. policy in the region. The Somocista economic model that we experienced here is now being replayed in El Salvador, Guatemala and throughout Central America under U.S. influence.

Z: I wonder if it's really fair to call the Somocista model "capitalist"? It seems more like the story of a Mafia family dominating its piece of turf. Ideally, in capitalism, such awesome power is not supposed to be concentrated in a single family.

RAMÍREZ: I think this is simply, or realistically, the model capitalism assumed in Central America and, in particular, in Nicaragua. The only response was to destroy this abuse at a terrible cost in human life and destruction, and to make basic reforms in the structure of this society so that such a dictatorship could not be repeated. We've tried to construct a society that's not separated from its political and economic base.

Under the Somoza model Nicaraguan capital did not exist except within a framework of dependence. No one sought forms of investment within the country and no one worried about basic social necessities. Other capitalists also benefitted from this Somocista-North American domination. They enjoyed a capitalism dependent upon a military dictatorship. Other Latin American countries, certainly Chile today, for example, have more or less similar structures.

Z: Just how much of the economy was in the hands of Somoza and his friends?

RAMÍREZ: We've already spoken of per capita income and the concentration of capital. Look at land. Fifteen percent of the population controlled 70-80% of the land. And the reverse, 80% of the population controlled less than 20-25% of the land. The Somoza family itself had 20-25% of the arable land. You can see that it was not only Somoza but also others without conscience as well who benefitted from this model of accumulation. The whole economic policy of the past came to us debased. The base of the economy was agro-exportation. The agricultural sector directed toward internal consumption, to feed the people, was left absolutely abandoned. The system was aimed at exporting solely to gain foreign currency. The internal economy was attended to only minimally.

For example, under this system, the small producer was never able to get state aid or credit. The small producer began to receive credit only after the Sandinista Revolution. This internal abandonment meant a great disarray in the supplying of basic needs. In fact, there was no concern for trying to provide for basic needs at all.

For example, 1977 was statistically the most productive year for Somoza. In 1977, nearly 12,000,000 gallons of milk were produced and, under Somoza, milk was exported. In 1982, we produced almost 20 million gallons of milk and we had to import still more milk because the policy of this Sandinista government is to provide basic necessities, like milk, to the great majority of the population. The policy under Somoza was exactly the opposite—an export economy that was never directed at supplying basic necessities but rather to administering luxuries to those few in control. For this reason, the Sandinista Revolution has established control over the administration of foreign currency gained through exports. This enables us to create a model of investment that permits social investment with the little we might be able to earn with the global income of Nicaragua, which comes from cotton, coffee, etc. [sugar, corn, bananas, tobacco].

Z: Could Somoza have maintained himself in power longer if he had more generously shared the wealth with the smaller capitalists?

RAMÍREZ: It's possible, but that's a hypothesis that's a little absurd, because the model doesn't really consist of that. Small property ownership has grown rapidly under Sandinismo. Now, if this had happened under Somoza it wouldn't have been Somocism, by definition.

Z: In the last years of the dictatorship even business people came to oppose Somoza. Why was this?

RAMÍREZ: Somocismo is a model of domination which is quite old, an old model that through the years developed old rules of the game. These rules of the game, recognized or unrecognized, allowed a certain sharing of business among an elite group. For example, Somoza never established a private financial mechanism; instead, the banks were left to others. However, after the 1972 earthquake Somoza broke even the accepted rules of the game. He created a Bank of Central America, his first bank ever, and he began to meddle in investments, things he hadn't done before. He became completely avaricious and grabbed money after the earthquake that was aid earmarked for clean-up and reconstruction, which never took place. This tacit pact was broken. Everything was affected. He was caught with his hand in the money bag.

This time he didn't need the private sector because he had his own bank. And at this time, when he no longer needed the private sector for financing because he had created his own bank and his own businesses from the earthquake with only his closest associates, that's when the other capitalists began to resent him. Then began a deterioration in relations between pure Somoza capital and other capitalists. The other capitalists showed timid disagreement. This was only the tip of an iceberg showing above the surface, but the popular sector could take advantage of this surface contradiction. The underlying popular sector wanted a new model of society different from the one then existent rife with malnutrition, illiteracy and poliomyelitis. Contradictions surfaced. The private sector and the popular sector began to come together to oppose Somoza. But the private sector joined this struggle not because they were bothered by the Somocista model of capitalism but because Somoza had broken the rules and now they couldn't continue business as usual. The private sector was not a strong force against Somoza but was able to act in certain situations. Only the FSLN had the capacity to analyze this situation and to use it to their full advantage in the political struggle against Somoza.

Z: How would you describe the economic model of development in Nicaragua today?

RAMÍREZ: Today we have a mixed economy. The structure of the economy is such that 55–60% of the economy is in private enterprise. People's enterprise, the state, has 40–45% of the economy. In the area of agriculture, small private entrepreneurs do 25% of the total business. It's not often recognized that the Sandinista Revolution has aided the growth of small private enterprises, which before almost didn't exist.

This mixed economy is always spoken of as something abstract, but we have the figures to show that the percentage of participation of private enterprise in the internal production of the economy is larger than the public sector. This is not what bothers COSEP [the Supreme Council on Private Enterprise]; it is that the small private enterprise now has a precedence that never existed during the tortured times of Somoza. This sector was also previously a victim.

Those who benefit from the agrarian reform are not only the few small farmers who existed under Somoza but also newly created small ownerships and the cooperative system. All of this has social benefits and raises production for all. This is the base of the economy. This is the theory: to try to share. It's a different model of accumulation: to provide basic necessities for the population and to invest in defense. We understand that if we don't invest in defense the small gains we've made will be for nothing. Defense becomes an obligatory investment. And so it has to be that we have a war economy. We hope this war economy won't be necessary for long, but this is the great cost of aggression. It ought to be added that our economic model tries to ensure independence: to break dependency by diversifying foreign commerce. We don't want to be controlled by one country or a certain group of countries. For example, last year 13% of our exports went to Socialist countries and 18% to the United States. International aid received by Nicaragua last year was $1.8 billion. Twenty-four percent of that came from the Socialist countries and the rest came from the West. It's important to see the accurate measure that the Communist Bloc, or the Soviet Union in particular, supplement the Nicaraguan economy. It's important first because it's important to tell the truth and to erase the negative point of view generated in the U.S. that Nicaragua is totally dependent on Socialist countries. Certainly we maintain natural relations with those countries. However, we receive aid from all of Western Europe and Latin America. The only country that could help us but doesn't is the U.S. In fact, it does the opposite with its blockade and its refusal to maintain its quotas of sugar and beef purchases. But all of the other countries of the world help us including, of course, the Socialist countries.

The external component of a mixed economy is a political pluralism. This means having many external ties and the diversification of foreign commerce and credits. We don't want to be overly dependent on anyone. The Nicaraguan Revolution doesn't accept help, commerce, or loans with political conditions. This is fundamental to the defense of our sovereignty.

Returning to the economic model: we establish investments within the country to supply the basic needs of the population. And we try to invest in goods that produce capital from foreign countries. To accumulate technology and to be independent are our goals. Because right now we depend on the technology of the U.S. or U.S.S.R., or other developed countries in the East or West for machinery. The important thing for us is to produce, accumulate capital and develop.

In 1983, according to a CEPAL report, the economy of Nicaragua was more dynamic than that of the majority of the countries in our region, and more dynamic than in preceding years. In spite of the aggression, internal production increased 5.1%. CEPAL reported a growth in agricultural exports of 2%. In spite of the economic, political and military aggression, and the costs of that aggression, there was an increase in production.

Z: In the U.S. our government has said that the mixed economy in Nicaragua is merely a transitional stage, or propaganda, and not the real goal of this Revolution.

RAMÍREZ: The mixed economy is not propaganda. It's part of the objective conditions that define the reality of Nicaragua today, which calls on all sectors to produce and to raise the standard of living for the whole population. In this mixed economy that part that is private enterprise doesn't exist only to be self-enriching but also with the purpose of serving the general population. The theme is that to have the right to make profits they have the obligation to put part of it at the service of the population. This is a model which leads to socialism. I would call it "Nicaraguan socialism."

Z: Are there guarantees of economic liberty for the private sector?

RAMÍREZ: There exist such guarantees but there also exist real limitations. The primary limitation is the control of foreign currency. Let's say a cotton grower wants to invest his profits in a Mercedes Benz or a trip to Europe. Foreign currency has another destiny now than it did under Somoza. This might cause irritation. Foreign currency goes to production and to development. Private enterprise doesn't manage foreign currency. This is a limitation and it implies a permanent intent to defend salaries (real buy power) by making sure that prices can't fluctuate in a free mark as before. This limits and controls traditional capitalism. Without a doubt there are productive sectors that have understood that primary now are the necessities of the great sectors of the population that were marginalized for years by Somoza and other employers. It's also possible that some private enterprises in this system are gaining much more than in the past.

Z: What's your response to COSEP and others who say that the private sector can no longer operate here and that it's necessary to change the government and the economic model once again?

RAMÍREZ: This is a political, not an economic, point. And it's a lie. More than 50% of production is in the hands of private enterprise. And this private enterprise, what does it do? Does it enrich society for all or does it only gain profits for some? They produce more than 50%. What are they doing, earning money or not? The question would be for them.

Z: What are the most difficult problems facing the Nicaraguan economy?

RAMÍREZ: The most difficult problem is the aggression. The aggression costs hundreds of millions of dollars every year. In 1983, the aggression cost this country $130,000,000. That figure was 31% of all of our exports and 6% of all of our internal consumption. Only the recent mining of our ports had an effect in blockading goods destined for our people that was truly incalculable in dollars. There are other aspects of aggression: the contras interrupt peasant production, disrupt cooperatives, destroy health centers (which is very costly), destroy centers for storing grain (which complicates food supply problems in many regions), and destroy centers of popular education (which has a very large social and economic cost). The contras have killed 135 adult education teachers, which is beyond a dollar value. This aggression has seriously affected our economy. A large number of people have to be involved in defense instead of production. This aggression causes us to invest money, people and scarce resources into defense instead of production.

We are in the crisis of a crisis. International inflation, fed by the rising price of oil, became unmanageable. Inflation set a record of 17% in 1982, but in 1983 rose to 38% here. A measure of our success in dealing with this inflation was that the price of basic necessities rose only 9%. Less basic products rose more and became subject to a black market in such goods. For example, a liter of milk costs seven cordobas to produce, but the consumer buys it for three cordobas because this government is committed to providing milk for its people.

The economy is not 100% satisfactory, but we try to protect the real salary (buying power) of the workers. The aggression affects everything. I would add that we've only had this new government for five years after 50 years of Somocism. We have a young government, which makes mistakes in managing certain things. We lack experience at all levels of government. The people who are working here have never governed before. And five years, in which we've been involved in a war, is not, I believe, enough time to learn everything.

Z: When people have enough to eat they begin to want things like tape recorders, jeans and cameras. How do you meet such demands?

RAMÍREZ: It's a problem but the people have a high level of consciousness about our economic situation. Our government shares the facts with them. For example, we have a program, "Cara al Pueblo" ["Face the People," broadcast on national TV, but filmed each week in a different neighborhood, where Nicaraguans question and confront the highest leaders of their government, who talk to the people, and frankly confront the problems of supply and scarcities. The people understand the problems and support the policies that are necessary in this situation of aggression.

Z: The contras, supported by the U.S. government, are waging war on Nicaragua. And it seems that part of that war is economic just as an economic war was waged in Chile to destroy the government of Salvador Allende.

RAMÍREZ: Clearly the U.S. has chosen to fight on many war fronts. It's made a financial war on Nicaragua in international terms. It has tried to separate us from the European markets, tried to neutralize the Contadora process [the peace efforts of Colombia, Venezuela, Panama and Mexico], taken away its own credits by not buying our sugar, mined our ports, and supports mercenary troops on our northern and southern borders. One of their goals is to strangle the economy and to confuse and discourage the population. But the main problem for this plan is our own knowledge of our history of successive U.S. interventions from William Walker [a Tennessee freebooter who had himself installed as President of Nicaragua and reintroduced slavery in 1854] to Anastasio Somoza [Debayle]. They do all this to destroy us, but they can't succeed, because our people remember and will not allow this to happen again.

Even in Chile, with everything they did, they couldn't have gotten rid of Allende simply by squeezing the economy. Because with every such move the popularity of Allende increased. Allende only fell because the military turned against him. Therefore, our primary fear is not for the economy but of a military invasion. The economic route to our overthrow will not work.

Z: What will Nicaragua face in the future?

RAMÍREZ: The future is sacrifice. There may be a total war. But the U.S. could not win a war that would set all of Central America ablaze. There could be a war against Nicaragua from Honduras, but Honduras couldn't do this without U.S. help, and so such a war would eventually involve the U.S. and the rest of Central America, and the U.S. would be facing a Central American "Vietnam." Certainly, Nicaragua wants to avoid such a war. I think this year will be a year of sacrifices, economic hardships and aggression unless the people in the White House change their policies.

Z: Is there currently an internal war here between the government and COSEP? For example, Ramiro Gurdian told us that his land was confiscated because of his words in a newspaper.

RAMÍREZ: The internal war with COSEP is not economic but political. They want to run the state so that they can profit from an economic model much like the one of Somoza's day, and the state won't permit this. In all of this there is an element of casuistry, or one or another's land has been confiscated for nothing more than talking. But this economic war is being fought with more than just words. Here nobody takes away anything for just talking.

* * *

RAMIRO GURDIAN, 40, is president of UPANIC, the Nicaraguan Union of Agricultural Production, and vice-president of COSEP, the Supreme Council on Private Enterprise. In both positions he speaks authoritatively for the private sector in Nicaragua today.

PHILIP ZWERLING: To begin, would you please tell us a bit of your background?

RAMIRO GURDIAN: I was born in León and studied in Granada in the Jesuit high school there. Then I went to London for a year and a half to learn English. From there I went to the United States to

Ramiro Gurdian, Photo by Philip Zwerling

study economics at Rochester University. I returned to Nicaragua to attend law school. And then I worked for 12 years managing banana plantations in partnership with the Standard Fruit Company. The banana plantation had been purchased by my father in 1950 when it was a cotton plantation. I made it a banana plantation in 1970 and it became the largest banana plantation in Nicaragua. That farm has the capacity of exporting 1% of the total exports of Nicaragua; not 1% of the bananas, but 1% of *all* the exports of the country by dollar value.

During that time, in partnership with Standard Fruit, I was in different positions. In turn, I was in charge of the total budget for all of the farms, I was in charge of all the banana exports, and during the war, on these 16 large farms, I was in charge of payroll for all 4,000 employees. Including these workers on the plantations themselves, we estimate that this partnership with Standard Fruit generated 25,000 jobs in all. We were so successful in protecting the farms during the war that ten days after the Revolution we were able to put the first bananas on ships for export. That was the first export of the Revolution.

During the war I was the guy who represented all of the owners in negotiations with the government and the opposition. UPANIC represents agri-business of cotton, bananas, cattle, sorghum and dairy farmers. COSEP represents and includes the agricultural producers in UPANIC and private enterprises in industry, commerce, banking, etc.

Z: Since the founding of UPANIC in 1974 and COSEP in 1978, I would imagine these private sector representatives would have had internal political divisions depending upon whether or not they supported Somoza?

GURDIAN: Not really. At our convention in 1974 we attacked Somoza. And in 1978, you know, we called three strikes against Somoza. These were not strikes by the workers against business. We paid the workers not to come to work to make a general strike against Somoza. Unfortunately, Somoza was so stubborn that didn't make him quit. We backed the Revolution. And our participation was so strong that in the original "Plan of Government" out of 33 planned seats in the Council of State, COSEP was to have six seats and the Frente Sandinista was to have six seats. They recognized our participation. We helped write the original plan of government before the Triumph and it became the first law of the new government. But these people have totally deviated from the original plan. They increased the number of seats from 33 to 47 and they reserved all of the new seats for themselves [new seats went to mass organizations of women, youth, unions], which gave them an overwhelming majority. Shortly thereafter, the non-Sandinista members walked out, including the COSEP representatives. If they had not deviated from the original plan of government there would be no war today. We would be very happy. There would be no reason for Mr. Reagan to be so hard on Nicaragua. There would be no reason for the contras to exist.

Z: Let's go back a little bit. Could you explain why business people opposed Somoza? Wasn't he good for business?

GURDIAN: Somoza was a dictator. He pushed the law around to get his way. He tried to get along with us, but often he pushed on us too. He repressed people, the labor unions and then he killed Pedro Joaquín Chamorro [editor of the opposition daily *La Prensa*, assassinated January 10, 1978]. To me that was the spark that set off the Revolution. We could not back Somoza.

In a pragmatic sense, Somoza was not bad for business. You could do business if you didn't get involved in politics; if you didn't get involved in any economic activity he liked. But if you were involved in an activity and he got interested in that activity, you were in trouble. But normally he left you alone. That's not the case today.

Z: How are things different today?

GURDIAN: I don't like to compare two evils to decide which is worse. I didn't like Somoza and I don't like the Sandinistas. A dictatorship of the right lets you do business as long as you stay out of politics. But these Marxist-Leninists get involved in every activity of your life. They want to control everything. They want to push you around. I'll give you an example: the draft law. Somoza had an army, he had a war, and he never had a draft law. These people today put on a draft law. And they're so popular, and people are so enthusiastic for them, why do they need a draft law? The problem is that people are not backing these guys.

They want to control every aspect of your life. They don't want you to drive too much so they give you coupons for gasoline. They want to control your food. The first thing they rationed was sugar. But we export sugar. It was not to save sugar, because we have sugar. It was a political decision so they could say if you don't behave, you don't get a card and you don't get a food ration. And they'll try that in the elections. They'll say if you don't vote for the Sandinistas you won't get a card. And then people will say, "Hey, man, that's too much!"

They say rationing is to assure fair distribution of goods. But look who gives out the cards to people: not the government but the CDSs (Committees of Sandinista Defense), which belong to a political party, the Frente Sandinista. What they want is to control everybody. And they are tightening up now for the elections. Through the food they will control people.

I was talking to a parliamentarian from West Germany last week. He said to me: "Ramiro, the balloting is going to be secret, who can know how you vote?" I said to him: "That's true." But each voting box is designed for the ballots of 300 people. What's to stop the head of a CDS in the neighborhood from saying to people: "I don't care how you vote but out of that box better come a Sandinista majority or in this neighborhood you don't eat for the next three months." So you don't have to see every vote. There's no way these are going to be fair elections. A Marxist-Leninist will never play fair in any aspect of life. If they're having elections it's not because they want to, but because international pressure forces them.

Z: If there were a free and fair election, how do you think the Sandinistas would do in the voting?

GURDIAN: Very badly. I don't have any doubts. Three years ago *La Prensa* ran a poll showing that only 30% of the people backed the Sandinistas. Now the situation is worse. Now there's a draft law and people are angry about that. If you ran that poll today the Sandinistas would do even worse than before. Right after that poll came out they passed a law that no one can print public opinion polls. Don't you think that if the Frente Sandinista really thought they were popular they'd be inviting newspapers to run public opinion polls? They know they're very unpopular, so they made polls illegal. Now, in any country in the world where a government has been in power for five years and the economic situation is bad, that government is going to be voted out of power if there are fair elections. Because that's how people express their feelings about a bad situation.

Z: What about the other side? The Sandinistas point to the Literacy

Crusade, increased health care and land redistribution. Aren't there good things they've done?

GURDIAN: Let's go one by one. That Literacy Crusade was good, but I don't believe they accomplished what they claimed. Maybe a peasant can now read "Carlos," but he can't read a book or a newspaper. That's a lie. This lie makes them happy, OK. But it's a lie. The truth is that you cannot teach someone to read in three months and that was the whole length of the campaign. There was no followup. But I always try to give them the benefit of the doubt. We're supposed to have what, now, 88% literacy? I can guarantee you I can take you to the countryside or to the market in town and you're going to find more people than they say who can't read or write.

Health care? They have a program of prevention that's very good. Vaccinations. That's a program that was going on before the Revolution and they've increased it through a U.N. program. It's a successful program. But I cannot tell you that health is better in Nicaragua now than before. That's a big lie. Go to the hospitals and sometimes you cannot operate because you don't have surgical thread, because you don't have blood or the plastic bags to put the blood in. In the drugstores here it's very difficult to find medicines. How can you have better health if you don't have the materials? When you get sick here, forget it, you're in trouble.

Land reform? If ever there was a country that didn't need land reform it was Nicaragua. The problem here is not land but lack of people. We have five million manzanas [1.7 acres] of land in this country and we plant less than one million manzanas. We're talking about good land. We have three million population. Density is 25 people per square kilometer. In El Salvador, by comparison, it's 268 people per square kilometer. There's plenty of land. What do they do? They take land away from people and what happens to that land? Nothing. They took 1.4 million manzanas of land from Somoza and his friends right after the Revolution. But to this day, the Agrarian Reform has only given out 300,000 manzanas of land. They haven't given away all of Somoza's land yet but still they go on confiscating. I'm not against the Agrarian Reform Law. It's a good law. But there are two things I don't like. Sometimes they take land without paying compensation. I'm against that. And the other thing is that decisions of the Agrarian Tribunal cannot be appealed to the Supreme Court. The executive branch decides to take your land and an executive branch organization judges your appeal. The separate judiciary can't get involved. It's the same with these special Anti-Somocista Tribunals; they're part of the executive, not the judiciary. So the two most important things in the country, land and politics, you can't appeal to the Supreme Court. So why have a Supreme Court?"

Z: The government says that more than half the land is still in private hands and that this is a demonstration of the reality of the mixed economy.

GURDIAN: That's not true. The government owns nine million manzanas of land, called "national land." Besides that, they have two million manzanas they've confiscated.

Z: Where do you think this is leading, to a political dictatorship, to a socialist economy?

GURDIAN: That's a very good question. Do you have the answer? They want to push us hard for a Marxist-Leninist regime, but they can't. That's their goal. But they know now they can't do it. I believe their goal now is to install a system like Mexico, where one party, the PRI [the Institutional Revolutionary Party in power since the Mexican Revolution] goes on forever. I believe they would love to do so. But they have a big problem. First, they have lied to everybody and now nobody believes them. And another thing is that the Mexican revolution was for the Mexicans and they never thought about invading Guatemala or helping any groups overthrow El Salvador. Mexico was for the Mexicans. But these people here say everyday that they cannot turn their backs on the international proletariat movement. You will have all the time, "Nicaragua venció, El Salvador vencerá" ["Nicaragua won and El Salvador will win"]. What are they saying in that? If "Nicaragua wins for Marxism-Leninism, El Salvador will too." They're saying they support the guerrillas in El Salvador. Who are these guys to export revolution? I've told Bayardo Arce, Jaime Wheelock [commandantes of the Revolution and members of the FSLN National Directorate] two years ago, the last time I saw these guys, I said: "If we have enough problems in Nicaragua, let's be Nicaraguans and solve those problems." And they told me: "We are first internationalists and second Nicaraguans." Bayardo Arce told me so. And I say, what can I expect from these guys? For what is best for Nicaraguans I can't expect nothing from these guys. So it's very difficult to see what will happen. But I can say that the danger of becoming another Cuba has passed. That danger is gone.

Z: Why are you so convinced that the Sandinistas can't last?

GURDIAN: Because their system can't work. Everything they've tried to push in Nicaragua is a failure. The economic situation is terrible.

Z: Is that because of their policies or because of the U.S. reaction?

GURDIAN: Because of their policies. They've destroyed the economy of this country from the very beginning. They began to take people's land at the very beginning. They scared business people. They killed this guy [pointing to a picture on the wall of Jorge Salazar, killed in November 1980 by state security forces in a shootout when his car was stopped and found to be filled with smuggled arms]. He was the president of COSEP and the leader of the private sector. There was no contra activity then. There was no Mr. Reagan then. There was no excuse for his murder. All the time they're talking about "Peace, peace, peace." That's for outside. But inside the country it's "Hate, hate, hate." "Hate the bishops." "Hate the bourgeoisie." They're always trying to stir up a clash of classes in the country. The only kind of peace they want inside is, "Leave me alone so I can kill everybody inside."

Look at who overthrew Somoza: the independent political parties, the independent labor unions, the private sector, the church and the Frente Sandinista. Today all of the others are against the Frente Sandinista. How can we be all wrong and the Frente Sandinista right? No matter how you look at it, if you're objective you come to the conclusion that the Frente Sandinista cannot survive in this country. Cannot survive. Unless they change. We never say we need to overthrow the Frente Sandinista. We just say, "Hey, follow the original Plan of Government." That's our position. We don't want to go back to the past, to Somoza. They say that we are so blind we want to go back to Somoza. We fought against Somoza. We don't want to go back.

Look at who's fighting. Who are the contras? Adolfo Calero? [Leader of the Nicaraguan Democratic Force (FDN)] He was here until a year and a half ago. Why did he leave? Because the last time he tried to leave the country they wouldn't let him. So he got pissed off and left. He was the political secretary of the Conservative Party. Alfonso Robelo? He resigned the Junta. Why did Doña Violeta [Chamorro] resign the Junta? Why did Arturo Cruz have to go? You can make a long list. Why did Edén Pastora, a Sandinista, leave?

Z: Why are these people working with the former Somocistas, former member of the National Guard today?

GURDIAN: That's another big lie. The Frente Sandinista always projects that for propaganda reasons. Look at the facts. How many

Guardsmen did Somoza have? 10,000? 8,000? Around that. Four thousand are in jail right now. So that leaves 4,000 or 5,000. Let's say half of them got killed in the war. Somebody got killed! They say that 50,000 people died in the war. Of those 50,000, let's assume that 3,000 were National Guardsmen. That leaves just 2,000. And you think that 100% are back with arms? Don't you think that some of them are working or farming or too old now? Let's assume 50%—1,000—are fighting. But how many contras are there? 15,000? 18,000? 10,000? And 1,000 are Guardsmen. They can call them all Somocistas, but they're not. Look at Pastora. First he's a Sandinista, now he's a Somocista?

Z: You've described for us the situation in Nicaragua today as you see it. How do you think the United States should respond to this situation?

GURDIAN: I believe the United States should try to export democracy. But let's be realistic. Mr. Reagan is going to do what he thinks is best for the United States. He's not going to do what Ramiro Gurdian thinks he should do.

Z: But let's suppose for a moment that President Reagan would follow your advice. What would you tell him to do?

GURDIAN: I would love to answer your question if Mr. Reagan listened to me and the Frente Sandinista was not listening to me.

Z: Should the CIA mine the ports? Should the CIA support the contras? Should the U.S. boycott Nicaraguan products? Should we put troops in Central America? Should we support Honduras in a war with Nicaragua? Should we send U.S. troops into Nicaragua? People in the U.S. are arguing these questions right now.

GURDIAN: Unfortunately, if I answer any of those questions in Nicaragua today, I go to jail. They're going to call me unpatriotic. They called me unpatriotic when they confiscated my farm [May 1983] because when the U.S. cancelled their sugar quota I said in the press that they had every right to do that. So, those issues are very difficult. I would like for my government (I don't like those guys, but it's my government even if they're not elected) to stop all of its ties with Russia and Cuba and try to reapproach the West. We are in the U.S. sphere of interest and it's stupid to think we can stand up and fight the U.S. But these guys believe that if the Marines come here everyone's going to fight. I don't think so. The Frente Sandinista believes that attacks against them are attacks against Nicaragua. I don't believe that. I believe that the contra activity is a civil war between Nicaraguans. So how can they say we must defend the country? They mean defend the Frente Sandinista. Because Nicaraguans are doing the fighting on both sides. I say to this government, this war is against the Frente Sandinista, not against Nicaragua, and the people say the same thing.

If the U.S. goes to war, it would be a war against the Frente Sandinista, not against Nicaragua. But if there was a war I couldn't say that. You have to look at history and what happened in Grenada. I would not like something like that to happen here. But we don't want the Frente Sandinista to stay here forever either. I want a civil way out. The best way would be through elections. But that's difficult. The only thing the Frente Sandinista believes in is arms. It's very difficult to fight in a civil way when the only thing your opponent believes in is arms.

6. Educating the People

Carlos Tünnermann
Lucía Casco
Father Fernando Cardenal

CARLOS TÜNNERMANN, 51, has served as minister of education for the five years since the Triumph of the Revolution. Educated in Catholic schools (and today a leading Catholic layperson) and trained originally as a lawyer, Tünnermann reacted to the corruption of the judicial system of the Somoza years by becoming an educator, serving as rector of the School of Law of the Nicaraguan Autonomous University (UNAN), secretary general of the Federation of Central American Universities and president of the Union of Latin American Universities. Holder of a Guggenheim Fellowship, he also served for two years as director of UNESCO programs in Colombia. Shortly after this interview he was appointed ambassador to the United States.

* * *

PHILIP ZWERLING: Would you speak a little bit about the quality of education and the state of the schools under Somoza?

CARLOS TÜNNERMANN: We had a very deplorable situation, not only in the small number of schools, but in their quality as well. The teachers themselves were poorly trained. The educational system was designed to marginalize the great majority of the people and to keep them outside the functioning of society. In the countryside and the rural areas the peasant received little education and rarely completed the primary grades, even first or second grade. These rural schools had untrained teachers, perhaps one teacher for two or three different grades, and no materials. In effect, most peasant children were condemned to no education at all, because if they weren't being taught in the schools, their parents—usually illiterate themselves—certainly had no resources to educate them.

Carlos Tünnermann, Photo by Connie Martin

For these reasons better than half the population of Nicaragua, some 50% of the people, were unable to read or write. This was so widespread that the teachers were often little advanced over the students. Of the primary school teachers, 40% had no training and no education beyond primary school themselves.

The method of teaching had no context within the reality of daily Nicaraguan life and consisted of little more than memorization of facts and figures. School libraries were either poorly stocked or simply nonexistent. Laboratories had old or no equipment. Textbooks were obsolete. The teachers were without training or study plans for teaching their subjects. There were no state preschools, only private preschools that served those who could pay. These preschools existed only in the major cities, and no more than 1,000 children attended throughout the country.

In Somoza's time a child had to be seven years old to enter the public school system. Prior to seven, there were no free educational facilities for these children.

Secondary schools and the universities were concentrated in the major cities as well. Peasant children, without funds or needed by their parents to help in the fields, were unable to leave home to attend school. There was no equal opportunity for these children.

In this way the schools reflected the pyramidal form of the larger social hierarchy, where the wealthy and urban people had access to educational services that others did not.

Even where the schools were "free" the parents still had to make payments to maintain the school buildings and facilities, so even these were private schools in a sense. This was something that we changed within weeks of the Triumph on July 19, 1979. It's a fine thing for parents to contribute to repair a school building or to buy a book for the school library, but this has to be the choice of the parent, and not a requirement of the school administration. So this was made entirely voluntary.

Z: What other changes have been made?

TÜNNERMANN: The state assumed responsibility for a preschool education for every child, and today we have a preschool facility in every neighborhood. This is something that was unthinkable for the countryside, rural areas and poor city neighborhoods, which once had so little. These schools have trained and better-paid teachers than ever before, and they now prepare the young children for a real education. Children begin attending at the age of three. And for even younger children, we have infant centers as well. They are for children from a few months old to three years. We now have 60,000 children enrolled in free, public preschool centers. These are children for whom there was nothing before. These facilities are wholly a creation of the Revolution.

Z: Charges have been made that education has become an ideological weapon under the Sandinistas.

TÜNNERMANN: All education responds to the interests of those in power. All education carries an ideological message. Everything depends on what this message is. In Somoza's time education responded to certain ideological needs. It transmitted the values inherent in a political dictatorship, in an underdeveloped country committed to capitalism and an agricultural economy. Any teacher, even at the university level, was chosen not by standards of competence but by loyalty to a system that stressed individualism at the expense of communitarian values. These ideological needs distorted the teaching of history as well. The very history of Nicaragua was changed. Our anti-imperialist struggles disappeared from the history books. The struggle against William Walker [U.S. "filibuster" who invaded Nicaragua, had himself elected president, and introduced slavery in 1854] disappeared as if it had never happened. Our sense of nationalism was destroyed with the falsification of the history of Sandino, who was presented to school children as a bandit instead of a patriot. And Somoza had himself presented as a man of the people, as a man of peace. History was turned on its head for certain ideological goals.

Even the poor quality of the schools in Nicaragua had not only a financial, but an ideological cause as well. It's said that when Somoza was visiting Costa Rica and being shown their new schools and their literacy program, he responded, "I want oxen, not men in my country," meaning that uneducated people, little more than beasts of burden, were the more malleable material of his dictatorship.

In the past, the peasants had value only insofar as they worked and produced in the fields. This was the definition of who they were as human beings. But the Revolution changed all that by including them in the process of social change. The Revolution said that Nicaragua will not be fully liberated until people are educated. For that reason the Literacy Crusade was the second war of national liberation. This time the enemy was ignorance, also a product of the dictatorship. The goal was to liberate people to be full human beings, conscious people empowered to build their own future. Without a conscious, committed people there could be no Revolution.

The attainment of literacy was not simply the gaining of an academic skill, but the empowerment of a people who became aware of their reality and gained the tools, reading and writing, to affect and determine their future. The Literacy Crusade was not a pedagogical undertaking with political effects; it was a political undertaking with pedagogical effects. It was a political mobilization with political goals. In only two countries in Latin America have such Literacy Crusades been undertaken: in Cuba and in Nicaragua. Such a crusade is only possible as part of a process of political revolution.

The Literacy Crusade was planned prior to the Triumph and put into affect within months of the victory. For six months [March through August 1980] Nicaragua was a single large school. And don't forget that the crusade continues today with special programs and classes for adults. For us, the crusade was also a cultural revolution. Not only did the peasant learn to read and write, but the *brigadistas* (kids from high schools in the cities) learned for the first time about life in the countryside. They learned about peasant life. They learned peasant songs, art, history and customs. They were also educated. We now have recordings of songs, and art work and crafts, all done by peasants, along with recordings of oral histories, all of which are now displayed and used in any study of Nicaraguan culture.

Out of this came a new commitment of Nicaraguans to Nicaraguans. For hundreds of years peasants had been dying of easily preventable or eradicable diseases for lack of medical treatment. In some cases, brigadistas found they could not begin their classes because their students were too ill. The brigadistas shared their medicines with the peasants and called upon their families and leaders to send medicine and doctors. It was easy then to recruit medical brigadistas to follow the literacy brigadistas. The educational or ideological lesson was that Nicaraguans are one people and that those who are healthy, or have money, or live in the cities, have an obligation to stand with their less fortunate brothers and sisters. Teachers and students learned equally during the crusade.

This mutual education has caused some problems too. The peasants were exposed to a different way of life as lived by the brigadistas. They developed a taste for the city consumer products the kids had; for the sugar and eggs the brigadistas took for granted. Now the peasants are becoming educated consumers and want more. These rising expectations are a challenge to the development and resources of the country.

The peasants' taste for education was whetted as well, and now there is a desire for classes and schools and adult education. Right now we have a deficit of 6,000 teachers for all of the classes people want. These expectations are also a creation of the Revolution, which we are now challenged to meet. Because now the people want to learn and advance. Now when one adult completes a primary education he or she then becomes a teacher to the other adults in the neighborhood. In the past it was impossible to conceive of a peasant as a teacher; all of the teachers came from the city. But now peasants are both teachers and students, and this is a revolution in how the peasants see themselves.

Adult classes, in the form of Collectives of Popular Education (CEP), take place in every town and village—morning, noon and night—to fit the work schedules of the people. The CEPs build on the base established by the Literacy Crusade and help the people continue their education. There are now 150,000 adults enrolled in the CEPs. And these are not kids' classes for adults; these are classes designed for adults, touching upon adult concerns in agriculture, agrarian reform, health care and all the other aspects of the Revolution, so that they are integrated into the ideality of Nicaragua today.

Z: What programs are planned for the future?

TÜNNERMANN: We hope to professionalize the level of teaching. The teaching of adults, for example, requires not simply a master of the subject but also a style or approach suited for adult students. So far we have been too deficient in teachers to be able to reach the kind of standards we want for teachers, but this is a goal. We want to keep up with the adults as well. Once they've mastered the basic skills of literacy, or graduated from primary levels of school, we want to make sure there are increasingly higher levels of classes for them—at the high school level, for example. This would mean more teachers trained in more subjects. The door to education at all levels has now been opened to all of the people.

In the future we hope to have every child in school. Perhaps 1,000 children are still outside the school system. But 1.1 million Nicaraguans are enrolled in some form of educational program today. That's one in every three.

We are forming more teachers colleges to train teachers for the future. We have nine more today than we had in 1979, when we had only five; now we have 14, located in all the different regions of the country. We are developing technical schools for agriculture and industry to train needed personnel in these fields. All of this aids the economic development of the country.

Z: What's the role of private schools today?

TÜNNERMANN: This year we began for the first time the distribution of notebooks and pencils free to all of the children in primary schools, both public and private. The Revolution has kept private schools and supplies aid to them. The public schools are still attended by 35% of the children today. Most of these private schools are religious schools but, as we say, between Christianity and the Revolution there is no contradiction. When we have congregations that offer private schooling to the children, including children of the poor, then our ministry offers aid to pay the teachers and buy the books, even though the private administration hires the teachers and chooses the books. If the school teaches the approved curriculum, they are then free to teach whatever religious subjects they choose, and the state will pay for everything. So, in reality, the parents are free to choose the education they want for their children.

Z: But what happens when there are conflicts between the church and the state over the schools, as happened recently at the school of the LaSalle Fathers?

TÜNNERMANN: This conflict arose after a new director of the school was appointed and he tried to force out teachers there who had already been approved by this ministry. This new director sought to develop a center of opposition to the Revolution at the school. As long as a private school covers the minimum standard curriculum we don't care whatever else they chose to teach in addition to this. But this new director wouldn't allow information about the Militia Service. This was part of the curriculum for every school. Militia Service is a law of the land. So we had to insist that this be included. After we discussed it with the school administration these problems were resolved.

Z: President Reagan tells the North American people that Nicaragua today is a totalitarian Marxist state. Yet you are a well-known Catholic layperson here. How would you respond to these idealogical charges?

TÜNNERMANN: These charges are made from a political motive to attack the Revolution. They have no reality in truth. How else could you explain the free operation of religious schools here? For example, the Christian Brothers run a school in Barrio Fuentes, a very marginal barrio with many poor people. They could only accept a certain number of students and only offered classes in the mornings. We gave them more money to enable them to offer two sessions each day, morning and afternoon. So twice as many students could attend. This school used to be only for the rich, but with a state subsidy poor children are now accepted as well, and taught in the same building by the same teachers. Three hundred more students now go to that school. There's no way that you could call what these children receive in these religious schools a "Marxist education." If the aim here was a Marxist education, I don't think I would have been chosen to head this ministry for the last five years.

Z: How do you understand the role of your religious faith in your work here?

TÜNNERMANN: This work in education is totally compatible with the Gospel. What could be more Christian in intent and practice than the Literacy Crusade, which was an immense act of love. It involved thousands of Christian students from the religious schools who volunteered to teach their illiterate brothers and sisters. This was a mobilization of the whole nation without distinction. And the goals of the Revolution in the crusade: to teach people to read and write, and to empower them to be creators of their own world, are goals of the Gospel as well. In this work Christians lived out their faith. Christianity understands an obligation to the poor. And in this, Christian principles are part of the Revolution.

Z: Please tell us a little about your role in the struggle against the dictatorship.

TÜNNERMANN: I was only a lawyer very briefly. In 1956, when [Anastasio] Somoza García was executed by the patriot Rigoberto López, I volunteered to defend Tomás Borge, who was arrested at that time. Other lawyers, out of fear, stayed away from these cases. The trial was before a military court. Somoza's sons (Luis and Anastasio II) reacted violently to the death of their father. Many hundreds of people were in prison, tortured or killed. They were taking their vengeance. The trial was held in a Guardia barracks. To be charged was the same as being convicted because the Somoza sons pulled all the strings. Comandante Borge was convicted although he had done nothing. It became clear to me that a lawyer could not expect justice under the dictatorship or have any faith in its legal system. So I returned to the university and a career in education.

At the university, as a professor and later as rector, we struggled to preserve the integrity and autonomy of the university as a center of learning and critical thought. In reality, the university and the paper *La Prensa* were the only consistent critics of Somoza that were able to survive.

I studied in Washington on a Guggenheim Fellowship and wrote a book on the universities in Latin America. Later, I directed UNESCO programs in Colombia. I was in Washington and Colombia when I developed contacts with Miguel D'Escoto [a Maryknoll priest who is now Nicaragua's foreign minister] and Sergio Ramírez [member of the three-member National Junta], and we put together an opposition group of prominent Nicaraguans to speak against Somoza at home and abroad. (This became known as the Group of 12) This group returned to Nicaragua in July 1978 to massive demonstrations by over 100,000 Nicaraguans. Only this support protected us from Somoza's wrath. Once in Managua, we traveled to Masaya even though the Guardia tried to stop us. But so many thousands of people came with us that we made it to Monimbo [an indigenous barrio of Masaya renowned for its opposition to Somoza] as a symbol of the kind of opposition Somoza would face in the entire country. It was very dangerous because it looked so bad for Somoza to see this outpouring of opposition. From Masaya we traveled to Estelí, León and Jinotega. When fighting broke out again we had to flee the country or seek asylum in the embassies. Our group got together again, first in Mexico and later in Costa Rica, to form a government in exile. After the Triumph I returned and began work here as the minister of education.

When I first entered this particular office on the day after the Triumph there was an enormous life-size photo of Somoza on that wall because the previous minister was the wife of one of Somoza's military leaders. I called the vice minister in, and the first thing we did was to throw that portrait out the window over there. Thousands of people were out demonstrating and destroying remnants of the dictatorship. It was a great celebration!

* * *

The small country town of Yalaguina is in an area classified as a "war zone." In the Department of Madriz, it is 220 kilometers north of Managua and just 20 kilometers from the Honduran border.

Here, at Coronel [Colonel] Santos López Elementary School, we visited with 34-year-old teacher LUCÍA CASCO. She has 36 students in her fourth-grade class.

* * *

LUCÍA CASCO: I have been a teacher for 10 years and I've been working at this school for four years. The school is about 10 years old, and since the Revolution many classrooms and a preschool have been added. We have 230 students in all. This is a very poor area. The students' parents are peasants and the children attend school from 8 a.m. to 12:45 p.m. each day and then go home to work in the fields or in their houses.

During the Literacy Crusade of 1980 I was a technical worker there. Before the crusade 90% of the adults were illiterate. Today it might be 20%. There are Centers of Popular Education (CEPs) for adults. The majority of people here are poor peasants who have to work during the day. So these classes are at night for them.

The people here are farmers and quite poor. They grow vegetables, corn and beans. What they grow goes to feed themselves.

The school uniforms in our country are white and blue but not many children here can afford them. Some of the children are so poor that they come to school barefoot. In past years we had very few materials, but now the government buys one notebook and one pencil for every child. Materials for the classroom are still difficult to find. The parents help us by contributing days of work to construction of classrooms or as aides in the classroom.

Our school is in a war zone and this has been very hard. Last week we had to close the school and hold classes in people's homes. The school buildings had to be used to shelter people from the community of San Ramón, which is in a valley near here. The contras passed through San Ramón at 6:30 in the morning and began killing people. They killed three people. They killed two peasants, one of whom left nine children and the other eight children. And they killed a teacher who had two young children. The people of San Ramón fled in terror and many are now in Somoto, afraid to return to their homes. In this area the contras always pass. Teachers are their favorite victims because the teachers support the Revolution, serve in the militia and the CDS, and are leaders in the community.

Lucía Casco, Photo by Philip Zwerling

Of course, this affects the children. We have guards and everyone is armed. In the front yard of the school we have a large trench dug into the earth to use as a shelter if the school is attacked. The children have to live with these fears. We expect our children to be the forgers of the new society. In the future the children will not suffer. With the Revolution they will walk forward, and they will not walk barefoot as in the past.

I have my home here and my husband and three-year-old daughter. We are required to live where we teach—not to work in one place and live in another—but to be part of the community. We try to immerse ourselves in the lives of the people so that we can teach more fully.

* * *

FERNANDO CARDENAL, 50, is a Jesuit priest whose three major roles in the revolutionary government have involved him with young people and education. Two weeks after the Triumph, he was named national coordinator of the Literacy Crusade. In the fall of 1980, he was named vice-coordinator of Sandinista Youth movement and served in that post for four years. In February 1984, he was named national vice-coordinator of the Sandinista Defense Committees (CDSs). In July 1984 he was appointed minister of education to replace Dr. Tünnermann. Resisting Vatican demands to leave the government, he was expelled from the Society of Jesus in December. However, he continues as a priest and government minister.

PHILIP ZWERLING: Would you please explain how a Nicaraguan Jesuit priest came to identify his life's work with the poor of Latin America?

FATHER FERNANDO CARDENAL: I believe my training and preparation for the priesthood were the same as for Jesuits all around the world. I attended a Jesuit college, the University of Central America here in Managua, and received a classical education. I entered my novitiate in 1952, studying Catholic doctrine in Ecuador and philosophy in Mexico. After 17 years of study I was ordained a priest. My most important education, however, came in 1969, in my last year of training, when I served for a year in Medellín, Colombia.

Certainly I had studied the "social problem," the problem of the poor mass of people in Latin America, in an intellectual way. But these problems of the poor, the majority of the populations in Colombia, Mexico, Ecuador and Nicaragua, were made manifest and real in my work in a poor barrio in Medellín. In my contact with these poor people, victims of oppression and exploitation who were yet alive and vital, I was changed in a profound way. And I decided that my life and my priesthood lay in working with and for the poor.

Z: And you returned to Nicaragua and began your priestly vocation under the Somoza dictatorship?

CARDENAL: I returned to Nicaragua in 1970 and began working for a revolution because it was clear that here such a revolution was the only hope for the poor. I had seen in Colombia that we could help the people, we could serve some of their material and spiritual needs. But I also saw that this aid was limited by the system of oppression under which they lived. And I understood that it was this system that had to be changed. Charity could help a few, but the system always produced new victims and only a revolution could change that.

Now I must say that this realization came to me gradually and I went through a process of developing a revolutionary consciousness. What I had seen in Colombia opened my eyes and what I saw in Nicaragua continued this internal process for me. For example, I was a great admirer of Mahatma Gandhi and Martin Luther King and my orientation was for nonviolent action for social change. I participated in actions like a hunger strike, protesting conditions of FSLN prisoners who were being tortured, public demonstrations and church sit-ins. This was a nonviolent movement.

Very early after my return to Nicaragua I was appointed vice-rector of the Central American University. The administration of the college simply wanted things to run without problems, but I became a problem. The students initiated a strike with the participation of some of the professors. Their demands seemed reasonable. The day the students took over the university there was a large meeting of the students. Student leaders spoke. And then the students asked me to speak as vice-rector. I was taken by surprise, but when I spoke I had to say that their demands seemed just. For that I was dismissed as vice-rector of the university.

Father Fernando Cardenal, Photo by Boyd

But the time came when we realized that there was no other choice but armed struggle. And, in 1973, I began work directly with the FSLN. This work was both clandestine and public and involved the risk of arrest and torture.

In 1977, Comandante Daniel Ortega asked me to become part of the "Group of 12" [12 prominent Nicaraguans in exile who worked with the FSLN in opposition to Somoza]. This was a year after I had gone to Washington, D.C., to testify before a Congressional committee against U.S. aid to the Somoza dictatorship. I went as a priest and as a founder of the Nicaraguan Commission on Human Rights.

This was very important to us as an opportunity to present the truth to the world. In the time of [Augusto César] Sandino, Somoza [García] had been able to present Sandino as a bandit and the Guardia as the protectors of order. But now I was able to go, as a Sandinista, to testify that Somoza was a bandit and that the Guardia were terrorizing Nicaragua. My testimony was very strong and I named 25 officers of the Guardia by name who were known to be torturers and murderers. I named them, general by general, as the assassins they were. The Guardia was furious. But I was too public for them to kill me then. So Somoza forbade me to leave the country after my return. To join the Group of 12 in 1977 I had to leave Nicaragua clandestinely and cross over the mountains to Costa Rica. And I wasn't able to return until the insurrection in 1978.

Z: And after the Triumph your first assignment was as director of the Literacy Crusade?

CARDENAL: Yes. I was in charge of putting together all of the staff for this, all of the preparation and then the crusade itself. The crusade began as a name only and we had to build everything from scratch. This took a whole year of my life.

Z: In the past I've read that you referred to this Literacy Crusade as a revolution of love. How is that so?

CARDENAL: Every act of education is an act of love, because it involves an intimate relationship between two people, teacher and student, in giving and receiving. And the Literacy Crusade was an act of love on a national scale because all of the people were involved. There were 100,000 volunteer teachers and 500,000 students. During those first five months Nicaragua was a single huge school, with part teaching and the other part learning. And illiteracy was reduced from 50.2% of the population in the time of Somoza to 12% at the completion of the first stage of the Crusade. Since then adult education classes have continued to lower the illiteracy rate.

It must be remembered that literacy, the ability to read and write, is not simply a collection of academic skills. Literacy is what separates human beings from the beasts of the field and empowers them not only to understand but also to change the world around them. Literacy makes people participate in their Revolution and the building of a new society.

Z: I understand that historically literacy has always been a concern of Nicaraguan revolutionaries like Sandino and Carlos Fonseca.

CARDENAL: In the time of Sandino [1927–33], even when he was fighting the U.S. Marines, his army had a Department of Education. He made sure all of his generals learned to read, and when recruits joined his army they were taught to read before they learned to handle weapons. He said, "First, teach them to read."

And Carlos Fonseca [a founder of the FSLN, killed fighting

Somoza in 1977] always instructed his guerrillas to teach the ants to read. So we have been completing this desire of Carlos Fonseca in a revolution he did not live to see triumphant. We never forgot this history of Sandino and Fonseca and within weeks of the Triumph we began to complete this mission with the national Literacy Crusade.

Z: In all of these various tasks you have undertaken and government posts you have held, how have you understood your role as a Roman Catholic priest?

CARDENAL: In revolutions like the one in Nicaragua the word "politics" recaptures its primordial meaning. As Aristotle said, "Politics means taking care of the common good of all the citizens." In a revolution this action is born from a great act of love, like the Revolution itself, and I, as a priest, am obliged to live out, in the real world, the primacy of love. In my whole life, nothing but the Revolution has given me the opportunity to live out this love. The literacy campaign was based on love. It was a revolution which never killed anyone.

The Revolution coincides exactly with the Gospel. The heart of the New Testament is the message of Jesus in Matthew, Chapter 25, where we are instructed to feed the hungry, clothe the naked, shelter the homeless and comfort the prisoners. This has been the work of this Revolution which has transformed life for the poor people, the hungry, naked and the homeless of this country. Because I have been working for the poor there has been no divorce between my priestly and revolutionary work.

Z: The Catholic hierarchy has forced other priests to leave their government posts. Father Drinan, a Jesuit like yourself, was forced in my own country to resign as a congressman from the state of Massachusetts. How has your situation been different?

CARDENAL: The Pope states a general doctrine, but circumstances vary in every case. The Gospel cannot be lived apart from a real time and a real space. I know Father Drinan and I have visited him in Washington. Drinan withdrew from politics because in normal times a priest should not be in politics, but in Nicaragua these are not normal times.

In 1972, when the great earthquake leveled the city of Managua, I drove a truck to the Jesuit farm, loaded it with vegetables and then drove through the city taking food to people who were still trapped inside of the buildings; people who had lost everything they owned. Now, in normal times, it is not a priest's job to drive a truck, but in that time it was my priestly function to drive a truck and not to stay behind in a church praying because that would have been a betrayal of the Gospel.

In the United States there are thousands of people just as prepared, or better prepared, than Father Drinan to serve in the government. In Nicaragua our society was so underdeveloped that we did not have people of adequate preparation. My 17 years of Jesuit education made me one of the few who were prepared to serve in a government.

Another great difference is that in the United States politicians and government officials receive a handsome salary. Here we are paid so little that it is a financial sacrifice to most of us to serve in this government. There is no material advantage to service here. I have seen the large and well-furnished offices of congresspeople in the United States. You can see my office here in contrast. [It is small and sparsely appointed.] Another difference is that the work here is dangerous. We don't know what might happen to us from day to day, with the contras and the CIA. Here any day could bring us a bullet in the head. Our work here is great and tiring, but we are content with it because we know how much we are needed.

Z: It's a strange thing to say that in a supposedly "Marxist-Leninist revolutionary regime," according to President Reagan, a Catholic priest should be put in charge of the youth organization. How do you answer these charges after four years of serving as vice-coordinator of the Sandinista Youth?

CARDENAL: What do names mean? It's a mistake to call this a Marxist-Leninist revolution. If you had to choose a name it would be the name Sandinista. Because this is a revolution in the tradition of Sandino, a nationalistic, anti-imperialist revolution. Here we have a mixed economy. Sixty percent of the economy is in private hands. In Bolivia, the government has taken 70% of the economy and no one calls Bolivia "communist."

Here we have 10 political parties. Here we have the participation of Christians in the Revolution. They are a concrete sign that this is not a Communist revolution. This is a revolution which puts its children, the future of the Revolution, in the charge of a priest. "Sandinista" is the only label that can be applied to this Revolution.

They accuse the Sandinistas of indoctrinating the youth. But what do we teach them? Sandinism, which is love of national sovereignty and independence. This is the dignity of Nicaragua. In the poor countries the people need to know, and need to be proud of their history and their heroes. To learn about Sandino and to learn the truth about Somoza is to learn the reality of your country. So many poor countries allow their people no dignity at all. Like Honduras. There is a country that exists only at the service of the United States. The people have no history or country to be proud of.

Sandino cried, literally cried, over the way the United States dealt with Nicaragua, over the way Moncada, Sacasa and Somoza sold this country to the United States. The message of Sandinism is a message of pride and independence. This is a revolution made by Nicaraguans for Nicaraguans. It's absurd to speak of Cuban influence here or Soviet influence here. Certainly we accept help from any country, but we didn't make this Revolution to surrender our independence to anyone ever again.

It's stupid to call this a Marxist-Leninist revolution as the government and media do in the United States. It's a Sandinista Revolution. Every country has its own history and makes its own unique revolution. Ours is different from any other. You've read the report of the Kissinger Commission? It's a joke! Kissinger spent eight hours in Nicaragua! Suppose I went to the United States for eight hours? Would I understand your revolution or your society in that time? Kissinger comes for eight hours and meets with the industrialists, with *La Prensa*, the newspaper of the bourgeoisie, and with [Managua's conservative archbishop] Monsignor Obando y Bravo, and then he writes a report without speaking to the poor people in the barrios, in the countryside and in the factories, who are the people who made this Revolution.

In 1978 I was invited to Mexico to a political celebration. At the airport in Mexico City we guests were met by air-conditioned limousines and taken to a beautiful air-conditioned hotel. Cars took us to the theater, to meetings and back to our hotel. Could any of us think we had seen or understood Mexico? For in Mexico we never saw the poor barrios of the city or the poor peasants of the countryside who never experience air-conditioning. I had lived in Mexico years before, as a student, and I knew we were not seeing the real face of Mexico on this short trip. You can only understand a country by learning its history and by encountering its people. And the government of the United States has never understood the Nicaraguan people.

Z: Last month you were chosen vice-coordinator of the national organization of Sandinista Defense Committees. In the United States, the CDSs are presented as sinister organizations spying on ordinary citizens. How do the CDSs function?

CARDENAL: Well, it seems our enemy has a different mentality, an odd imagination, to think this way. The CDSs, organized in every barrio in every town in Nicaragua, are concerned with the health of every neighborhood. They help carry out vaccinations and clean up litter. They take responsibility for the neighborhood parks. They help to distribute food. They help construct schools in the neighborhood. And they help combat delinquency in the neighborhoods. The CDSs are simply the people organized. A small, poor country like ours needs the hands of all of its people to raise itself up and to develop itself.

This small country faces the very real threat of North American attack. Our airport has been bombed. Our ports have been shelled. Our harbors have been mined. Armed bands attack across our borders. Defense has to be our first priority. And the CDSs function for defense and vigilance. And because of them, in spite of all of these attacks, no Fifth Column has organized and no attacks have occurred behind the lines. The people protect their own neighborhoods.

Nicaragua is a people in arms. Everyone has a gun. This should be a paradise for delinquents and criminals because it's so easy to get a weapon. And this is a country which used to have a delinquency rate of 40%. But because of this organized revolutionary vigilance such crime has almost disappeared. Now some 200,000 Nicaraguans are active in neighborhood vigilance committees, but it's a caricature to present these CDSs by emphasizing only the aspect of defense. They have simply organized communities so that people can work together to improve their own neighborhoods. The CDSs are the people and no other organization combines people of each sex, different ages, different professions, in a single organization for the betterment of the whole community.

Z: Let's speak of the future. How do you see the future for the Catholic Church, for Nicaragua and for yourself?

CARDENAL: In Nicaragua today there is one church, not two, and it is with the Revolution. Some of the bishops are in opposition, but they are living in the past when the Church stood on the side of the oppressors. This type of church has no future at all. The future is with fealty to Jesus, with the humble and the poor, not with great churches, but with great service to people. The church of the poor and of Jesus has a future. It's a caricature to speak of this as a Popular Church. We are simply Christians with a faithfulness to Christ and the poor. This is the church of the future because it is the real church of Jesus. The Church hierarchy has always stood with the powerful. In Nicaragua in the past they have sided with the King of Spain and the U.S. industrialists, each in turn. Now they side with King Reagan.

In Nicaragua in the future we will see the complete transformation of society for dignity, development, independence, peace and love. All of this costs much: lives, blood and money. We want to be able to make all of these changes in five or 10 years. This is a weak country. Our economy is very weak. For example, all of our petroleum must be imported and this puts us at the mercy of other countries. It will be the work of 20 years and more to transform Nicaragua.

We can only hope that your powerful government will leave us alone to develop our country. I believe that our cause will succeed. We may not construct a biblical land of milk and honey, but the cause of justice will succeed. Because the cause of justice is the work of history. The idea of liberation is growing throughout Latin America. The United States holds Central America in its grip but this subjugation cannot stand against the force of history. We are in a process favored by history. We stand in a line of liberation extending around the world. The same line of liberation that saw the end of colonialism in Africa. We are in a process of revolution and liberation, and I hope and believe that Nicaragua will develop and will live with love, dignity and justice.

I share my own future with my country's future. I could be killed as others have been killed. I have contributed 30 years of work. There are many possibilities for me. But what is sure is that the cause of the people goes forward. That is the only thing that's important. Death is the end of life, but it's not failure, because the cause continues."

7. Rebuilding the Country

Samuel Santos

Forty-five years of Somoza dictatorship, numerous earthquakes, and the insurrections of 1978 and 1979 that left 50,000 dead have made Nicaragua a plundered and underdeveloped but potentially rich land.

Since July 1979, the new government has been struggling to develop agriculture, industry, social services, and the infrastructure of roads and telecommunications—all in the face of escalating covert military action directed by the United States.

This legacy of underdevelopment, of high hopes for the future now threatened by a growing war, can be clearly seen in the capital city of Managua, home to one quarter of Nicaragua's population of 2.9 million.

In this interview, SAMUEL SANTOS, the 44-year-old mayor of Managua, discusses the task of national reconstruction:

* * *

SAMUEL SANTOS: You cannot call me the mayor of Managua, both because I was not elected—I was appointed by the national government junta—and because my job is different from the usual tasks of a mayor. I share those usual tasks of governing a city, but have the additional job of reconstruction of the capital. Therefore, my real title of minister of the Junta of Reconstruction for Managua is quite accurate.

To understand where we are now and the situation that confronts us, it is necessary to look at the history of Managua. Managua was founded on the shores of Lake Managua in 1856 and was designated the capital of the country in 1872. Up until that time there had been two capitals: León, home of the Liberal party, and Granada, home of the Conservatives. When the Liberals were in power, León was the capital; when the Conservatives ruled, Granada. But in 1872, to put an end to this feuding, Managua, then smaller than either León or Granada, became the official capital.

In 1885, the first recorded earthquake struck Managua. In 1931, there was another devastating quake, and in 1972, the third earthquake. The dates of these earthquakes are significant because in 1931 U.S. Marines were here, having come in 1927 to fight against the independence movement of General Augusto Sandino. The Marines stayed until 1933.

Samuel Santos, Photo by Connie Martin

With the marines in charge they decided that the only way to avoid a plague following the quake was to burn the city, and so Managua was completely destroyed and reconstruction begun. However, this reconstruction took place under the shadow of Somoza. Anastasio Somoza [García] was made the first Nicaraguan commander of the National Guard, which was founded, trained, and armed by the U.S. in 1927. In 1933, the Marines left Nicaragua and, in February 1934, Somoza had General Sandino assassinated as he left the Presidential Palace, where he had come to discuss a truce under promises of safe conduct. Two years later, Somoza staged a coup and used the National Guard to make himself president of Nicaragua.

The first Somoza [Anastasio García] was executed by the patriot Rigoberto López in 1956 and he was succeeded first by his son Luis, and then by his second son, Anastasio [Debayle], who was overthrown by the Triumph of the Revolution, July 19, 1979. The Somoza dynasty ruled for 45 years.

The third earthquake destroyed 70% of the city. Ten thousand people were killed. Again, reconstruction took place under the shadow of a Somoza. Millions of dollars of international aid came into the country after the earthquake, but 99% of all this aid was stolen by Somoza.

So, see what happened to the city over those 40 years? First, Somoza turned Lake Managua into a garbage dump. This large lake had given birth to the city on its shores. It gave food, in the form of fish, it was a means of transportation and communication, and it was a center of recreation. But Somoza made it a dump for the city's garbage. Because it was cheap, all of the city's sewage was directed into the lake. And industry was attracted here to use the lake as well. Penn-Walt, which had to move its factory from Pennsylvania because of environmental regulations, built an auto battery factory on the shores of the lake and dumped mercury wastes into the water. This is how Somoza attracted development to Nicaragua while enriching himself. His family became the richest in the country and he held an interest in almost every company. Outside of the city his family owned 20% of the arable land in the country. Here in Managua the level of contamination in the lake rose, it was like an open garbage pit and the people began moving away from the shores of the lake.

When the third earthquake struck, in December of 1972, Somoza had a large wall built around the central part of the city that had been destroyed. People were not allowed to return to that area, and the National Guard was turned loose and stole everything. They stole personal belongings left in the houses and they stole any building materials that could be used again.

And with the center of the city walled off, people had to go to other cities to live: to Masaya, Granada and León. But although the people moved, their workplaces remained in Managua. They had to travel back to the capital to work. The traffic back and forth was incredible. The highways were inadequate and the system of transportation unprepared for these numbers. And, so what would have been a trip to commute to work of 30 or 40 minutes became a trip of three hours, and people were spending six hours a day to commute to and from work. This was an impossible situation. The people wanted to return to Managua, to live on their land. But the center of the city had been destroyed and had not been cleared or rebuilt. The international aid for this purpose had all been diverted to Somoza's pockets.

Land for the people had to be found on the outskirts of Managua. There the land was owned by Somoza, his family and his friends. There was a gigantic exploitation of this land without any law or control to protect the people. Somoza grew rich again selling the land at exorbitant prices. The population of the capital was dispersed into little settlements all around the outskirts in areas like OPEN 3 [Operación Permanente Emergencia Nacional 3; Permanent National Emergency Operation 3], which became Cuidad Sandino after the Triumph. These were like little nuclei settlements all around a city which no longer had a center. This is the demographic situation we have today.

In these outlying new barrios there was no safe drinking water, there was no sewage system, and there was no electricity. Again the people were exploited. Because drinking water was so distant, entrepreneurs would buy or rent trucks, fill them with water and make the rounds of these barrios selling the water at exorbitant prices. There were no government controls on these capitalists and there were no plans to develop city services in these new centers of population.

So, at the Triumph of the Revolution we found a city in Managua that was completely dehumanized. In 1979, 60% of the neighborhoods were without drinking water, 60% of the neighborhoods lacked sewage facilities, and 60% were without electricity.

One of the few public works projects Somoza had done was to construct vehicular bypasses—like short freeways to connect different parts of the city. But he adapted these from North American models. This was how he thought. He built these bypasses without sidewalks, because he built them thinking only of the dominant class who had cars, and not about the people who had to walk. So we inherited a city without sidewalks.

Given this history, our central task after the Triumph was to humanize Managua and to make it livable. This has been the work of reconstruction. Today we can say that there is drinking water in every barrio. There is a sewage system, or latrines, now in every barrio. There is electricity now in every neighborhood. First we put electricity or running water into a barrio—in the centers—and then we work to bring them to each house. And every time we build a new street or road, we build a sidewalk. Now we have planned bus routes so that there is an access route for transportation to every barrio.

Before, in Managua there was not a single center of recreation for the people. In the past four years we have built parks, like Caranyo Park and Velásquez Park, where before there was only a desert. We have developed public beaches for the people on the ocean (Pacific) at Pochomil and at Laguna Xiloa outside the city. In the center of the city we have a beautiful lake, Laguna Tiscapa. In the past this was entirely closed to the public and it was used only by the Guardia and their women, who washed their clothes there. Today, we have built two restaurants and an amphitheater for cultural events, and everyone in the city can walk or take a bus there to go swimming.

We have a great campaign today to plant fruit and shade trees in public places and in all of the neighborhoods—with all of the population participating. We have great plans to clean up Lake Managua and we've had expert help from all over the world for this. Various plans have been proposed, but the costs are between $500,000 and one billion dollars, which is simply beyond our means. We are looking at various plans for canals and also at filtration plans. We've stopped all dumping of sewage and factory wastes into the lake. We hope to reintroduce fish for recreation and food, and to surround the lake with green parks and access roads so that people might come to the lake to walk, swim, fish and go boating.

We now have 400 buses serving the city, but we need 800 more for good transportation. But now we have an integrated plan, so that when we build, we build roads, sewage, water pipes and electrical wires together. And we have an integrated development plan for the entire country. Before, whatever development there was was only in the cities, and the countryside was totally ignored. But now both go hand in hand. This means Managua gets a bit less in resources, but developing the countryside prevents a problem of urbanization where people leave their farms and go to live in the cities and overwhelm the resources of the urban areas.

The population of Managua today is 750,000. In our development plans, we discovered that we needed everything. We had to start a complete system of public telephones from scratch. In Somoza's time there were eight public telephones in this city. Isn't that incredible! But, of course, he and his friends and supporters had private phones, so there was no need for public phones. Today we are trying to make public phones available in every neighborhood.

But, as with every project, the economic blockade works against us. The telephone parts, switching stations and the main plant were all to have been purchased from a company in West Germany. Their government loaned us money to buy this equipment, but now they say they can't loan us more and so we have had to stop installing new telephones.

In all of our work and plans for reconstruction it's clear that the attacks of imperialism, the covert war financed by the United States, have their impact. Today so many resources have to go to defense simply to defend the country when all of those resources should be going toward reconstruction. We don't have enough iron or steel for construction. We don't have enough plywood or cement. We don't have enough people power for our projects. In Somoza's time unemployment in Managua was 28%, but now we lack construction workers. The tractors and the trucks we need have to be diverted to the war zones for defense and these are all resources we need here. Trained engineers and workers have to take up guns to defend the country.

There haven't been any contra attacks in Managua except for those planes that dropped bombs out at the airport. And it would be difficult for the contras here because of the high level of popular participation in the vigilance committees [Sandinista Defense Committees]. Today people guard their neighborhoods and workplaces and parks because they know and feel that these belong to them. For example, right downtown, along one of the earthquake faults where there was nothing but rubble, we built a park. Because it was on a fault we built open spaces and no buildings—for both recreation and safety. We built fountains, basketball courts and flower beds. We named the park as a memorial to Luis Alfonso Velásquez.

Luis Velásquez was a street kid. He sold fruit to people on the street. He lived on the street. But he opposed the dictatorship. He organized other street kids in demonstrations against Somoza: to carry messages for the guerrillas to aid the insurrection. In time, the Guardia placed a price on his head and sent hired killers to find him. They assassinated him in April 1979. He was nine years old. This park was opened on the first anniversary of his death in 1980. This is both a park and a memorial to the history of a struggle for independence and freedom. People do not forget.

As a mayor, I see the city and often it seems dirty to me. Not so dirty as in the past, when there was garbage everywhere, but it doesn't seem clean. But other mayors come here from other countries, like the mayor of Amsterdam [Netherlands], whose city council voted to become our sister city, and they tell me how clean the city seems to them compared to their own. I can only think the difference is that here the people try to keep the city clean because now they know it is their city.

As minister of Managua I have traveled all over the world to visit other cities and to attend conferences. Last year, I went to Puerto Rico to attend a conference of Latin American mayors. And there I met New York City's Mayor Ed Koch, who was present representing President Reagan. We were sitting at breakfast one morning, many Latin American mayors around a large table, when Mayor Koch joined us for the first time. He sat down and almost immediately began talking to me about the Revolution in Nicaragua. It became a debate between the two of us. At first the other mayors seemed to be on his side and would say things in support of Reagan's policies. But Koch's attitude, with his talk of U.S. rights in Central America and U.S. perogatives there, was the attitude of a modern-day conquistador [conquerer]. I spoke about our Revolution and our independence and I could see the change in the other mayors and their pride in this Latin country. When Koch rose to leave, I was the only other mayor who rose in respect to shake his hand.

National independence is what we struggled for all of those years. My grandfather was a general in Somoza's National Guard, and my father was jailed many times for opposing the dictatorship. He was a lawyer in León and active in politics there. His death was caused by the Guardia. Following the assassination of the first Somoza in 1956, all opponents were rounded up and jailed, including my father. Although he was ill they kept him in jail without any medical attention. When they released him, he died of cancer a few months later. That was in December 1959, and when he died I was in jail for being part of a student opposition movement. When my father died, my mother took our family to the U.S., to safety. She remained in exile for 20 years, until the Triumph.

But I was in Los Angeles with the family for only six months when I had to leave. It didn't seem like any kind of a life to me to work only to earn money to buy things. It had no meaning for me, and in 1960 I returned to work in Nicaragua. I had all kinds of jobs here in order to eat. I was a waiter, a factory worker, an office worker, a land salesman, a press agent, a student and then a professor of economics at the Central American University. And I was involved in opposition politics, in strikes and demonstrations.

At first I simply wanted a change of government, an end to corruption and the dictatorship. Most of us had no sense of the kind of new government we wanted. That ideology developed for us over 20 years. And while I led this public life as a businessman who was occasionally politically active, I led a clandestine life as well—for two decades.

I gathered arms and money for the guerrillas in the hills. I remember on my honeymoon in 1962 we went to Honduras and El Salvador. We drove a Carmen Ghia in which I had installed a special suspension to hold extra weight, and I brought back rifles in that car. My wife didn't even know about it. I continued smuggling arms in the early '60s. Until one day in 1965 the arms were discovered in the home of a friend and the servant denounced us both to the Guardia. I was arrested and spent a month in jail. But my friend confessed sole responsibility and I was released.

In 1967, I was present at one of the great outrages of the dictatorship. I had an office as a press agent in the Grand Hotel. It was a time of an election campaign and another electoral fraud for the dictatorship. The people marched in protest and were massacred by the Guardia. From my office I saw them killing people. And then the Guardia withdrew. And more people came to the Grand Hotel, in the center of town, to see what had happened and to join the protest. I left my office and walked around the hotel. The streets were full of people, but I could see that no one was on guard as the hours passed and that the Guardia would return again to kill the people. When I pointed out this danger, Pedro Joaquín Chamorro [editor of *La Prensa*, assassinated by Somoza in January 1978] asked me to see to the defense of the Grand Hotel, and so I became the "military chief" of the Grand Hotel. When the Guardia returned, we fought with pistols and old rifles. We fought for three days and kept the Guardia out of the hotel.

Officials of the church were involved as intermediaries and negotiated a truce. We were to leave the Grand Hotel in return for safe conduct and a promise of no reprisals. The truth was, that night I was an idiot and went home to my house, tired, went to bed, and the Guardia came and dragged me off to jail. Again I spent several months in jail.

After several other instances like that I had to flee the country. I went into exile in Honduras and El Salvador for two years. When I returned to Nicaragua in 1969, I became a student and later a professor at the university. Publicly, I was identified with the student movement, but secretly I ran a safe house for combatants in Managua, in my home, and became a member of the FSLN. During the insurrections of 1978 and 1979 I transported arms to the people again until March 1979, when a truck full of arms was captured by the Guardia and traced to me. I had to go underground and flee the country. Four months later, with the Triumph of the Revolution, I was able to return and begin this work of reconstruction.

So you see, for 20 years I have led many lives. But I can tell you that during all of those years, in jail and out, when the level of struggle was high or low, I was always confident of victory. As a child, in the home of my father, I always knew we would win one day. And, because of this, no North American conquistador, no Mayor Koch or President Reagan, can ever destroy our victory.

8. Women in the Revolution

Glenda Monterrey
Amada Pineda
Dr. Maria Lourdes Bolaños

GLENDA MONTERREY, 36, elected in July 1981 secretary of AMNLAE (Association of Nicaraguan Women/Luisa Amanda Espinosa), is the highest ranking officer of this national organization of 50,000 members.

* * *

GLENDA MONTERREY: Our women's organization came out of our involvement in the struggle against the Somoza dictatorship. As early as 1969 the FSLN had tried to organize women in the Revolution. This began as the Patriotic Alliance of Women. But there were problems at the beginning and this attempt failed. But women were active at other levels: a few as combatants, and many more within the students' movement, which attracted many women students from 1969 to 1974. Also during this time, women were active in the neighborhoods organizing demonstrations, meetings, and petitions for the release of political prisoners who were being tortured and murdered in Somoza's jails.

It became obvious that an organization of women was necessary to unite this work and, in 1977, AMPRONOC (Association of Nicaraguan Women Confronting the Nation's Problems) was founded. AMPRONOC united bourgeois and peasant women in many Nicaraguan towns and cities to struggle together. It became a great movement.

After the Triumph of the Revolution, July 19, 1979 there was so much to do: clean-up, reconstruction, health needs. It was clear that now the women's organization had a new goal—to involve all women in the work of rebuilding. And so a new mass organization, AMNLAE, was formed and named after Luisa Amanda Espinosa, the first woman FSLN combatant to die fighting the dictatorship. Luisa Amanda was killed by the National Guard on April 3, 1970. She was 21. We knew her as both brave and humble, dedicated to the struggle and identified with the people. The organization's name honored her and carried her memory as an example to all women.

AMNLAE was meant to be open and inclusive of all women, and its first objective was to represent women in all revolutionary work. With the Triumph our task was to raise the level of involvement of women in every aspect of reconstruction, and to ensure their equality with men. And

Glenda Monterrey, Photo by Connie Martin

so women have been active in every aspect of revolutionary work. Women were active in the Literacy Crusade. In the cities, housewives who could read and write taught their neighbors who could not. In the countryside, 60% of the 60,000 teenagers who went out as literacy brigadistas were young women. Mothers were teachers in the city and their daughters teachers in the country. The brigadistas had never paid attention to the country people before. Now they lived three, four or five months with the peasants, working in the fields, teaching at night, and becoming a real part of these families. They experienced the terrible conditions of peasant life, and a new sense of solidarity was built at the same time, as these young women were able to take charge of their own lives, make a valuable contribution, and feel that they had made a difference in other peoples' lives.

In the same way women were active in the Health Crusade—giving classes in public health and going out into the barrios or the countryside to offer vaccinations to the children. Women knew they were part of this struggle to develop Nicaragua. This active, visible participation of women had its effect, as well, on the women who received their literacy or health lessons. Because they were models to these women of what all women could do. And, in the countryside, peasant women had never before seen women active and as leaders before.

The same is true of defense. Forty-five percent of the people in the volunteer militia are women. And when they have faced contra attacks, they have fought and died for their country. In the revolutionary vigilance committees [CDSs] in each barrio the majority of the participants are women who take turns walking the streets at all hours of the night to protect their neighborhoods. And there are women in the regular army and women officers. When the draft law was debated in the Council of State to make military service compulsory for men, we argued that it should be the same for women. Women may be excluded from various fields for considerations of ability, but the mere condition of biology should never be used to keep them out. In the end, the Council of State made military service compulsory for men and voluntary for women, but we thought we had made our point.

We have worked also to make sure women are represented in the police force and at all levels of national and local government. Women serve as members of governing *juntas* [councils] in many municipalities. Women serve in the Council of State, on the Supreme Court, and a woman, Amada Pineda, has just been appointed to the Supreme Electoral Commission. We are about to begin our first free national election campaign. Perhaps this year, or in the future, there will be women candidates for president or vice-president.

All of this is in contrast to the terrible status of women under the dictatorship. Women then had no access to any life other than working in the home. Very few were able to study in the universities or work in the factories or in professions. Education then was only a dream for peasant women. There were no schools in the countryside. There were no health centers or hospitals in the countryside, and women saw their children sicken and die from preventable or curable diseases. Women had no political role at all. Women who could find no other way to support themselves had to sell themselves in the streets. Women and children had to do this.

There was a general problem of unemployment and almost no work for women. But the Triumph meant new opportunities for women to work. Women work now in the factories and in the fields. They harvest cotton and drive tractors. And gradually they have risen to leadership positions in their unions.

Before, there was a general low level of culture and education for everyone, but especially for women. Now women have learned to read and write, and can still attend the CEPS [Centers of Popular Education for adults] at night. They serve in the militia and they have a life outside the home when they go to work. In every way women have helped to develop our society and themselves at the same time.

When a woman gets out of the home and a traditional role, when she works and gets an education, she forms a new vision of the world around her and she has a new sense of herself. She sees herself as a person of ideas and accomplishments. She sees herself as equal to men. And women are developing a collective sense. Before, under a capitalist system, people worked to get money, to become rich. But now women work not only to earn a living but also to benefit our whole society.

Seeing this changes the ideas of our children. Our little girls are changed, too, and their ideas and possibilities are expanded. Women are seen taking charge, making decisions, contributing to society, and this affects the whole culture.

Of course, some men have difficulty with these changes. This is a problem. For centuries men have developed traditional ideas of the role of women. In Somoza's time women were seen as the property of man, to serve them in the home and to produce children. It was terrible. Women were servants to be beaten, or even tortured, if they protested these roles. We are changing men's ideas, however. The roles and relationships of men and women are not simply personal problems. They are social, political and ideological issues. They are a priority of the Revolution, and work and education on these issues are being done across the country. Eventually, we'll develop a new mentality to match the new reality.

Our organization is different from feminist organizations in other countries, which see the problem as the personal exploitation of women by men. We understand that, but we think this is mainly a political problem. In 10 years, in 20 years, we hope to create a society where women are fully integrated into the political, military and every other field in the society.

In AMNLAE we understand that we are struggling to defend the Revolution, which is still under attack. Perhaps in time our goals will change. But right now our first priority is to protect the Revolution, which is our only guarantee of future changes. Our roles are in military defense, in economic development and in feeding of our people. These are basic to our survival.

The upcoming electoral campaign offers a great opportunity for educational outreach for women. Because, before, women never voted. In 1955, women were legally given the right to vote. But under the fascist regime, the elections were a joke and a fraud. The people didn't vote or pay attention to the two traditional parties. There was no open objective discussion of issues that affected men and women politically. In Latin America, and especially in Nicaragua, the two traditional parties, Liberal and Conservative, had made a joke of political life.

But in the coming election we will discuss issues and candidates, and vote freely. People will have the opportunity to choose or reject the candidates who helped make this Revolution. Political life becomes important and educational then as people see the value of their participation, openly and democratically. The elections are an opportunity to legitimize and endorse the work of the Revolution. In AMNLAE, we know this work includes all of the new opportunities for women. And women will struggle to defend what they have won. Women and men will vote for the party and candidates who represent the interests of the majority of the people, and this will represent a break with the past.

AMNLAE is a national organization but we try to develop regional bodies and grass-roots organizations so that we can involve and respond to women in the situations in which they live and struggle. Really, we have no great structure. We are more a movement than an organization. We have 50,000 members who carry membership cards, but feel that every woman who identifies with the Revolution, who makes a contribution in vigilance, defense, health or education is also AMNLAE, and that includes thousands and thousands of more women.

What I've told you of the women's movement in Nicaragua is also my life, too, for I have lived through this history. My life is simple to tell. My parents were very poor. My father was a tailor. My mother took charge of the business. I have three other sisters. It was a hard time and we were very poor. Fortunately I was able to graduate from high school and be licensed as a teacher in 1966. In the university, I was involved in the political movement and exposed to the social situation in my country. I was in the university, but I realized that thousands of others couldn't attend. And when the FSLN came to our university I learned from them and became involved. I joined the teachers' union, and after several years became an official of the union. I held that office during a great teachers' strike in 1969, which was met with great repression by the dictatorship. The movement was destroyed. I lost my job as a teacher.

But then I went to work full-time for the FSLN, first as a collaborator and then as a militant. I had to first work to support myself, so I got a job at the university as a secretary. A few years later, I became president of the secretaries' union and then president of the Union of University Workers. It was a very active life in the union. There were two great strikes at the university in 1976, one of which we won. But again the response was repression—arrests and beatings—and I had to leave the university.

I was active then publicly in the Movimiento Pueblo Unido, a coalition of left political parties. After the triumph, I was secretary general of the CDS. In October 1979, the FSLN sent me to work on the Atlantic Coast, an incredibly rich experience working with revolutionary women in northern Zelaya around Puerto Cabezas. In July 1981, I was democratically elected secretary general of AMNLAE. Three years. Three years I have held this office with AMNLAE! All of my life I have worked for the Revolution and for the liberation of women. And I will continue that work for the rest of my life.

* * *

AMADA PINEDA was a peasant and wife in the hills of Matagalpa. When she became active in union activity, she became a victim of Guardia repression. I interviewed her the week after she was appointed one of the three members of the newly formed Supreme Electoral Commission, which will act as a fourth branch of government to decide all aspects of the new Election Law and to oversee the first national elections since the Triumph.

* * *

AMADA PINEDA: I'm 40 years old now, but for the first 35 years of my life I lived and worked as a peasant women in the mountain lands outside the city of Matagalpa in the north of Nicaragua. Our lives as peasants were very hard and we suffered all the persecution of the Guardia. In those days we were totally at the mercy of the *patron* (landowner). We were paid five cordobas for a day's work, which was not enough to support a family.

My husband was active in union work, organizing to demand a raise to 12 cordobas each day. Unions were supposedly legal, but the *patron* denounced the organizers as subversives because he didn't want to have to pay more, and the Guardia came in and arrested people and murdered the leaders.

After a while I became active with the Democratic Women's Organization of Nicaragua, formed by the Socialist Party, which was active in the mountains and in the cities. After the Revolution, this group joined AMNLAE.

In those days before the Triumph, comrades from the FSLN would visit us, help us to pick the coffee, and talk about politics with us. When the guerrillas came, we would feed them and attend meetings with them. When the Guardia heard of this they came and arrested and tortured people, and raped the women. This happened to me.

In those days you struggled to save your own life and the lives of your children. But sometimes you couldn't save the children. Once, when the Guardia came to arrest us, my husband fled in one direction and I fled with the children in another. And there in the mountains, in a great rainstorm, as we fled, my little baby, a boy of two months, died of pneumonia.

I have given birth to 11 children, but only six are still living. My son, who would be 22 now, was murdered by the Guardia on June 29, 1979, just before the Triumph. He was 17 years old. They wounded him, tracked him down, and then shot him in a woodpile.

In 1974 the Guardia came and arrested me along with other peasants. I was beaten and tortured. And then I was raped. This went on for six or seven days in jail. It seemed like seven centuries spent within those walls. They would beat us anytime. They would rape us at any hour of the night. They put me into a pit filled with mud and animal excrement. And after the beatings and the lacerations they caused, I had terrible infections and I was very sick for a time.

These things happened to many peasants and included the men. I remember the case of the peasant woman Mary Castil. The Guardia killed her. They tortured her and raped her. She was five or six months pregnant and they cut her baby out of her belly. Her children saw all of this happen and it has affected them to this day. My daughter, who is 11 now, was a baby when the Guardia came for me. She was very ill then, and she has never gotten over what she saw them do to me.

Peasant women took part in this struggle through the years, and after the Triumph of the Revolution the role of women in this society became very important. Because now we have the right to work, the right to be in charge of our own lives, and the right to hold important posts in this government. I think of women like Comandantes Monica Baltodano, Dora María Tellez and Leticia Herrera.

Now a woman can be anything: a student, a worker, a peasant or a leader. Before, women were marginalized. We were just taught household chores because it was thought to be useless to teach women other skills. We weren't educated. In the countryside we spent our lives marginalized, first subject to our fathers, then to our husbands and then to having heaps of children. Now

Amada Pineda, Photo by Connie Martin

we can be useful in anything. Women are everywhere, even in the army, learning all kinds of productive skills. Oh, the men still may have a sense of *machismo,* but they're just going to have to adapt to all of the things we are doing today.

Since 1981, I have been one of three magistrates on the Agrarian Tribunal. We act as judges under the Agrarian Reform Law. At the time of the Triumph all of the land owned by Somoza and his friends was nationalized by the government. But this still left two-thirds of the arable land in private hands. For the past three years land has been distributed to the peasants if private landlords are not producing, if they've abandoned the land, or if they've engaged in "decapitalization" by taking their profit out of the country instead of reinvesting in production. Under this law we magistrates hear cases brought by the peasants who are seeking to expropriate land to form cooperatives of their own. We visit the land and spend perhaps 22 days of every month out in the countryside. When a case is brought to us we hear three witnesses from the peasants and three from the owner and then make a ruling.

As a peasant myself, it's hard to rule against other peasants, but sometimes we do. When we do decide for the peasants, the government agricultural agency, MIDINRA (Ministry of Agricultural

Development and Land Reform) buys the land from the owner and lets the cooperative pay back the money as a loan. In this work I've been able to see the better life the peasants have today. Under the dictatorship the owner would pay workers five cordobas a day, which was not a living wage for a worker with eight or 10 children. Now in the countryside the workers form cooperatives and work together for the good of all. Now they have schools and health centers nearby.

Under the dictatorship we had no rights. Worst of all, our children lacked milk, clothes, all of the necessities. They suffered from all kinds of diseases. But now we have vaccination campaigns in the countryside to protect the children. Really, it's a total change, greater than anyone could have imagined in the past. Now we have more of a will to work because we can make our own decisions. Now the peasants understand more, read and question what is best for them. The adults go to school at night because now they only work eight hours a day instead of 12 as before. Now they have time to learn.

Next week I begin my work as one of three members of the Supreme Electoral Commission and I will be leaving my work at the Agrarian Tribunal. This will mean more work and I will need to learn my new job. In Somoza's time we always had elections but they never meant anything. I never bothered to vote then. But now everyone is committed to free elections because we know the whole world is watching.

The Council of State [interim parliament] has passed an Electoral Law of 126 articles and called elections [last November 4, 1984] to choose a president, vice president and 90 members of a National Assembly. Everyone over 16 years old has the right to vote, and instead of two political parties, as in Somoza's time, we now have 10 who will participate in the two- to four-month national campaign and receive equal government subsidies and have equal access to the media to present their candidates. The Electoral Commission must apply the law and ensure that the election is democratic. I serve on the commission with a university president and a prominent lawyer and I was surprised to be chosen by the Chief Justice of our Supreme Court for this new task.

Under the dictatorship if peasants didn't vote they knew their land would be taken, they could be put in jail or killed. I remember one time the Guardia came to our area and promised everyone something to eat and drink and transportation to the city of Matagalpa if they would vote. They took them into the city and they voted. But then they left them without anything to eat or drink or a ride back to their farms. It was a long way to walk back and people were really mad. They came home tired and hungry.

This job will be something new for me. It will be very public and very political. But for my country I will do everything I can.

You ask me my hopes for the future. I only hope that we can live in peace, without aggression, without the Guardia and without traitors like Edén Pastora. Because we are still at war here in Nicaragua. The war is in the countryside and the peasants are dying. The contras kill women and children. They attack at night and kidnap people. Sometimes they enter a village pretending they want to buy food, but then they kill the cows and the chickens. People abandon their farms in fear. Whole areas have become like deserts because of these attacks. The contras can kill people but they can never win, because almost all the peasants support the Revolution because they know they're going to have money and land and be able to live better. Today the peasants work their land with rifles in their hands to defend themselves.

So, my hope is for peace: peace in Nicaragua and also in Guatemala and in El Salvador, and peace in all of Latin America.

* * *

DR. MARÍA LOURDES BOLAÑOS, 40, practiced as a lawyer during the Somoza regime. Following the Triumph of the Revolution she was appointed first to the Appellate Court and later to the Supreme Court. After two years of service on the Supreme Court, Dr. Bolaños resigned when the court was reorganized and the justices were reduced in number. Today she is director of the legal office of the Association of Nicaraguan Women/Luisa Amanda Espinosa (AMNLAE).

* * *

PHILIP ZWERLING: How have issues affecting women been dealt with in this new legal system?

DR. MARÍA LOURDES BOLAÑOS: On the Supreme Court I was responsible for the committee which was revising the family code. This work was supported by AMNLAE, which had a commission concerned with family justice. This commission consisted of women lawyers, sociologists, psychologists, child psychologists, social workers, doctors, pediatricians, etc. It was a small group, but very well composed.

We came out with two laws. The first law was introduced by AMNLAE into the Council of State in 1980. It was the New Law of Adoption. Its objective was to respond to the needs of children left homeless by the earthquake and by the Insurrection. Their needs were not met under the old law, which was written in 1970 under Somoza. Under the old law, a child was not really considered the son or daughter of an adopting couple. Also, few couples met the economic requirements necessary to be adoptive parents according to the old law. We wanted to transform the intent of this law and to respond to the number of children who needed homes at this time. That's why it's called "the First Law of Adoption."

Z: And for that reason the government offers help to a family wishing to adopt a child?

DR. BOLAÑOS: Yes, the law presents more favorable conditions for adoption. There are few economic limitations. An adoptive parent needs to be able to give the child that which is necessary to live and to be morally capable of raising a child. Single people may also adopt a child.

Z: Yes, but does the government give material aid to the family?

DR. BOLAÑOS: No, the family assumes complete responsible for the child. The second law that AMNLAE introduced into the Council of State was a law concerning relations between mother, father and children. The previous law had been structured so that the man had exclusive rights as the head of the family. The AMNLAE commission felt the law should reflect the reality of life in Nicaragua. Normally here, mothers are entirely responsible. They assume economic and moral responsibility and take care of most family needs.

Z: In the majority of families in Nicaragua, is the woman head of the household.

DR. BOLAÑOS: Exactly. And there was a contradiction between the responsibility a woman assumed and her rights under the law. Under previous law women didn't have the right to make decisions concerning real estate and household property because the right to make all decisions belonged to the father. With this law we sought to equalize the relationship between the mother and father. Before AMLAE brought this law before the Council, it brought it to the women of Nicaragua. We held meetings all over Nicaragua, and we had women read the law.

Z: These discussions were in AMNLAE. Were they also held in the CDSs?

DR. BOLAÑOS: In the beginning it was discussed only in AMNLAE, but later there were discussions in the CDSs and at the Council of State, because the law has characteristics which affect all Nicaraguans. We are almost all either mothers, fathers or children. This law required much preparation and also had a considerable economic cost. It was approved by the *Junta de Gobierno* on July 3, 1982. This law was made by the people themselves to answer their needs. We don't consider this law to be "eternal." It is passing through stages of analysis and testing. If necessary, it can be changed in the future in response to the people.

After this we began working on the Law of Nourishment. In September 1982, we presented this law to the Council. We had a much bigger struggle on our hands because we were touching men's pocketbooks. For the law equalizing family relations, AMNLAE held 89 consultations throughout Nicaragua. For the Law of Nourishment, we held about 400 discussions and consultations. Part of the law, for example, says that the work of a woman who doesn't work outside the home has to be recognized; that it has to be computed, because there are women who wash, iron, clean, cook, shop, etc.—not in the same conditions as a developed country—but in the conditions of an underdeveloped country such as ours. This work is done by the woman's own strength and without the help of vacuum cleaners, refrigerators, washing machines, etc. It is work that is very difficult and heavy.

Z: Are women going to receive a salary for their work?

DR. BOLAÑOS: No. What we believe is that the value of the work should be calculated. How much is child care and maintaining a household worth? A couple in which both work outside the home has to hire a person to care for the children and run the house. And both pay her.

In contrast, a woman who works at home is belittled by the man: "You don't do anything here. I'm the one who brings money to the house." He often gives her scarcely enough to survive on. With the Law of Nourishment a woman can say what her daily work is worth, and take from him what is necessary. Clearly the situation is difficult, as is the economic situation of Nicaragua. In our war economy, salaries barely reach that of a living wage. And when a man is badly educated, and with children on all sides, and *macho*, he is not likely to recognize the value of a woman's work. Another section of this law recognizes the right to support children born outside of a marriage as well as within a marriage. It

Dr. Maria Lourdes Bolaños, Photo by Martin

gives equal rights to all children, in and out of marriage. In the past only those children born within marriage were protected.

Above all else, the Law of Nourishment is an economic law concerning relations between mother and father. This law was passed by the Council of State, but still hasn't been approved by the Junta. This law is also a law made by the people, and even though it is not formally a law of the Republic, it is in the minds of the people.

In November 1983, we introduced another law, the Law of Filial Relationships. This law would eliminate any kind of discrimination because of so-called illegitimate birth. However, at the exact moment the law was introduced, aggression escalated and we were afraid of an invasion at any moment. Discussion of this law had to be postponed. Right now the fundamental work of the Revolution is the elections. So the Council of State began working to produce laws regulating political parties and elections. The Law of Filial Relationships is important, but we will have to wait for it for a while.

We are halfway through with our work. We have made advances, but we need to continue and that is why we have this office. The people recognize the need for social transformation and they know that AMNLAE is responding to and backing the Nicaraguan woman. They realize that the laws which AMNLAE asks for are not abstract laws, but laws to resolve the problems of women.

Here is this office we are oriented principally to the legal problems of women. We help with problems of housing, divorce, child support, etc. These are usually civil, not criminal cases, and problems can often be referred to various government ministries. In some cases it is necessary to go to court. These are usually criminal cases. If a woman has been physically abused we have a serious problem.

The first line of support in these cases is the police. However, they often have a sexist mentality, too. They say if she was beaten she can leave her husband. It's true that she could leave, but we're concerned with who is going to protect her at this moment. We don't have a law that exclusively protects a woman from physical abuse.

Z: But it's a crime?

Dr. Bolaños: In general. If a man brutally beats a woman in bed and leaves her completely beaten up, her wounds usually heal in eight days. So there's no penalty; because for minor lesions there's no punishment. This is a situation which greatly concerns AMNLAE, that the physical abuse of women is treated so causally. The executive committee of AMNLAE has suggested that we acquire a method of dealing with this emergency, and has stated to the government that we need to transform the article dealing with beatings so this crime is punished.

Z: In the U.S. we have a few homes for battered women. Are there any here?

Dr. Bolaños: No, we don't have any. We have extended families. The women can get help from an aunt, a sister, a grandmother, etc. For this reason we don't have refuge houses.

Z: Also, in the U.S. there's a movement to understand rape as a possible crime within the state of marriage. Are there discussions of this here?

Dr. Bolaños: No. We have not yet dealt with rape. There is a problem with rape in that it's considered a private crime. If the women doesn't go to court, the crime is not prosecuted. If she is willing to go to court, then it is possible to act. Usually the crime doesn't get to court because it's an embarrassment for the family. We haven't evolved to that stage yet.

Z: How is it possible to say that these four laws changed the thinking of the Nicaraguan people?

Dr. Bolaños: The law only reflects the feelings of the Nicaraguan people; it has not transformed us. We were transformed by our struggle. During the Insurrection women fought in the mountains and at the barricades. Today, women are playing a very important role in the frontier zones, in production and in defense. This is what has transformed us and continues to transform us—not a law, but this. Even before the Triumph AMNLAE had its predecessor in AMPRONAC, and at the time of the Triumph they had certain points concerning the equality of men and women that they wanted to see expressed in the new government. They asked for equal pay for equal work. The goals of the women involved in the Revolution were very specific. And now we are fighting to be included and to advance the Revolution.

Z: Are you familiar with the project in León sponsored by the Ministry of Social Welfare? It's a restaurant run by a collective of former prostitutes.

DR. BOLAÑOS: I don't know of that one in León, but I know of such a project in Corinto and another here in Managua, a very good one. These women have great conviction. They worked as prostitutes before to support themselves in a bad social system. The problem after the Triumph was that they had no specific work training. Now they have learned skills and have been integrated into the productive system. Nicaraguan society has not yet risen above treating these women in a discriminatory manner. These women often have profound problems with society, and sometimes within themselves. We would like to play a larger role in solving these problems, but we have limited money and personnel. The projects we are sponsoring now are working very well.

Z: What was your work as a lawyer like during the time of the Somoza dictatorship?

DR. BOLAÑOS: By the time of the Triumph I had worked 12 years as a lawyer in my hometown of Masaya. As a lawyer I began to see the enormous inequalities that existed within our system of justice. To become a judge at the time of Somoza was to become a very powerful person. To become a judge one had to have a great deal of political influence, or to pay Somoza well. I served the exploited classes. I didn't have power or political influence. I would prepare well, but the rich would always win. The only time when there was a chance for a poor person to win was when both parties were equally poor, because neither party could pay the judge. The judge dominated everything and he served "El Señor" of Masaya.

Z: Who was "El Señor?"

DR. BOLAÑOS: Colonel Orju. He was the "owner" of Masaya. He was famous. He was president of the Congress of Nicaragua. He was famous for his repressive laws against the campesinos and against the Sandinista Liberation Front. It was a very specific law against the progressive forces in Nicaragua. It was through this law that Pedro Joaquín Chamorro [editor of *La Prensa*] was imprisoned. "El Señor" was very influential. He was a great friend of Somoza. When Somoza was ill with heart trouble Orju accompanied

Somoza to the U.S. He was the owner of almost all of the Pacific Coast. He accumulated a tremendous amount of money. At the time of the Triumph he was killed by the people. His family left the country. They are all very rich and living in Miami.

Z: How was life for you during this time?

DR. BOLAÑOS: We lived more or less well. We didn't need to borrow money, but on the other hand, I didn't have any desire to be an exploiter. My husband and I were two people from the middle class, one trained as a lawyer and the other as a doctor. We didn't have a lot of capital. We served the exploited class. Very few lawyers left the country during the Insurrection. We are here today working for the Revolution. A number of doctors left. Why? Because as a lawyer injustice was easy to see and difficult to combat. The judges were all corrupt. At the end of the Revolution not one judge stayed here.

Z: During the time before the Triumph did you defend political prisoners, too?

DR. BOLAÑOS: Yes. However, very few ever arrived in front of the judge. They were killed or they disappeared from their jail cells. I was a member of the Human Rights Committee of Masaya. We looked for prisoners and visited them. We talked and we hoped, but in practical terms we couldn't do anything. Masaya played a large part in the Insurrection. The FSLN was well organized there. My husband and I helped. My husband founded a clandestine hospital in Monimbo. It was because of our ideals that we got involved: because of the dictatorship and a need for social change. As middle-class people, we had a standard of living which was more or less good. We had a son and a daughter at this time and we all came out of it well.

Z: How many children do you have now?

DR. BOLAÑOS: Three, and we are all working for Nicaragua.

Z: What do you think the future of Nicaragua will be?

DR. BOLAÑOS: We will eliminate the obsolete laws which are discriminatory. We will reach a better level of economic development. As feminists, we want men to receive what they merit, and women, too. Our principal objective is that our children will live better than before, have better health care, education, etc. We will continue to work for these goals.

9. Health Care for the Nation

Dr. Fernando Silva
Dr. Mayra Pasos

DR. FERNANDO SILVA, 57, a pediatrician, is director of the Hospital Infantil de la Mascota in Managua. He is also a poet and novelist.

* * *

PHILIP ZWERLING: Tell us a little bit about your childhood and education.

DR. FERNANDO SILVA: I was born in Granada and my mother died when I was a very young child. I lived with my father in the region of Río San Juan. All of my infancy was spent in that region. It's a jungle region. It's a type of Nicaraguan countryside that is earth and water. I'm a writer, too, and my second book is called *Of Earth and Water*.

After Río San Juan I studied in the primary and secondary schools in Granada. I began studying at the school of medicine there, but when Somoza closed it I finished medical school in León. I did my residency in Managua. Then, with a scholarship from the French government, I studied pediatrics in Paris. Later I returned to Nicaragua and began to work.

Z: Why did Somoza close the medical school in Granada when it was one of only two in the country?

DR. SILVA: What Somoza did could be seen as curious and diverting, I suppose. It had its origins in the rivalry between Granada and León and between the two political parties, Conservative and Liberal, respectively, that were associated with them. Somoza was leader of the Liberal Party and had married into a wealthy family of León. When his wife, Doña Salvadora Debayle, asked him for a birthday present, he gave it to her. She said, "For my birthday, give me the closing of the medical school in Granada, and he did.

Z: When you were young and a student, did you have problems with the dictatorship?

DR. SILVA: When one is very young, one may not be very perceptive. With Somoza, it was a curious thing; he had a certain manner, a drowsy atmosphere and a dullness about him, so that one didn't completely understand the man. There was a flavor somewhere between honey and the taste of failure.

My father, for example, was a Liberal, an old soldier and an enemy of Somoza. As a Liberal, he was caught in the rivalry between the Liberals and Conservatives. Personally, he was against Somoza, but he held an important post in the Liberal Party and Somoza played on this. Because if you were a Liberal Party official, you had to keep your post or a Conservative would take over. Somoza played all these cards. Old Somoza was a very cunning man. He had the reasoning of a fox, a malicious fox. He knew how to handle many things.

Now, the youth who were developing in this atmosphere didn't really understand the situation. Little by little, as we came in contact with the outside world, we began to understand things better. And the struggles in the universities, because they were first, were very important. In the beginning all were against Somoza and the system belonging to Somoza. But Somoza had a way of co-opting people. He had power over the upper class and the dictating class because many people with money saw him as their protector and backer. Furthermore, Somoza permitted them more profits than ever from Nicaraguan capitalism. It was important for Somoza to keep the favor of the very rich so they would support him. The youth were developing in this type of mix. Their understanding had to meet and to comprehend contradictions like these.

In the university we began to struggle, but some were more serious than others. Carlos Fonseca was the principal leader of this group of ideological youth who had real knowledge and opinions developed through study. I was a doctor, and in all of my time of study for that vocation I always wanted to find out who Sandino was. Somoza struggled to keep Sandino hidden. Carlos Fonseca studied Sandino totally, and then presented to the youth a real, historical man who truly had feelings in favor of his people, a fighter who was sincere and honest. We had all been taught that Sandino was a robber and a killer, but in the history of Nicaragua

Dr. Fernando Silva, Photo by Connie Martin

there was never anyone like Sandino. I hadn't known the real man because the histories had been written to malign him.

We doctors entered the struggle in one way or another. There were many styles of struggle. We began by not participating in anything of Somoza's. We were doctors and we didn't want to deny care to the people. We worked in the hospitals, in Social Security clinics, and in private practice, but the vast majority of doctors refused to work for Somoza in any way.

Z: What was practicing medicine like under Somoza?

DR. SILVA: Doctors were the servants of the bourgeoisie. In the hospitals we worked with patients who came to receive free attention. But this was difficult. Even though Somoza always had the aid of the Yanquis for all orders, there were many limitations because of scarce supplies. Often people who ran the hospitals were thieves. The tremendous thievery that went on was a terrible thing. But the result was that doctors gave what there was to the people who could pay. The people who could pay were the bourgeoisie.

It's evident that a sick person is not a bourgeoisie but only a sick person. However, the dilemma of a doctor is this: the sick person who is a person of the humble classes manages himself perfectly, but the bourgeoisie is always behaving and acting in a way that the doctor has to submit to him. This tires and bothers the doctor. The bourgeoisie is rich and simply paying to be served. The poor person who is waiting for the doctor for a cure sees the doctor as his friend. This is a different thing, a different relationship between doctor and patient. Therefore, in the past, the practice of medicine was tiresome, although undoubtedly a source of income.

Z: What role did the doctors play during the Insurrection?

DR. SILVA: Many different roles. Some went to the countryside to fight and die. Others struggled clandestinely. For example, in the resistance here in Managua I was the doctor who cared for the children whose families fought in the struggle. I took care of guerrillas, too. We also had a network of those of us who worked in hospitals who would gather needles, syringes, penicillin, gauze, and other medical supplies to send to the countryside and the fighters.

Part of the struggle, as well, was our decision not to accept anything from Somoza. Out of this came something he really hated: the great strike of all health services. In this strike some doctors continued working. This bothered us all. The Revolution, however, is very generous, and many doctors are now working in spite of the fact that they continued to work during the great health strike.

Z: Did you face repression from the National Guard during this struggle?

DR. SILVA: In the beginning I was very careful. I was very fearful—terrified, really, of the Guardia. They were truly beasts. But little by little one becomes more and more committed and convinced, and begins to contribute in spite of danger. At that time I was working in the Social Security clinic. I would get into my car, a Toyota Corolla, and drive to the clinic. My license plates were attached to the car by wire. My contact would take off the plates and put them on her car, which was also a Toyota Corolla. I would make sure Dr. Silva drove in his car with plates "26-26." Then I left, but it wasn't my car that left. Anyone who checked cars would think Dr. Silva was at the clinic.

However, the day came when the medical director arrived. I was working and he stood in front of me. How uncouth that was. He said he was convinced I was working with those "sons-of-bitches Sandinistas," and how disgraceful that was. This really shook me up because my jacket was bulging. In treating the guerrillas I was in the habit of traveling armed, and I still had the weapon. "We will have to settle it in this way," he said. "After you finish, come to my office so that we can talk." I didn't know what I could do. I needed to get rid of the gun. I was in great anguish that I would have the misfortune to be shot. I was trembling. There was a man nearby holding a baby in his arms covered by a blanket. He touched me. "Don't worry," he said. And he took the gun and put it under the blanket. So I was saved from certain death, at least.

That night they attacked my house here in Managua. I hadn't arranged to take anything from my house. I had gone with my wife to Granada with nothing but a little money. I was afraid we were being watched, so my wife left by the side door and I left by the main door. We didn't take the car, but went to the corner and took the bus to Granada. Later I returned with a truck to take things from the house. When I got out of the truck a neighbor ran up to me and said, "Doctor, you're alive. I'm so happy. I can't believe you're alive." She told me the following: late in the night two Guardia arrived on motorcycles. One of them opened up with a blast of machine-gun fire. The neighbor thought I had been killed. But I had already left. The Guardia had thought, because of the dim light, that he saw me standing fixed against the wall, and with a beard. So he opened fire. But in reality what he saw was a postor of Charlie Chaplin on my wall. There were four bullets in Charlie Chaplin's chest.

Z: In Somoza's time, was it possible to publish your novels and poems?

DR. SILVA: In that time there was only one thing that wasn't touched, that was the true newspaper *La Prensa*. And we had *La Prensa*'s literary supplement, whose director, Pablo Antonio Cuadra, was a man who was with us, a man who was with the great coalition, a man with a lot of prestige. All else was repressed. My poetry at that time was not overtly political. My poetry was a poetry that contained something of Nicaraguan humanity, of the Nicaraguan mind, and it was cyclical. I began with a book, *Earth in the Blood*. It was concerned with the formation of the land, and how the land was united, and how the people formed their feeling of love for it and their defense of it. And when the Revolution came I wrote another book, *The Blood in the Earth*. Here the blood returns to the earth for the glory of the people and the salvation of the people. My second book, a collection of stories, refers to my life in Río San Juan; it is *Of Earth and Water*. It's about earth, love of Nicaragua, its life and its reality. But not in a form that is foolish or pretentious, but directly and seriously using authentic Nicaraguan language in a vital, useful manner.

Z: Is it true that many doctors left the country after the Triumph?

DR. SILVA: Yes, some of them. Some left because they were middle-class doctors who were never with the Revolution and whose families were never part of it. Another percentage thought that a doctor has to have a major commitment to his people and that that meant renouncing certain privileges and liberty in the exercise of the profession. Because they thought the Revolution was to receive all of their work. But it was never like that. Some were counterrevolutionaries or disaffected from the Revolution. Others had families who were involved with Somoza.

Z: How many left?

DR. SILVA: About 200 of the 1,000 doctors in the country. And perhaps more. A few are still leaving today.

Z: Was it a difficult decision for you to remain here?

DR. SILVA: No, no. Above all, I like the work. There was a reality that I would earn less. And now I say, "Never have I worked so much. Never have I earned so little. Never have I been so happy." Because I am totally with the Revolution. I am a doctor. This is a Revolution of the poor, and so our salaries have to conform to this. But it is a very satisfying, beautiful experience to work directly with the people when the people also contribute to the work.

My specialty, social pediatrics, has served me tremendously. After the Revolution I went to the mountains in the center of the Atlantic Coast, in the jungle. The people never in their lives had seen a doctor. After the Triumph of the Revolution we brought medicine to the whole country. And then I began to be useful and to teach hygenics and nutrition, and about innoculations. From there I went to work in Ciudad Sandino and was director there. I worked in community development. It was a beautiful time with marvelous people. That's what I like: the land and the people. Next, I went to work in my own line of social pediatrics, and here I am, director of this pediatric hospital.

Z: What can be said about the change in the level of health care now as opposed to the past?

DR. SILVA: There is a great difference, a great difference. The first change is that Somoza invented statistics. His facts were wholly inventions. One could perceive this in the normal relations with the people. There were epidemics, horrible, beastly epidemics. In November, the hospitals would be full of children with poliomyelitis. When I was a resident, for example, in the time of Somoza, I was solely responsible for that ward. Seventy children were afflicted. Managua had at this time a population of 400,000. What barbarity! What cruelty! Measles were also terrible. And the mortality from these diseases was truly immense. There was nothing I would call decent attention. For example, in the health center there was always a heap of people. The doctor would arrive and begin writing prescriptions and handing them out one after the other. All that mattered to the people was to get a prescription. After the Revolution the first thing that happened, and it was a great idea, was the participation of the people in the struggle, in the defense of their health, and with great results. Because the people understood that it's an obligation to care for and conserve their own health.

Really, we have limitations because of the present aggression. Materials are scarce. But there is true growth in health care. We have programs for the people in areas such as nutrition, but we do them very simply, without much money. It is with a series of courses and instruction that we have achieved things without much money and without many resources, but with the desire of the people to defend their health.

In the past measles epidemics were tremendous. The population was terrified and people were at the hospitals grasping for services. But there were robbers and thieves in the hospitals. I remember arriving at the home of the hospital director at his suggestion that we get together. In his bathroom I found towels marked "General Hospital." Illicit behavior at the time of Somoza was normal. It was very clear and vivid to people that "so and so" was the chief thief. There were many sayings and jokes to that effect.

Z: What are the biggest problems facing health care workers today?

DR. SILVA: We are a poor country. The biggest problem is obtaining the foreign credit with which to buy medicines. We have a limited quantity of instruments and medical equipment. We also need more trained medical technicians. These are great problems. Our resources are few. It is very difficult because these things cost so much and we need them so desperately. We have a constant struggle around the allocation of what we do have. All equipment is in great demand. We have to make agonizing decisions about foreign currency and what to spend it on because we have so many needs. The resources we do have are used up very quickly.

With this Revolution, open in all aspects, the people have great access to hospitals and health centers and everything else. The number of people seeking services is huge. For example, a doctor in a health center sees eight patients in an hour and works eight hours a day. That's 64 patients. The people who need services, who want to be in that group of 64, sometimes begin arriving at two in the morning to be placed on the waiting list and to await the dawn and medical care. The number of people who want attention is three or four times the number that can be seen. It's very difficult because we don't have a sufficient number of doctors. Within four years, more or less, we will have the first group of doctors educated here in the Revolution. These will be trained to care well for the people.

Z: Are there limitations now in private medical practices? Is it necessary, for example, for a doctor to work in a hospital or health center to have time for his private practice?

DR. SILVA: No. Absolutely nothing is demanded of the doctor. Some work totally in private practice or in private institutions. Some work with us half-time and half-time in their private clinics.

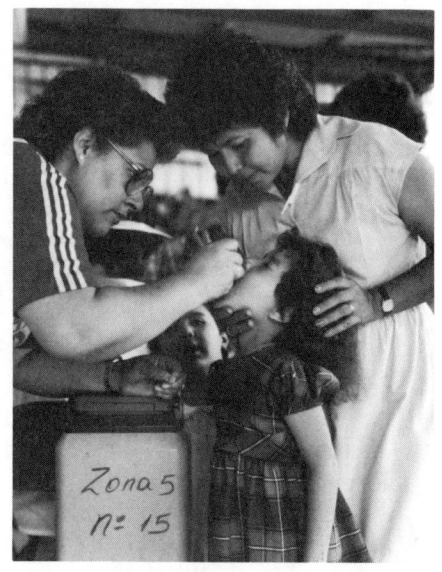

Neighborhood health care, Photo by Zwerling

Z: What is in store for Nicaragua in the area of health care in particular and progress in general?

DR. SILVA: The future of Nicaragua in the area of health will be very difficult because we have very little relief from the constant aggression. We also have an underdeveloped country. In spite of this we are doing great work in popular education, in raising people's consciousness concerning health.

Now we are beginning to realize the fruit of our vaccination program. In a very few years we have vaccinated almost all of the people. We will have healthier children, and diseases like poliomyelitis, measles, and malaria will be eradicated. And in a few years we will have more revolutionary medical personnel. These are the major advances in the health sector. Because of these advances there is much hope. I am completely optimistic about the development of the Revolution because I see with the "whole eye." Let me explain what my "whole eye" is. Generally, we see the Revolution with half an eye, the part from the middle of the eye and above. We see what is most visible, the bourgeoisie, the petite bourgeoisie, people who in some cases are disaffected with the Revolution. But from the middle of the eye down we see the rest of the people, and these are the revolutionary masses who struggle. This is the Revolution I see with the "whole eye."

* * *

DR. MAYRA PASOS, 37, serves as vice minister of health. Once one of the few trained psychologists in Nicaragua, she was a leading activist in the women's organization AMPRONOC, the forerunner of AMNLAE. This interview was conducted in her office in one building of the sprawling new National Health Center located at the entrance to the 1st of May barrio in Managua.

* * *

PHILIP ZWERLING: What was the health care system and delivery of service like before the Revolution?

DR. MAYRA PASOS: Here in Nicaragua, before the Triumph of the Revolution, the health care system was a capitalistic system. There was a health care system, but the mass of people had no access to it. . . . Services for poor people were minimal. It was a mercantile system of health. There were 17 large for-profit hospitals that made millionaires of their owners.

Social Security clinics served a small proportion of the population although many workers were taxed to support them. They existed not to save lives, but to make money for people in the government who ran the system. There was a very high rate of infant mortality, 121 deaths per 1,000 live births, and a national average life expectancy of just 52 years. Sixty-eight percent of the children under five years of age suffered from malnutrition. The children died of diarrhea, measles, parasites, and all kinds of other preventable diseases.

At the Triumph of the Revolution, we faced a critical situation in every sense in health care. The basic decision of the Junta was to declare that health care was a human right of the Nicaraguan people and an obligation of the State. Then we could begin to consolidate all of the separate areas of the health care system under the Health Ministry. This was a complicated matter in itself. The whole business in medicines had been riddled with corruption and this had to be cleaned up. This internal organization was the first step.

Then we could reach out to the public through an emphasis on public health. For example, technical aid for community latrines, programs to combat infant diarrhea with special local clinics for this ailment, special programs for pregnant women, child vaccinations, health brigadistas who went out into the countryside and were then followed by rural clinics, and new hospitals like Bertha Calderón Hospital for women. Health care became free and available to all. Primary health care facilities increased from 172 in 1977 to 446 in 1982; rural hospitals increased from 37 in 1977 to

46 in 1982; the number of doctors per 10,000 inhabitants increased in that same five-year period from 5.37 to 6.47, while the percentage of the national budget allocated for health care increased from 8% to 11%. The number of vaccinations given quadrupled over those five years. Polio, once a major killer, has claimed not a single victim in the last two years in Nicaragua. Seven of the top 10 causes of death in Nicaragua were either preventable or parasitic-induced diseases. All are declining in mortality due to these efforts.

Dr. Mayra Pasos, Photo by Peter Kelly

Because this system is now at the service of the people the people are part of the system of health services delivery. The thousands of health brigadistas, like the Literacy Crusade brigadistas before them, are all volunteers. They're trained in different tasks, like innoculations. Because they are volunteers, they take the initiative in bringing health care to their neighborhoods. During the vaccination programs if parents in a barrio didn't bring their children in to the health center, the brigadistas and CDS workers would identify the missing families and take the vaccinations directly to their homes—something doctors never did in the past when they were part of a mercantile system.

We are building new hospitals in Bluefields, Rivas and Chinandega, and new health centers in areas where they never existed before to take primary health care to where the people are. We have a commitment to preventative medicine, not only in terms of vaccinations but also in nutrition, public health and the health education of the people. One of the first tasks of the Revolution was to organize campaigns to clean up the cities to remove health dangers. In the malaria crusade, brigadistas went door to door in every community to kill mosquitos and to remove the standing water that bred them.

Of course, with this expansion of services we find that our medical personnel are insufficient. The brigadistas fill part of the gap, but more doctors are needed. Every day more Nicaraguans are going to health centers or hospitals in search of services. We have to train more new doctors. The single, excellent medical school in León is insufficient, and we hope to open another medical school. In the meantime, volunteer doctors serving in Nicaragua from Germany—East and West—Cuba, the Soviet Union, the United States and France are saving lives daily. A German doctor and a French doctor have been among the many health care workers who have been assassinated by the counter-revolutionaries.

The contras have also attacked health centers, destroyed medicines, and murdered young health brigadistas in the countryside. Our efforts have also been hampered by the CIA mining of Nicaraguan ports, which in several cases caused ships loaded with medicines to turn back and unload their cargos in Costa Rica, which resulted in delays in arrival and increased transportation costs to truck the medicines across the border. The U.S. blockade of international loans to Nicaragua has denied us the hard currency to buy medicines on the international market.

Z: I've heard about the "House of Blood" that existed under Somoza. This illustrates, in part, the role of health care within a for-profit system that existed in the past. Could you say more about this?

DR. PASOS: Somoza had a plasmapheresis center here where the unemployed and the starving could sell their blood for a minimal fee, I think for about 15 cordobas. It was a business Somoza ran with a Cuban exile in Miami. The blood was sold in the United States for a huge profit in dollars. This business of Somoza was also called the "House of Death" and the "House of Dracula." It was the most literal example of a dictator sucking the blood of his people. When Chamorro was assassinated and everyone looked to Somoza as the culprit, he tried to divert attention by speculating that perhaps his Cuban exile partner was responsible. The people in the streets marched to the "House of Blood" and burned it to the ground. This business of exporting Nicaragua blood for U.S. dollars epitomized the concept of health care under Somoza as a mercantile system. Today, free health care is the national right of every Nicaraguan.

Z: What other kinds of changes are taking place in health care today?

DR. PASOS: We've opened state-run pharmacies to make medicines available to poor people. A medicine that might cost 60 cordobas in a private pharmacy costs five cordobas in a state pharmacy. The idea is to allow people to buy medicines without picking their pockets at the same time. The Atlantic Coast is a good example of these changes. This was a marginal area under the domination of foreign companies. Most people lived and died there without ever seeing a doctor. Today we have hospitals in Puerto Cabezas and Bluefields, and health centers in areas like the mines, for example, where many people were made ill by that work. Health workers go out into the villages by jeep and canoe, and over new roads and trails that have been made there. On the Atlantic Coast, as in other areas, we have tried to build houses of "child development," where the children of a village receive food and milk each day and are near a health center equipped with a small pharmacy and visited by a doctor or nurse each week. With this kind of care the level of health, generally in the country, and especially for the children, has improved greatly. These successes have made the doctors, nurses and brigadistas special targets of the contras as they try to destroy this service of the Revolution to the people. In the last two years, 15 health workers have been murdered, 11 wounded and 17 kidnapped by the contras.

Z: What plans do you have for the future?

DR. PASOS: By 1985, we hope to have health care centers sufficiently dispersed to really have primary health care services available to everyone wherever they live. Our other major emphasis is to improve the level of health care. That means more doctors, nurses and technicians, and more equipment and medicine. The government has made this commitment to the Nicaraguan people. But we can only fulfill this pledge if the agression ceases and peace allows us the funds and time to move ahead in the health field.

10. Working the Land

Tomás Cruz Díaz
Santo Pedro Martínez

Gregorio Váez
Father Peter Marchetti

Nicaragua's economy and prosperity are based upon its success in agriculture. Once dependent on imported foodstuffs, the country now struggles to feed its own people. The 40% of the arable land once held in large farms of beef, tobacco and cotton (mostly for cash export) by the Somoza family and their associates has been nationalized. Today, public presentations of land titles to previously landless peasants are regular events. Still more than half of the land remains in private hands. However, state farms and cooperatives are growing steadily under the Sandinista government's encouragement.

To understand the changes this has brought to the peasants themselves, I traveled 11½ kilometers from Managua on the old road to León to the "Luciano Vílchez" Cooperative. Here 14 families, totaling 114 people, work 27 hectares (1 hectare equals 2.471 acres) of land and raise cabbage, corn, watermelon, tomatoes, beans and onions. The cooperative is an interesting mix of Nicaraguans and Salvadoran refugees. In all, the Nicaraguan government has sheltered and resettled some 25,000 refugees who have fled from the violence in El Salvdador.

Here we spoke briefly with two Salvadoran refugees, 56-year-old TOMÁS CRUZ DÍAZ and 25-year-old SANTO PEDRO MARTÍNEZ; a Nicaraguan, GREGORIO VÁEZ, 31, the son of a peasant family from Juigalpa in Chontales; and with an American Jesuit priest, FATHER PETER MARCHETTI, who works with the Nicaraguan government as an agrarian expert.

* * *

TOMÁS CRUZ DÍAZ: Many of us are from Morazán Province in El Salvador where there has been heavy fighting. We came to

Nicaragua three years ago and have been at this cooperative for two years. We have been very well received here and have formed good friendships, but when we can, when peace comes, we wish to return to El Salvador. Members of my family died in the violence there. A married couple, who were relatives, were both killed. Many of my friends died fighting with the guerrillas. After a while, the army was just massacring everyone and my family had to flee to save themselves.

At first we were in a refugee camp, but since we worked the land in El Salvador we asked to work on a farm in Nicaragua and we were integrated into the cooperative movement. This farm was confiscated from a Somocista and now we have title to the land for as long as we are working and producing. Farming is the same whether here or in El Salvador. But here we have the right to live, to work and to enjoy the fruits of the land. There's a school for our children, and evening classes for adults as well. Everything is calm here.

* * *

SANTO PEDRO MARTÍNEZ: I am from the Department of Cabañas in El Salvador and my family and I are refugees. Here my children are learning to read and write, but in El Salvador illiteracy is very high. We hope we can succeed at this cooperative. The government banks loan us money to buy seeds and to rent machinery. When the crops come in we repay these loans with 2% interest. If the crops fail, the banks give us more time to repay. The land is rich and we have water for irrigation, but right now it's very hard to buy seeds for planting because of the mines in the ports and the blockade. It's time to plant now and we don't have enough seeds.

In our country we were workers on other people's farms, or owned small plots of land that we worked individually. Here we work cooperatively. We work eight hours a day, six days a week. On Saturday, we all gather in an assembly to discuss the problems and make work assignments. Not everyone can produce equally because not everyone has the same capacity, but we keep track of how many hours each person works and they are paid accordingly.

This land belongs to us as long as we are here working. We can't sell the land. If we leave it reverts back to the state, although we can be paid for whatever improvements we've made. If our families grow in size, the government will find more land for us in another part of the country. This was one of the first cooperatives in Nicaragua after the Revolution. We produce enough to live, but we really haven't yet turned a profit to be able to buy things with.

* * *

GREGORIO VÁEZ: During the dictatorship of Somoza we worked even though it was difficult to get land to work, not like now. To get land then first one had to make a labor commitment to the owner of the *hacienda*—the landlord. The landlords had a system. The landlord would let you live on the land, but you had to agree to do his work first; to clear and prepare the land and all of that. And when you finished all of his work then you could do your own. So you had to work quickly to have time to do some work for yourself.

In the planting, we worked up to the last minute. First we had to plant for the landlord, corn, *frijoles* [beans], etc., and then we could plant for ourselves. At times we would be late in our own plantings and the best time for planting would have passed. So often our small plots of land didn't yield much corn or beans because we had planted late. The landowner, however, had a large amount of land planted and therefore a large harvest. So the landlord would give me corn or beans to pay me for my work. That's the system that was used. He gave me corn and beans in exchange for my work—always. We were paid with a little rice and beans. We were always exploited by this system. The landlord would always make a profit, but we never received more even if he had a very good harvest.

But now it's not like that. We are in different times. We make our own decisions about what to plant and when to plant. It's a great change. We have the right to get land from the government. Now the campesinos have land that before could only belong to the rich and the military. Now the majority of campesinos of Nicaragua all have land. The government is giving people title to the land through Agrarian Reform to make cooperatives. It's been three years since the government gave us the right to work this land, and two years since we have had title to it through the Agrarian Reform. I believe that with work and struggle and new methods and equipment, we campesinos will move forward.

In the time of the dictatorship there was little. There was hardly anything one could earn with his work. It was enough to try and feed the family. There was nothing left over. Now we have help because the government guarantees the prices of basic necessities for the whole population—so that no matter what happens we will all have the necessities. Before, it was often impossible to even find basic necessities. Now there is a perfect distribution of these basics.

Today all of the campesinos support the Revolution. We see the changes and we continued going forward with the struggle and in support of the Revolution. The aggression cannot change things here now because the entire people of Nicaragua would struggle to prevent a return to the past. This would become a country without people because all of us would struggle and die before we would return to the past. We would never give up our land. This is now *our* land. We would go to jail or fight in the mountains. We would never think of returning to the way things were in the past.

I would say to the people of the United States that the people here do not want another war. We are being oppressed now by an unjust war. We would ask the people of the U.S. to be one with us and to oppose this unjust war against Nicaragua. I would say that we people of Nicaragua, a country so small and poor, are not a danger to them and that their government is imposing a war on us. We don't want to anger anyone. We just want a better life. . . . We believe that the people of the U.S. are against the war because many *compañeros* from the U.S. have visited us and have told us that they are united with us and against the wars in Nicaragua and El Salvador.

It used to be very rare for Nicaraguans and Salvadorans to work together like at this cooperative, because there wasn't the unity that exists now between the Nicaraguan and Salvadoran people. Now the Salvadorans and Nicaraguans are one people. Now Salvadorans are struggling and fighting for their liberation as we did, and we are struggling against aggression. We are struggling to develop our country. We are fighting against a war of destruction. We are in a crisis. Everything we build they are trying to destroy.

All of us Nicaraguans and Salvadorans want that the war be ended. We want to be left in peace. That would be enough for us. We want to walk our own road and to continue going forward.

* * *

FATHER PETER MARCHETTI, a North American Jesuit priest, works with CIERA. Born in Seattle, Washington, he went to school in Omaha, Nebraska, joined the Jesuits in 1963 and entered the priesthood in 1977. As a priest, agrarian expert and government agricultural employee, he's in a unique position to give an overview of agricultural developments in Nicaragua today.

* * *

CONNIE MARTIN: Why are you in Nicaragua?

FATHER PETER MARCHETTI: I came here in early 1980 to give lectures on land reform strategy from what I had learned in my previous experiences in Chile. I had wanted to stay in the U.S. . . . for five years, [but] my friends were saying, "Come down here and give these talks," so I came down. I was invited to stay and take on the job of advising the Ministry of Agriculture here on land reform. I took it. So it was basically in being disenchanted with where the U.S. was going—knowing there would be a long wait before things in the U.S. would look better—and old friends inviting me to come here.

M: You said you had previously been in Chile?

MARCHETTI: I worked there for four years. In 1968 and from 1970 to 1973. I was there doing research on the Allende land reform. I studied land reform in Latin America for many years. Yale University gave me a degree in that field some years later.

M: What work are you doing in Nicaragua?

MARCHETTI: Here I do research on land reform, research that empowers the peasants to further their land reform. I've done a lot of work on agricultural planning, and how the agricultural sector fits into the economy and economic problems around those two issues.

M: How does this work fit into your religious work and priestly vocation?

MARCHETTI: It seems to me that the Christianity of the Gospels speaks of hope for the poor; it speaks of a reversal in which the poor, who have been forgotten and exploited by the rich, take over what the rich had and take over the basic thing the rich had in their hands, which is dignity. As a Roman Catholic priest what I'm involved in working for is a group, a mass of 15 million people in Central America whose basic problem is that they don't have land. That's the basic thing they need to have their dignity, to be able to feed and clothe their children. It seems to me that's what the Gospel is about.

For me, there's a distinct link between what I do and what the Gospel says. Moreover, when you're living here in Central America, sooner or later you realize that what the U.S. State Department, our President and our Pentagon can't get through their heads is that in these people there is a powerlessness which becomes powerful—and becomes something that is not efficient, it is clumsy and uneducated—but it's a power with which the U.S. mechanism is not going to be able to deal.

When we speak about our faith and when we talk about the power of the cause, you can see that here. What we're witnessing here is the passion of Jesus again and we're witnessing the power of this passion. That is, the U.S. can kill 100,000, 200,000, 300,000 Central Americans and all that does is create a new strength in the people.

You have an opportunity to live as a Christian here, but there's more than that. What there is is an important time in Christian history when it's very easy to see the revolution of God in struggle. If you're here long enough, like all of the Jesuits who've given their lives here, you know they're not perfect people, they're people with all kinds of weaknesses. And yet, at a given time, they live in such a way, they die in such a way, that their death becomes a part of a living tradition of faith. I think the Pentagon is clear that they have enough arms and diplomatic savvy to be able to win the war in Central America. But what they don't have is enough of the will to win. And that will to win comes down to having religion on their side or against them. That's why they've talked about bringing the "free churches," or the sects to replace the Roman Catholic Church, which they feel they can't trust anymore in Central America. The problem is that they have the idea that this is simply a political reality; that all you have to have is the right kind of priest or minister around to say the right things and the people will follow that. They're tremendously wrong. I think God is a God of justice. The poor have a sense of justice. At times in history when the mold of ideology and repressive thought patterns are broken, a revolution begins to occur and it's a revolution in spiritual terms.

So it's not like the poor are just pawns out there being moved around. Poverty has two faces. The face that grinds people down, destroys their dignity and makes it impossible for them to think of a new world and get out of poverty. But the other face is that if poverty is chosen freely then poverty becomes a tremendous force for liberation and mobilization. You can see it in the case of Gandhi, for example. That's what happens with many of the Central Americans who lead the struggle among the poor, and that's what happens among the masses who follow them. They freely choose their poverty. And I think religion is the same way. We think of a religion as a tremendous opium, a tremendously repressive force. But it has another face, too. Religion has a face of liberation, and once that starts, religion and belief in God can be an amazing force for changing structure. It's a force that gives absolute meaning to relative projects.

I don't think the Pentagon realizes that those are not just psychological patterns or situations of explosive poverty, but that here something is happening: a people of God are standing up and trying to achieve their freedom. And that's what's going to create more and more death here until they realize that they don't understand this—that Central America doesn't belong to the Pentagon but that it belongs to the Central American people.

M: Are we seeing two different faces of the Catholic Church in Nicaragua, and can the conservative hierarchy hold a revolutionary grass-roots movement in check?

MARCHETTI: We see a conflict in the church and we tend to say it's a religious conflict, but it's really not. It's a political conflict. Most of us think that as this gets more and more defined as a political conflict, the church that is for this process of change is going to not only receive blessings from the rest of the churches in this hemisphere but also support from the hierarchy, for the poor and not for the conservative bishops. Seventy-five percent of the bishops in this hemisphere, in the U.S., Brazil and elsewhere, already support this process.

To oppose this the hierarchy, the conservatives, have to politicize religion to the extent of identifying specific political positions with religiosity. Then they lose credibility. Any way you look at it, from an institutional viewpoint or a popular viewpoint, it's not going to go well for those who oppose the process. I say that knowing that all the signs say, "Here's the Roman Catholic Church doing it again. What would you expect but for them to be against social change!" The new factor here, though, is the intensity of religious belief, the kind of transformation that has gone on in all of the Central American societies since Vatican II in 1965. I'm optimistic.

M: How has Agrarian Reform worked in Nicaragua?

MARCHETTI: Agrarian Reform is a very broad thing. It means the transfer of resources, usually to the peasantry, within a social transformation. Agrarian Reform is a change in the correlation of forces within a society whereby a new social class gains power. Agrarian Reform is usually one of the key elements in that transformation. It's not only the transfer of land but also the transfer of credit, technical assistance and investments—all of which works to displace an old class of people, an old group of social forces who were holding back the development of society.

Land reform doesn't always mean that peasants end up being the group that has power. Land reform and peasant movements are the forces that overturned China, the Soviet Union, Germany, England and Vietnam. In all of those cases you had very different groups coming to power. But in all those cases a land reform occurred and it's much more than just the transfer of land to peasants. The transfer of land is the most striking aspect of change, but what really happens is a society is overturned, relationships of agriculture and countryside are radically changed, and new groups come to hold power in society.

Here the land reform had three different phases. The first phase was, I think, the more creative phase of land reform in Latin America. The first phase was what I like to call the "market phase" of the land reform. During that phase the price of land was reduced by 89% so that peasants were able to rent an acre of land for about $7. The land was rented from any private owner, but the rental price was controlled so that peasants could afford to rent it and grow crops to support themselves.

The second part of this "market phase" of the land reform was to allow access to the formal credit schemes in the national agricultural bank. In Somoza's time about 16,000 of the 150,000 peasant families had access to formalized credit. The vast majority dealt with usurous middlemen who charged them 50% and 60% interest on the credit they would give them. The credit usually came as a bottle of cooking oil for the wife or a machete for the husband. The peasant has no money, so the merchant says, "I'll give you that and I'll buy your crop at such and such a price." When you work out the averages on that, it was about 60% interest.

The third part of this "market phase" guaranteed prices to the peasants. Under Somoza prices were carefully controlled. For example, between 1975 and 1978, when the prices of corn and beans were up on the international market, Somoza drove the prices down here for the peasants. There was control over the price of land, credit and products and what the Revolution did for the peasantry over the first several years was to open up the market, to make it possible for someone in an ordinary situation to farm if they wanted to farm. About 100,000 peasants ended up receiving formal credit. The credit expanded by 700%. Three thousand cooperatives were formed during this period, making Nicaragua the fastest "cooperativizing" society in the history of any land reform in Latin America.

What was really happening was something that was really crucial: the state was not paternalizing the peasantry; they weren't saying, "Here's Somoza's old hacienda. We're going to put a cooperative in here and a cooperative is such and such and leaders of a cooperative are a president and a secretary . . ." There was no urban bureaucrat dictating to peasants to form a cooperative within an old hacienda. That was crucial, because what the peasants were able to do was to form new farms as they wanted. If they didn't have land, they were able to rent land and begin their farming operation at the scale where they could handle it and understand it. If there were groups of 15 or 16 families, together they rented a piece of land which they had the economic capacity to handle.

What has happened in other land reform is a whole problem of putting new wine in old wineskins. The old wineskin is the hacienda structure. The new wine is the peasant cooperative. What usually happens is that this is a productive failure. The peasants don't understand the cooperative. They don't understand the old hacienda no longer exists. This is a typical land reform problem that the Sandinistas, luckily or perhaps intelligently, didn't fall into. This is one of the key reasons we had a 15% growth rate in the agricultural sector last year. That was a year in which immense transformation was going on. Land reform was speeding up during the year. Yet the agricultural output went up by 15%. That's unheard of. Agricultural sectors fell apart in Mexico, Bolivia, Chile and Peru with their land reforms. This is the first one in our hemisphere to work in the sense that output is increased, peasants are getting land, and power is being transferred to workers, peasants and middle-class people who had been excluded from power under Somoza.

It's all the more remarkable because the three main engines of agricultural development still haven't recovered from the war. We lost about one quarter of the cattle from 1977 to 1979. Owners were killing off their herds and selling the contraband across the borders to Honduras and Costa Rica. The guerrillas eating cattle; the people eating cattle. The cattle sector is extremely crucial. This is really cattle country, like Nebraska or Texas in the 1860s. That hasn't come back. Cotton hasn't come back either because of the world prices. Nicaragua is doing better in its recovery than the rest of the countries in Central America with cotton, but it still hasn't come back. And corn hasn't come back. Despite the fact that these three biggest crops have a problem of recovery, the whole agricultural sector grew by 15% last year.

This first phase of land reform constituted giving the peasants the freedom to do what they wanted with a freer market situation. During that time the state put back into production 20% of the abandoned land that belonged to the Somoza clique. That's part of the reason the state was not paternalistic with the peasants: they had their hands full trying to put these farms back to work.

The second phase of the land reform is really just going through and legitimizing what the peasants had already done. The peasants had already taken over the land, established credit and established that they were responsible producers. After November 1981, the state began to hand over title to this land to the peasants. Much of the land the peasants received was state land. Actually, the state sector dropped from 23% of the land in 1980 to 19% of the land now, because the peasants tended to move on to the old Somoza lands to carve out their new farms and cooperatives. Under this second phase about one quarter of the peasantry have received land. About 60% have received the benefit of being in cooperatives with technical assistance. About 75% of the peasantry have received new benefits in terms of market freedoms—having the right to go to the bank, the right to guaranteed prices, etc.

The third phase of the land reform is the one we're in now, which is a phase mixed with the war of aggression that is hurting the peasantry so much. It's more of a traditional phase of land reform with urban promoters and urban middle-class people out pushing the land reform further. It's not as spontaneous, calm and slow as the first phase.

In the first phase, people in the countryside and small towns had the chance to sit down and say, "How do we want the land reform to go?" People sat down and said, "Well, who really are the people who ought to be expropriated here, according to our law?" And the law gave four basic guidelines for expropriation: one, your land is idle; two, you rent your land; three, your land is deficiently exploited—like the lands of the Pastora family, the family of ARDE [Democratic Revolutionary Alliance] leader Edén Pastora, who had 30,000 acres on which they had 40 acres of corn and 100 head of cattle. It was good land. That's what you call deficiently-exploited land. And, fourth, if you're decapitalizing your land or you have indentured servitude or sharecropping mechanisms working on your farm, you can be expropriated.

The first clause of the land reform states that anyone who produces has guaranteed rights to private property. It's a very practical, productive land reform law—as the whole land reform has been. It doesn't start off by saying that anyone with more than 500 acres is going to be expropriated. That's what happened in Chile and it was too arbitrary. You always found that there were people who had worked themselves up from dirt poverty, who had land, who really weren't exploiting people, who had their land taken away. And, on the other hand, you found some of the worst exploiters, who had 20 pieces of property that they had stolen from peasants whom they had trapped in debt mechanisms, and all of these pieces of land, although they made a huge estate, were tied up individually (and since land reform laws were expropriating titles), [these people] couldn't be touched. Here, what's expropriated is the family, all of the landowning members of a single family. And that makes a very just land reform law. Those are the three phases of this land reform.

M: Ramiro Gurdian, of COSEP and the former owner of the largest banana plantation in the country, tried to convince us that there was no need for land reform in Nicaragua. The problem, he said, was not an absence of land to distribute but a lack of people. He said that there were thousands of acres of unused, arable land that made it unnecessary to expropriate anyone's farms. He said as well that an additional criterion for expropriation was political discrimination against opponents of the Sandinistas.

MARCHETTI: Nicaragua has a shortage of labor relative to its land. And there are a number of reasons for that. People estimate that in the 16th century there were 600,000 Nicaraguans. When the Spanish got through taking over and selling Nicaraguans down into the silver mines of Potosí [Bolivia] the estimate is that there were 46,000 left. That's the first reason this country is relatively depopulated in comparison to El Salvador. The second reason is that Somoza, and the other property owners in alliance with him, denied credit to the peasants and produced a peasantry who couldn't afford to farm. There was a lot of land out there, and it was all locked up in big, unproductive estates. In that sense, Ramiro is right—there's all kinds of land in this country and there is a relative shortage of labor. But that didn't mean that peasants didn't want land and need land to stop the poverty and disease in their families.

One of the things that has to be understood is that there was an alliance between the export growers, who had highly technical production, and the very extensive, backward cattle ranchers. The cattle ranchers who took over all of that land held about 10 million acres for cattle development and used about 1.6 million acres for export crops. What that huge acreage of cattle did was to act as a buffer so that the peasants couldn't develop their agriculture. It assured that impoverished peasants had to sell their labor for starvation wages to the export growers. So Ramiro told you the truth, but he didn't tell you how that truth hides an ugly fact about Somoza's agro-export business.

Another part of that ugly fact is Managua. Because peasants didn't have the right to farm their land under Somoza, there was no room for the small family enterprise in that society; they tended to wind up being workers on the agro-export estates or coming to Managua. Nicaragua is the most urban society in all of Central America even though it has the most land per person. Managua is far and away, in relative terms, the biggest city in all of Central America, precisely because people were driven off their land by these mechanisms.

One of the real problems in agricultural development here is two things. MIDINRA means Ministry of Agricultural Development and Land Reform. For agricultural development in this society to advance you need labor, and I think one of the hopes is that when El Salvador is finally free it's going to be very important for many Salvadorans to emigrate into Nicaragua and to work and develop their lives here because the land resources in El Salvador are horrible. One of the hopes for the future is that sort of trade-off between El Salvador and Nicaragua. The Nicaraguans would welcome the Salvadorans because they would answer a tremendous need in this society.

M: Wouldn't that set the scene for all kinds of tensions, like the guest-worker Turks in Germany or the Salvadoran peasants who were driven out of Honduras?

MARCHETTI: That depends on the type of government. You find throughout Latin America that peasants and workers share a very similar culture. It tends to be the middle and upper classes who differentiate into national cultures. I think also the cases you mentioned are cases where immigrant populations are being manipulated for a national economy. It wasn't a problem when European farmers moved into Minnesota and Wisconsin. In agricultural frontier situations as we have here, with a vast shortage of labor, the challenge is to develop agriculture by very hard physical labor, I don't see it as a problem.

M: Is the private sector still producing here in Nicaragua?

MARCHETTI: Well, what do you mean by the "private sector"? People make a mistake when they think the private sector is made up of large entrepreneurs. That's true in Guatemala and El Salvador. It's not at all true in Costa Rica or Nicaragua. The private sector here is the small producer. It's the man who has two or three hired hands on his farm, who perhaps learned how to read during the Literacy Crusade, who has no desire to go to Miami or to purchase anything from Miami. His only sign of being successful is to see how many cattle he controls or how many acres of land he can wrench out of the jungle and turn into coffee production. That's the private sector. They control, at this point, about 45% of the land.

As a whole they control 60% of the land, if we include all the small farmers who don't have anyone working for them. A person like Ramiro Gurdian would feel very uncomfortable sitting in 149,400 of the 150,000 homes of this private sector. Gurdian would feel comfortable with 600 members of the private sector. And of those 600 he would find three groups. Two hundred are patriotic producers who find the Revolution continues to give them a chance to make a profit, to continue to produce. Usually, these 200 have family ties. Their children are Sandinistas. They may not like all the revolutionary changes but they can't leave their family. Their wife might be a Sandinista. Or they might just be honest people who see the new schools and [the new] clinics and whose main problems might be U.S. mines blowing up ships in the port, which make it hard to get goods and cuts off their credit.

So here is Ramiro, able socially to walk into the homes of 600 of the 150,000 members of the private sector. Two hundred are patriotic producers and aren't going to talk to him. Another 200 of them are what we call the "climate seekers." If the Revolution gives them a good price for their sorghum, they produce sorghum and feel pretty good about things. If the Revolution doesn't increase the price of sorghum, they don't produce sorghum and go on strike and force the Revolution to increase the price of sorghum again in order to get the sorghum to feed the chickens to supply all of the people in Managua whom Somoza drove off the land. With that group Ramiro, or U.S. Senators, might be able to speak the same language.

There's another group of 200 with whom the majority of our U.S. senators, congresspeople and Ronald Reagan would be in full agreement: the people who are decapitalizing. These are people who want to see this Revolution destroyed. These are people who don't want to see a private sector be successful in Central America. What they want to see successful are the multinational corporations who will supply a fragment of the private sector with capital goods for development. They want to see that other private sector reduced to tenant farmers, sharecroppers or impoverished, small capitalists who have to sell them labor.

I think this is the most terrifying thing of this Revolution to people in Washington who know what's going on. There are a lot of people in Washington who are ideologically convinced that the world is divided into Communists and non-Communists. I think there's another group of people in Washington who are afraid of being tagged as unpatriotic because they're soft on the communists. But I think there's another group in Washington, people who are ruthless, who say, "We have to destroy the Nicaraguan Revolution because if it succeeds people will see that it's not a stereotypical Communist revolution, but a revolution that will appeal to an advanced private sector: farmers across Latin America. And if that happens, we could lose all of Latin America." That's the way those people think in Washington.

The big entrepreneurial sector in whose homes Ramiro Gurdian would feel comfortable now owns 12% of the land. They're not very important in terms of land mass. They might be producing 24% of the agricultural products. That's a lot. But when you have to look at what's important, you look at the people who hand you three meals instead of one meal.

The Revolution wants to work even with this sector, however, because they need their production. But the response of the big private sector producers is not a response dictated by production. It's a response dictated by politics. Part of the goal of this Revolution is not to eliminate their entrepreneurial sector and not to drive out the highly qualified professionals in this society. The leaders of the Revolution think something like this: "The rich have kept the poor alive, barely alive, so that the poor could work to keep the rich rich. Now that the poor have gained a slice of power in Nicaraguan society why should these people who have suffered and slaved drive the rich out? Why not keep them alive—'barely alive' in their own conception of what it means to be alive, to be alive as a rich person—so that they can help reconstruct a war-devastated country and move into the future?"

That's not only a tactical thing for the next 20 years of this mixed economy model, but the Sandinistas are creating a new socialist model in which they don't have to take over the means of production. They control finance and commerce, essentially, and leave the freedom in the productive sphere. It's a new type of model and it's proved to be very effective up to this point. I think when you produce a new private sector in Nicaragua of 150,000 members, they become entrenched as a new social base, one that's going to be with us long into the future.

The U.S. is not going to help Nicaragua. And the Soviet Union is not going to bail out Nicaragua, probably because they're over-extended. So Nicaragua is going to have to depend on its nonaligned course and this new economic model. I think a lot of people here wish that Reagan was right and that the Soviets wanted in here in a big way as he thinks they do—that would be a wonderful thing for production at this point. But they don't. I think part of that has to do with the fact that Nicaraguans are very jealous of their freedom. They're a very proud people. After having been run over for five decades they're not about not to run this society themselves. They paid 50,000 lives [in the 1978–79 war against Somoza] for that. I don't think any representative from a developed nation who comes to Nicaragua fully understands that. They think that because this nation is poor, because these people are in an out-of-the-way nook of the world, these people should all of a sudden roll over backwards because someone's come from the U.S. or Britain or the Soviet Union. I think that's a problem. It's the price these people are paying for their dignity. The poor continue to suffer because they have their dignity in Nicaragua today. That wouldn't have to be if any of the major nations of the world were willing to say, "We respect fully and support Nicaragua."

In 1984, our projections are that Reagan's war is going to stop Nicaragua's economic growth. In 1983, Nicaragua had the highest rate of economic growth of any country in Latin America. It was just a little bit behind the U.S. in terms of growth rate. But the war now threatens this growth and development.

11. Organizing Labor

Edgardo García

During the Somoza period the three major labor organizations represented less than 9% of the Nicaraguan workforce. Although such unions, unaffiliated with the Sandinistas, legally continue to function and organize, the largest present-day labor organizations support the Sandinista government. They are the Association of Rural Workers (ATC), with 42,000 members, and the urban-based Sandinista Workers Confederation (CST), which represents more than 100 individual unions.

For a view of union work in Nicaragua, we spoke with EDGARDO GARCÍA, 28, the elected secretary general of the ATC ever since he helped found it in 1978.

* * *

PHILIP ZWERLING: What relationship does the ATC have with the Frente Sandinista?

EDGARDO GARCÍA: We are an independent union, but we certainly recognize the Frente Sandinista as the vanguard and leaders of our Revolution. We are a union and they are a political party.

Z: Your union has a membership of 42,000 agricultural workers. Are there other unions in the countryside?

GARCÍA: No, only the ATC. There are a few community groups on some of the larger haciendas that are independent, but the ATC represents the mass of agricultural workers. This is because the union movement in Nicaragua developed in cities like Managua and León historically, and represented city workers. The peasant workers only began to organize very late, and the ATC was their first and only union.

Z: Who are your members?

GARCÍA: They're agricultural workers in the cotton, coffee, rice, tobacco and basic grain fields.

Z: Are these workers who own their own land?

GARCÍA: No, they are workers in agricultural enterprises on public and private farms.

Z: These are not workers on the cooperatives?

GARCÍA: No, these are workers on other people's land, and usually on the larger farms, with more than five workers.

Z: How did the ATC begin?

GARCÍA: Let me show you a magazine we put out, called *Machete*. This edition, well printed on quality paper, celebrates our sixth anniversary. We predate the Triumph of the Revolution. The ATC was founded in a national assembly on April 25, 1978, which met clandestinely in a convent in the mountains. Many of the founders were "Delegates of the Word," like myself, who were working in the countryside. And this is the first issue of *Machete* that we put out back then. [He shows me two pages of crudely mimeographed material.]

Z: So the ATC was an illegal union at its founding?

GARCÍA: Of course. It had to be secret because of the repression. We were risking months in jail and torture in starting this organization. We were organizing the most exploited workers. These peasants were paid low wages for long hours of hard work. Efforts to improve their lot were met with force by the government, which supported the landowners. Somoza even had the authority to set salaries. The standard was 20 cordobas and 10 centavos per day [about $2]. But that was an upper limit, and the various owners often paid their workers much less.

There were also the problems of poor food and housing for the workers, and the abence of medical care. There are places, for example, like the farm of Alfonso Robelo [originally a member of the Junta, now a contra leader] where, because the river was distant from the fields, the workers had to fill a single, plastic container with water in the morning to last them for a full day's work in the hot sun. The water was to wash their hands and face, make coffee and their water to drink. This one container of water had to last till the following morning. It was a brutal system. This is the way it was on Robelo's farm. The workers also had to buy their food in the store on the farm, and here the landlord charged them high prices. This was standard in the work centers.

Another problem was unemployment. People might work during the harvest and then be laid off when the harvest was over. Then there was no work for them and no salary. People traveled from place to place, as continuous migrants, looking for work. You can check the statistics and see that in the days of the most severe unemployment, the peasants began to seize land for themselves. People who had spent all winter without work tried to take some land. Days later the Guardia came in, destroyed the seed that they had planted, burned their shacks and arrested people. In this kind of situation it was dangerous to even talk of a union, let alone do real organizing. Many who tried were murdered. Every organization of the people was destroyed by the state.

Edgardo García, Photo by Connie Martin

Z: How was it that church workers, like the "Delegates of the Word" got involved in the plight of these peasants?

GARCÍA: This was a process that began in Honduras. In 1972 or so, several priests began this movement among the peasants there. It was influenced by theologians of liberation theology in Mexico and Chile. These priests preached about a God who was on the side of the poor, and of the value of a lifetime commitment of service to the poor. In Jalapa, on the frontier with Honduras, there were two priests who brought this idea to Nicaragua. They worked with peasants in Jalapa and trained them as "Delegates of the Word" to preach the Gospel to their fellow peasants and to lead exemplary lives of service among their people. In Solentiname [an archipelago in Lake Nicaragua where Father Ernesto Cardenal founded a Christian community] a similar process occurred.

This movement reached out to workers with a message of liberation. These humble, exploited peasants learned that Jesus had also been a poor worker like them. They learned that God had entered history on their side. This changed the way they saw themselves and their lives, and empowered them to act for change after living under repression and dictatorship for 40 years.

This was a new and distinct form of struggle. Before, people were taught that regardless of how bad their circumstances were in life, they could still work toward a tranquil mind and soul by worshipping God simply as an individual believer. But this new message was that it was impossible to live with God unless you lived correctly with your brothers and sisters. And you cannot live right with them when they are suffering oppression, hunger and disease. The work is to improve life for all. If you are not with them, you are not with God.

This was the thought behind this new movement. It transformed the "Delegates," and it transformed the people. It led them to discuss their situation and to plan to change it: to form cooperatives, small unions and newsletters. Sin was seen as not merely a personal error, but as a system of exploitation as well. If a thief was a sinner, then a landlord who oppressed his workers was a sinner as well because he was also a thief who stole the wealth of the people. It didn't take long for Somoza to identify these "Delegates of the Word" as enemies of the state, and many of them were murdered.

My family was Catholic, but my father, with whom I was not living, was a Baptist pastor. So my world was full of religion as a child. As a teenager I worked in a textile factory. Because of the poor conditions there, we workers went on strike. It was at that time that I first had contact with the FSLN. When we lost the strike I had to run from the factory because I had been too visible in the leadership. It was at this time that I first had contact with priests who were sponsoring the movement of the "Delegates of the Word" and the "Church of the Poor." I saw that this movement brought together the theological thought and ethical action that I had been looking for. I had found my faith.

With the help and training of these priests I became a "Delegate of the Word," and worked at this vocation from the age of 16 to 19. I studied the Bible and learned the Word of God. Then I conducted meetings, celebrations and religious services. I tried to apply the Gospel message to the reality of life in Nicaragua under the Somoza dictatorship. Concretely, this meant unifying the people and their organizations to work together and bring them a message of hope that strengthened them in their struggle for their rights.

It was a short step from preaching the Word of God to organizing labor unions, really. Because a labor union was merely a vehicle people could use to claim their rights. Also in this were Christian base communities in the countryside, which could cooperate as Christians with other revolutionary organizations like the Frente Sandinista. Christian organizations acted in this way decisively in takeovers of land and in public seizures of churches to make public and visible their plight. A literacy campaign in the countryside was also organized out of this Christian movement among the peasants in the mid-seventies. We were really making the Gospel come alive in ordinary people's lives.

By 1977, I was well known as a Christian who was committed to the Sandinista struggle, and repression was directed against me personally. Public work became too dangerous and I had to go underground. At first the dictatorship had been leery of dealing harshly with religious people, but it didn't take long for them to crack down. Of the five of us who founded the ATC, three were murdered by the Guardia.

Living clandestinely, I organized logistical support for the guerrillas—to supply food, water and weapons to the fighters. At times I was also, for all practical purposes, a guerrilla as well. In areas controlled by the FSLN we worked to feed the civilians as well as the guerrillas. We had to organize the people in an area so that they could survive the response of the Guardia to starve the guerrillas out. For example, when Masaya was under attack, we organized the peasants of Carazo to gather milk, grain, cooking oil—the basics—and to send them to the people of Masaya so that they could continue the struggle. In this way everyone was involved in the war long before the Triumph. The work brought together people in the city and in the countryside and in the different regions of the country, to offer support to each other against the common enemy. And, in all of this, religious people and religious organizations were involved.

Z: How does the ATC function today on behalf of its members?

GARCÍA: We have organized people in every field of agricultural work: basic grains, coffee, cattle, cotton, etc. We have dealt with problems of unemployment, health and working conditions. We've worked to make sure that women workers are paid the same as men. And today they are. We try to improve safety on the job. When we found that many pregnant women, who were tobacco workers, were being adversely affected by the nicotine—it was affecting their milk—we publicized this problem to protect them and their babies. We try to make sure that each large agricultural enterprise has a health center and a center for adult education classes, with classes through four levels of literacy. We are trying to improve housing conditions on each farm as well.

Z: Are the landowners resisting these changes?

GARCÍA: Of course. It's a long, hard battle. But now, for the first time, we have the power of the union and the power of the state on the side of the workers.

Z: Do you have problems with the state farm managers as well as with private landowners?

GARCÍA: Sometimes. There can be bad managers and the same kinds of problems.

Z: Are there times when a state farm manager, in a drive to increase production might, for example, pay less attention to the health needs of the workers?

GARCÍA: This could happen, but then we need only go to the health minister for the government to intervene and solve the conflict.

Z: What's the actual process if a worker has a particular complaint?

GARCÍA: First the local union official would meet with the farm manger to find a solution. It can continue to the next highest level if it comes to the assembly of the workers at that enterprise.

Z: There are such assemblies at each enterprise?

GARCÍA: Yes. The other thing is to call the Ministry of Labor, where there is a tripartite commission that will deal with the conflict. It's also possible to use a labor tribunal, where both sides can state their case, like a trial.

Z: We've spoken with Ramiro Gurdian of COSEP and UPANIC [see Chapter 5]. Has the ATC had problems with UPANIC [the association of private agricultural producers]?

GARCÍA: Oh, yes. Of course.

Z: He told us that in the past they never had problems with their workers, but now they do.

GARCÍA: That's too bad! But now the workers can do something about their situation and before they couldn't. For example, we're in a struggle right now with a big private farmer to force him to provide clean and safe water to his workers. This is the kind of trouble we make!

Z: In the U.S. we hear that Nicaragua is a totalitarian country, and that includes a work force and a union movement that is controlled by communists. How would you respond to that?

GARCÍA: They call us communists. They could call us progressives, Catholics, revolutionaries or democrats. We are all of those things. We are Sandinistas. I guess that's what Reagan doesn't understand.

Z: Have you faced problems of economic sabotage in the countryside?

GARCÍA: We've seen owners sabotage production. We have [seen] abandoned farms. Owners have taken government loans to buy equipment and then have sold the equipment over the border in Honduras or Costa Rica. Or they take their cattle and sell them across the border. The contras attack farms to disrupt production as well. We face many, many, many such problems. Union officials are targeted for assassination as well as literacy workers and medical brigadistas. Many have been killed. As long as this war continues the people in the countryside will be suffering.

12. Human Rights

Sister Mary Hartman

Human rights as an issue has taken on political as well as humanitarian importance. President Reagan has pointed to a lack of human rights in Nicaragua as a justification for U.S. intervention. For a greater understanding of the issue, Connie Martin interviewed 56-year-old SISTER MARY HARTMAN, a Roman Catholic nun from Pennsylvania who is head of the Social Services Department of the National Commission for the Promotion and Protection of Human Rights.

* * *

CONNIE MARTIN: I've met many North Americans working in Nicaragua today. How did you come to be here and how has this experience changed your thinking?

SISTER MARY HARTMAN: I was born in Altoona, Pennsylvania, in 1928 and made the decision to join the Sisters of St. Agnes, who have their headquarters in Fond du Lac, Wisconsin. I trained as a teacher and received my master's in education at Marquette University. I had expected to teach in the United States, but soon after I earned my degree I responded to a call asking 10% of all of the religious orders to work in other countries to evangelize for our faith. I was sent to Nicaragua in 1962.

I was quite unprepared for this assignment because I spoke no Spanish then and had no real background or understanding of the reality of Central America. However, in those days the only requirements were to have a college degree and I had big feet, and I figured that made me pretty stable.

I must admit that I came down here with the mentality that I was going to bring the True Word and the light of human progress to these poor, backward people. I was sent to the Atlantic Coast and worked among the Miskito Indians in Waspán near the Honduran border.

Medicines and food were sent down to us from the States so we could feel very virtuous in distributing these to the Indians. And these made a difference for some, but we couldn't really feed and care for everyone who was so desperately poor. We developed the feeling that we would do what we could but that, as the Bible says, "The poor are always with you."

Sister Mary Hartman, Photo by Zwerling

My own thinking began to change in 1970 when I was assigned to work in the poor Managua barrio of Riguero with Father Uriel Molina. This was after the Second Vatican Conference in Rome and the Bishops' Conference at Medellín, Colombia. In Riguero, we began to put into practice this new idea of an option for the poor, of incarnating oneself in the life of the poor. We lived with the poor, learned from them and suffered with them. It became clear that the poor were not intended by God to live in such subhuman conditions. Rather, they had the need and the right to change their situation. Just as the Israelites fled oppression in Egypt and wandered in the desert for 40 years, so the poor had to take that trek, too. For even if we don't reach the Promised Land perhaps our children will.

In 1972, a great earthquake struck Managua. The earth opened and at the same time people's eyes opened to the complete corruption of the government. In Riguero, one month after the earthquake the National Guard jeeps were in the streets selling canned goods and clothes to the people. These were contributions of international aid they were selling. I had occasion to return to my order's house in Wisconsin. Wisconsin was a sister state to Nicaragua and I spoke to the press there about how their aid was being sold in Nicaragua. And then I read in the papers that the statewide chairperson of this earthquake aid effort had denounced me as a liar. It turned out he was a friend of Somoza, and I learned more about corruption.

In our barrio most of the people had lost electricity and water after the earthquake. After many months only a small percentage had had these services restored. People circulated petitions to the government but received only unkept promises. So one night, after church services, the people walked through the barrio to protest the lack of electricity and water. It was a peaceful protest of women and children, families. But the National Guard jeeps rushed in and the Guardia attacked us, beating and teargassing people.

Why do people finally take up arms? And how can Christians undertake armed struggle? It takes a long time. It takes a long history of abuse and violence and oppression. There were 90 teenagers in the youth club in our barrio. Half of them had disappeared or been assassinated *prior* to the Insurrection. The corruption and violence of the whole system made people determined that they had to do something to change it. They began to organize themselves into study clubs to teach first aid, to study why Latin America was so poor, and to share their personal commitment to change.

In 1974, a group of university students came to live in our barrio. They were studying subjects like anthropology, economics and political science. These students, from wealthy families, had come to share their lives with the poor people of the barrio. They gave courses and led study groups. They helped me to understand social conditions and the work of the multinational corporations. These students had left an easy life at home to become involved with the poor. Their example gave me a concept of what it was to be a Christian. And their example gave me courage to act too.

I was living with a family in the barrio and I used the two small rooms I had there for meetings and for gathering medicines. I had an old Volkswagen which I used to transport FSLN cadre clandestinely. The university students slowly began to disappear from the barrio as they went underground to work with the FSLN. But through them I had begun to get involved. I started out helping to get medicines to the people in jail, and then I was asked to do more. I opened our home as a safe house and clandestinely transported workers in my car. By 1978, my work was coming to the attention of the Guardia. People who were arrested were questioned about me. To protect the family I lived with and their six children, I moved out of the barrio to the outskirts of Managua.

You know, those university students I met then are now in the revolutionary government. Luis Carrion is now vice-minister of interior, Joaquín Cuadro heads the army chiefs of staff, Salvador Mayorga and Roberto Gutiérrez are both vice-ministers of agriculture. They showed us what it was to be a Christian and they still do—by their generosity, sincerity and honesty. They weren't really trained or prepared for government positions, but they're learning, just as each of us has, as we go along.

M: And what has your work been since the Triumph?

HARTMAN: In 1980, the United Nations suggested that each country have its own human rights commission. Nicaragua was the first country in Latin America to respond to this call by establishing the National Commission for the Protection and Promotion of Human Rights. Our first President of this commission was Leonte Herdocia [who succumbed to a heart attack in Geneva in 1983], who had served on the United Nations Human Rights Commission. The commission consists of 12 members, each elected for a two-year term. They include two priests, two lawyers, a Moravian pastor and a Baptist minister, a doctor and a university president. The commission works independently of the government to investigate abuses of human rights and to educate the people at large to the sanctity of human rights.

I wasn't really prepared for this work, but perhaps because I had been involved in human rights work during the time of Somoza I was asked to head the Social Services Department.

You see, under the dictatorship the Christian community had organized around these issues. We had organized denouncements of human rights violations under Somoza. One time we drew up a list of 300 peasants who had been murdered, and brought their relatives secretly into Managua where we organized a public meeting to hear their testimony. Their charges made the front page of *La Prensa*.

Only once was I allowed to visit one of Somoza's prisons. We were 300 people trying to meet and visit in a single suffocating room. We would take food to the prisoners and a guard would meet us at the gate with a wheelbarrow to receive it. We would pay him, but we could never be sure the food would be delivered.

You talk about human rights, but to know what the National Guard did to our people here makes such words meaningless. Young people would disappear and parents would be called to go to the morgue to identify their children. There they would find the bodies of their sons and daughters without eyes or fingernails; horribly tortured. Then later, the bodies weren't even being returned anymore, and parents would go each day to the street where the bodies would be left. It was the road to the refinery outside Managua and it became known as the "curve of the dead."

Recently, the Roman Catholic bishops sent out a pastoral letter calling for reconciliation among Nicaraguans, revolutionaries and contras [Easter 1984], but these same bishops have refused to see the reconciliation I see between guards and prisoners in the penitentiaries. That's where my work is. In the rehabilitation programs the whole basis for the work is that each prisoner has worth. That each prisoner can learn a trade and return to live in this society when they leave prison.

I was at the prison at Tipitapa [just outside Managua] and talked to the prisoners alone, as I always do. One prisoner told me: "It's really great that 400 of us are getting courses in construction and another 400 getting courses in mechanics. We get three meals a day. It's not that I want to stay here, but life is pretty good." This was said by a former member of Somoza's National Guard and it reflects the difference everyone can see now from the time of Somoza.

M: How are prisoners treated and are there political prisoners in Nicaragua?

HARTMAN: Most of the complaints we receive are about the slow legal process, which is a problem. And there are some cases of physical abuse. This is not a paradise for prisoners. But we take these issues to the higher authorities and justice is done. For example, we discovered prisoners being held in an unlit cell without being fed. We took this case to Tomás Borge, minister of the interior, and named the guards who were responsible. Those guards are now in prison themselves. In fact, some 300 employees of the Ministry of the Interior or the Army are in jail now for violations of human rights. Working for this commission I have the right to visit any prison at any time without warning and to speak to any prisoner in private.

It would be accurate to say that here vengeance has been replaced by the Christian concept of pardoning the sinner. On July 19, 1979, with the Triumph of the Revolution, 7,500 National Guardsmen and Somocistas were in prison. Most served short sentences or were released immediately. Today there are only 2,000 such prisoners. And under the new *Ley de Gracia* [Law of Forgiveness] each of these 2,000 prisoners will have his case reviewed by lawyers from this commission on the basis of any new evidence or mitigating circumstances. And each sentence will be reviewed to be sure it was not too harsh. This has already begun, and of the first 200 cases reviewed, 49 prisoners have been freed or had their sentences reduced. No sentences can be increased in this process. One of the first acts of this revolutionary government was to abolish capital punishment. The maximum sentence for the most serious crimes is 30 years. If we didn't face the present armed aggressions on the northern and southern borders I think half of these remaining 2,000 prisoners could be released immediately.

I don't believe there are political prisoners here, although some of the counterrevolutionaries no doubt see themselves that way. These people are in prison because they've been convicted of smuggling arms or acts of sabotage—not for simply speaking out against the government. The difference between now and Somoza's time is the difference between night and day. Somoza didn't have many prisoners because he killed most of them.

The aim of Somoza's prisons was to brutalize and dehumanize the inmates. Tomás Borge was kept in solitary when he was a prisoner and horribly tortured. His wife was arrested and died under torture. But it was Borge who came up with the idea of the farms where prisoners live and work in the countryside without walls or barbed wire or armed guards. There's nothing else like these "open prisons" in all of Latin America.

M: As a member of a religious order I'd like to ask you about the charges of religious persecution against Catholics and Jews that have been made against this government.

HARTMAN: Charges of anti-Semitism had been made against the Sandinista government by individuals in the United States, and in response to a communication from the Anti-Defamation League of B'nai B'rith, our commission undertook an investigation of these charges. We found that Nicaragua had been home to perhaps 150 Jews. Two-thirds of them had left Nicaragua following the earthquake of 1972. Of the 50 who remained, almost all left before the Triumph in 1979 for various reasons: because the economy was in disarray, because they were in partnership with Somoza, or because they feared an anti-Semitic backlash for having helped arrange Israeli arms sales to the Somoza dictatorship.

One prominent Somoza supporter who is Jewish, Abraham Gorn, was arrested and his property confiscated, according to law, after the Sandinista victory. He was imprisoned for a week and then released. He sought asylum in the Costa Rican Embassy and a few days later was allowed to leave the country. He now has a factory in Costa Rica. On Gorn's confiscated land here in Nicaragua was a building used by the Israelite congregation as their synagogue. However, the congregation had never filed legal title to that property and it appeared as land belonging to Abraham Gorn.

Our commission's investigation found no examples of anti-Semitism, but did recommend that the synagogue be returned to the Israelite congregation. This the government has agreed to do, but the small Jewish community of Nicaragua has said they are unable to care for the upkeep of the building. In fact, they have appealed, without success, to Jewish organizations in the United States for financial aid to restore the synagogue.

Now even President Reagan has repeated this charge of anti-Semitism in Nicaragua [speech May 9, 1984], but it has no basis in fact, and is simply part of a propaganda war against this country.

The Roman Catholic bishops here will also say that they are persecuted. There have been incidents, but in each case we have investigated these have been the response of people in the barrios to a particular event and not part of any government plan. For example, in Barrio San Judas the people learned that Bishop Bosco Juvas was coming to their neighborhood to celebrate mass and that he planned to lead a street procession with political content after the mass. People in the parish, not all, but many, met the bishop before the service and told him he could not enter the neighborhood. And he left. Later, this was reported as the action of a Sandinista mob, but it was just the people of that parish.

The archbishop of Managua, Monsignor Obando y Bravo, used to have a regular television show of his masses. Only he spoke, and the program was pre-recorded. This didn't make for very good television, so the government-owned station [the Sandinista government controls the only two Nicaraguan television stations, having seized them along with all other personal property of Anastasio Somoza (Debayle)] suggested that the program be changed to include the other bishops or that the mass be broadcast live. The archbishop vetoed both of these changes and now he says that he has been censored.

But this same archbishop has removed over 12 priests and nuns from their parish assignments because they had in some way supported the people and the Revolution. He even tried to get rid of me. One day the archbishop met a member of our order in the street here in Managua. He told her, "I want that Sister Hartman out of Nicaragua!" When this was reported to me, I contacted our superior, who told Monsignor Obando y Bravo that such a request for a transfer would have to be put in writing. To this day he has not done that.

The hierarchy of the Catholic Church here has opted for Reagan's plans. In fact, there was a *Boston Globe* story of February 27, 1983, that the bishop received $600,000 from AID [U.S. Agency for International Development]. Such money is used to build homes for the poor, for example. This would be good if it were sincere, but it's used as a political statement so that the bishops can appear to be protecting the people from an atheistic government.

It's not really surprising that the hierarchy is in opposition to this government. I know the archbishop well. He was elevated to this position in 1970 and he has always been guided by an elite group of advisors. His friends were all part of the economic and political elite. He moved when this elite moved. In the last year [1978–79] even they came to oppose Somoza and decided to support the Sandinistas. The archbishop sent out a letter, just one week before the war started, saying that armed rebellion had become the only solution. But then, one week before the Triumph, he went to Venezuela to ask for U.S. intervention to forestall a Sandinista victory.

The archbishop maintains close ties with the U.S. embassy. When [Richard] Stone [U.S. ambassador-at-large to Central America] and [Henry] Kissinger [chairman of President Reagan's Special Commission on Central America] came here, they met with the archbishop and not with us. The archbishop has refused to meet with people in the Christian base communities [organized in the barrio parishes], and has refused dialogue.

The Catholic hierarchy is very powerful. The people have been taught—and I was taught this and had a hard time changing—that the bishops speak for God. And they have used this power. They have organized public street processions to show how many people will attend to support them.

On the last Good Friday they even used a supposedly miraculous statue, "The Blood of Jesus," that they had previously ignored, to get people into the streets to celebrate the statue. And then, when thousands of people had gathered, the bishop's talk was political. This was reported in the U.S. as an antigovernment rally when the people had gone to see the statue.

The bishop is trying to form an antigovernment front in Nicaragua around himself. The people will not turn their back on the bishop for fear of losing their souls. This feeling was reinforced and magnified by the Pope's visit here, when he repeatedly spoke about the "authority of the bishops."

M: Will people be forced to choose between their religious beliefs and their faith in the Revolution?

HARTMAN: There's a purification going on here and the church really needs it. The church needs to make clear its option for the poor. But the bishops haven't done this. They've never implemented the recommendations of the Medellín conference [which issued a strong expression of what has become known as liberation theology in 1968].

I think there's going to be a lot of repression by the hierarchy against religious people who believe in the Revolution. The bishops have refused to pray for Christians who have died defending the towns on Nicaragua's borders. They've never made the effort to visit the people who are on the front lines of these attacks. The hierarchy would simply like to see a counter-revolutionary victory.

Today Nicaraguan Christians fall into three camps. First, those who are very conscientious, especially the young, who are turning their backs on the bishops. They're writing themselves off from the bishops, but not from God or the church. Second, those who read the pastoral letters, who see the fruits of the Revolution, but who are not Sandinistas. These people are confused, but the moment for them to decide for one side or another is coming very soon. And third, those people who don't understand the pastoral letters or the issues, but who will simply believe and follow the words of the bishops.

I don't really know what the future holds. The bishop has access to shape international opinion against the Revolution. I think we're approaching a time of great crisis. I expect a final ultimatum soon that priests in this government will have to leave. Recently, members of our commission went to the archbishop to request a donation of 100 church songbooks to be used for religious services in jail. He refused to contribute a single hymnal because he refused to support in any way the work of the Sandinistas.

M: Isn't it true that there are two Human Rights Commissions in Nicaragua today?"

HARTMAN: Yes, ours, and the so-called Permanent Commission on Human Rights that was formed in 1977 and did a good job against the Somoza dictatorship. But now they've been making exaggerated denouncements. It's not possible to know, and they've refused to say, where their funding comes from. Their director went to Venezuela with [Archbishop] Obando y Bravo in 1979 to seek U.S. intervention against a Sandinista victory and he works closely with U.S. personnel. Right after the victory, he went to Europe with a list of 700 names of people he claimed had been killed by the Sandinistas, but an examination of the list showed that some were alive in Miami, some were in Honduras and that others had been killed in the Insurrection. Later he produced a list of Miskitos [Indians] who he charged had been buried alive. But we interviewed people whose names appeared on that list.

They were still quite alive. Now there's no doubt that there have been cases of human rights abuses here, but I can tell you that in each case we have been able to see that justice has been done.

M: What is the true story behind the charges of abuses committed by the Sandinistas against the Miskitos?

HARTMAN: I worked on the Atlantic Coast, where most of the Miskitos live, in the 1960s. The Miskitos lived a very isolated existence. Access to their territory from Managua was only by plane. They weren't part of the national picture and really didn't see themselves as Nicaraguans. Most of their contact was with English-speaking people. In fact, they had been used by English settlers to fight against the Spanish hundreds of years ago. In the nineteenth century their contact was with white missionaries, and then with the United Fruit Company and the North American mining companies. The Miskitos were used in the mines until they got siliocosis or tuberculosis and then they were sent home to die. Of course, living with their families everyone became infected, and I saw whole families suffering from tuberculosis. Eighty percent of the Miskitos had tuberculosis.

I met Steadman Fagoth [Muller], who has become a leader of the antigovernment Miskitos in Honduras, when I worked in Waspán. He was a student of mine at the university in the seventies. he received scholarships to both the UCA and UNAN universities. When the revolutionary government formed the Council of State, Steadman Fagoth was chosen by the Miskitos to represent them there.

But after the victory, the government began processing 35,000 of Somoza's files of collaborators and informers that had been left behind. Steadman Fagoth's file was among these. His scholarships to the universities had been arranged so that he could spy for Somoza. His file included the names of people he had reported and [the amount of] money he had received as payment.

Fagoth was removed from the Council of State and arrested. When the Miskitos reacted and demanded his liberty, he was released. He went to Miami and Washington and then to Honduras, where he began broadcasting to the Miskitos over a clandestine radio station. He told the Miskitos to come to Honduras to escape the Sandinista atheists who were about to send their children to Cuba and Russia.

In December of 1981 the Nicaraguan government discovered a plan called "Red Christmas" to take over a part of northern Zelaya province and to declare it a free territory with CIA help. The plot failed and to protect the Miskitos from the increased fighting there the decision was made to move the Miskitos away from their lands on the Río Coco south to relocation centers at Tasba Pri. This move was a traumatic experience for the Miskitos, who had to leave their traditional land, their lives on the river, and who saw the destruction of their homes. It was difficult, but it was necessary to save lives.

Accusations of government torture and executions that have been made have been proven false. But the people were forced to move. I've been in the relocation centers and they're real good. I've visited them for the commission. The people are safe and they have new homes and medical care. They have schools where the first four grades are taught in their own language, and they have buildings in which to worship. I think the older people want to return to their homes along the Río Coco and it's been promised that they will be allowed to return when the aggression stops. In the meantime, they are free to leave the camps to go anywhere else in the country to live. But the Río Coco area is a war zone now and they are not allowed to go there.

M: You've been in Nicaragua for over 20 years now. What future do you see for this country and this Revolution?

HARTMAN: Every country has a right to be free. But the United States has denied countries this right for hundreds of years and continues this denial today. The U.S. government has sought any weapon to use against the Sandinistas. Lies about human rights violations have been used to justify intervention.

People in the U.S. have been denied access to the truth. The government denied visas to Tomás Borge, Sergio Ramírez and René Núñez, leaders of the Revolution who had been invited to speak to prestigious universities and Congressional committees. All to cut off the flow of information to people in the States. You know, this is the only country in Latin America where the U.S. ambassador can walk down the street without fear. This government receives every delegation that comes down from the States.

Nicaragua is no threat to anyone. This Revolution is simply an expression of the poor struggling to develop themselves. They are the ones who have benefitted from the Revolution. As one peasant told me: "I have my own home now. I have title to my land. My wife is learning to read and write. We haven't reached the land of milk and honey. When I go out to work in the fields I have to carry a gun. As long as I have to do that we cannot say we are a free country."

If Nicaragua succeeds it will be a sign of hope for all of Latin America. This country has stood up to the multinationals, and the exploitation of former times is not allowed now. And I'm afraid that because of all of this, Nicaragua is destined to be condemned to death by the policies of Reagan.

* * *

During our interview I traveled with Sister Hartman as she made her rounds of two prisons near Managua. The penitentiary at Tipitapa is the usual prison: high walls, barbed wire and armed guards. Sixteen hundred prisoners are incarcerated here. Nearby, however, is the *Granja Regimen Abierta* (Open Prison). Situated on 70 acres of farmland, the Open Prison has no walls or barbed wire. The guards, called instructors, are unarmed. Fifty-one prisoners live here at any one time, and in its two years of operation 76 inmates have earned their liberty. One of six such Nicaraguan institutions unique in Central America, the Open Prison has had only one prisoner escape. I briefly interviewed both the prison's director and an inmate chosen at random.

* * *

FRANCISCO SILVA LEÓN, 32, has worked in prisons for the last four years and has been director of this Open Prison for the last ten months.

FRANCISCO SILVA LEÓN: We are learning as we go along here. No one in Nicaragua had experience in rehabilitation in prison work. In Somoza's prisons there was a torture room, a cold room and chains in the walls. They were torture chambers, not prisons. Here we understand that everyone is a Nicaraguan and everyone has rights. The prisoners receive newspapers and watch television. Their families can visit every week. Each six months the prisoners earn a one-week vacation at home with their families. Prisoners are also sent into town with money to buy supplies and return. The one escapee left because he was having trouble at home with his woman. We have a very macho culture and his response was not unusual. Now he is in a regular prison.

This is the only experiment of rehabilitation of its kind in Latin America. It is an extension of the Revolution and revolutionary values. Just as we are shaping the Revolution, so the Revolution is continually shaping us. We have a slogan here, *El pasado quedo atrás, hablemas del futuro* (The past is left behind, we speak of the future), and we hope the future of our country, in and out of prison, will be different from the past.

* * *

MIGUEL MORALES, 42, has served a year and a half in a regular prison and has been at the Open Prison for 9 months. He has one more year to serve.

* * *

MIGUEL MORALES: I was in Somoza's army. I didn't know anything about what the Revolution would be like, but now I am living in it and understand it. Now I consider myself a revolutionary. I work here in the prison kitchen. I've learned to cook and I've learned mechanics here, too. I'd rather not be here; I'd rather be home with my family. But I can live here and I can be free here. I have a good life. My family, including my children, can visit every Sunday. We have medicine here and a library; we make hammocks and purses and do painting. There are academic courses for those who need them, and vocational courses in agriculture and mechanics.

We grow our own beans and corn, and produce our own eggs and milk. We are not watched all of the time and the guards are unarmed. We have machetes to work in the fields and we drive vehicles. When I needed new glasses I was sent into the city to see a doctor. When my time is up here I expect to live peacefully in Managua. The prison will give me a recommendation to work as a cook in a restaurant somewhere in town. Production is part of the Revolution and now we are part of the Revolution, too.

13. The Atlantic Coast

Ray Hooker
Reverend Norman Bent

Zelaya, on the Atlantic Coast of Nicaragua, holds but 10% of the country's population while encompassing 50% of its national territory. Different in geography, history, language, culture, religion and ethnic background, the *costeños*—inhabitants of the Atlantic Coast—have presented a special situation within the Nicaraguan Revolution and are now a special target of the counterrevolutionaries.

Here, two prominent *costeños* discuss the Atlantic Coast from their different political and religious viewpoints. RAY HOOKER, a black, English-speaking, fifth-generation native of the Atlantic Coast, is a member of South Zelaya's regional government and is posted in the port city of Bluefields, a frequent target of contra attacks. Hooker was wounded and kidnapped by eighty members of the counterrevolutionary Miskito group MISURASATA on September 5, 1984, while campaigning on the Atlantic Coast as an FSLN candidate for the National Assembly. He was released fifty-five days later, on October 30, and was overwhelmingly elected to the assembly, receiving 82 percent of the votes cast.

REVEREND NORMAN BENT, forty-five, born on the Atlantic Coast at Tasbapauni—his family including both blacks and Miskito Indians—is now pastor of the large Moravian Church in Managua.

* * *

PHILIP ZWERLING: How can two areas of the same country, the Pacific and Atlantic coasts of Nicaragua, be so different in every way?

RAY HOOKER: Well, a lot of it has to do with history. The Pacific region of Nicaragua was conquered by the Spaniards. But the Spaniards were never able to conquer the Atlantic region.

Geographically, too, we're talking about different regions. Here we have lots of rain during the entire year. It rains from January to December on the Atlantic Coast. Sometimes we have two months of what we call the dry season in March and April, but usually we have precipitation the entire year. In fact, Bluefields has one of the highest levels of precipitation in the world. On the Pacific Coast, rainfall is not as abundant.

And our population is different. The native tribes of the Pacific were basically exterminated. The whole group was not completely exterminated only because Spaniards brought their sexual desires with them. Indian women became pregnant, and in this way, some part of the indigenous culture that existed before the Spaniards arrived survived.

Here on the Atlantic Coast the indigenous peoples fared better. It was very difficult for the European powers to really take over the Atlantic Coast. It's very difficult, for example, to build roads here. Communication is still a tremendous problem. Besides, many of the native tribes lived in very inaccessible regions.

Here in Central America you had two European powers, Spain and England, trying to weaken each other. The objective of British foreign policy in the sixteenth, seventeenth and eighteenth centuries was basically to try to weaken the Spanish empire. In order to weaken Spain, Britain tried to establish footholds in different parts of the Caribbean. First Jamaica was conquered and then other areas of the Caribbean were taken over. In 1631, for example, the British began their contact with the Atlantic Coast of Nicaragua. It was from the Island of Providence that British traders first began to establish contact with Indians living along the shores of the Atlantic Coast.

Interestingly, when you read the records you'll find the owners of the Providence Company telling their traders and ship captains to be very careful in their treatment of the Indians. "Do your best to gain their support, don't mistreat them." It wasn't because of altruistic feelings on the part of Britain. It was sound political and economic policy, because the support of the natives on the Atlantic Coast diminished the costs of British conflict with the Spanish. For example, in the historical writings you'll find the British commentators saying, "If we can assure the support of the Miskito Indians we can avoid having to send 10,000 British soldiers to the coast of Central America."

For Britain to have had to send 5,000 or 10,000 soldiers to the east coast of Nicaragua would have been too expensive. And so we read, for example, that when Nelson attacked the Spanish in San Juan, many of his soldiers were Miskito Indians. All of this was a very sound policy of establishing friendship with the Indians on behalf of Britain. For example, the Indians were very good fishermen and very good at harpooning. In the historical writings you'll read how one Indian harpooner was capable of supplying an entire ship with turtle meat for the whole voyage on British ships.

So, British policy was sound. It wasn't an altruistic policy. It wasn't that the British loved the Indians more than the Spanish did, because in the United States the British practically wiped out the original population. But here on the Atlantic Coast it was within British self-interest to gain the support of the natives living here.

Britain was greatly interested in the Atlantic Coast of Nicaragua and in the Atlantic Coast of much of Central America. The British were in Belize, on the Atlantic Coast of Honduras, and even on the Atlantic Coast of Costa Rica. It was Central America's geographical position that most interested Britain.

The idea of building an interoceanic canal connecting the Atlantic and the Pacific had become an obsession in Europe. It was obviously through Central America that such a canal would go. Since Spain had already taken control over the Pacific Coast of Central America, Britain tried to acquire control over the Atlantic.

This situation existed until about 1860. The United States declared its independence in 1776. Central America became independent in 1821. By the 1840s, you had President Monroe's doctrine, which basically stated that the United States should control the Americas and determine what should be done here. With the emergence of the U.S. as an important naval power, she came into conflict with Great Britain. So, in the 1860s, the U.S. and Britain came to an agreement that either of them might build an interoceanic canal and that whichever country built it would allow the other equal rights for its ships traversing the canal. They came to an agreement [Clayton-Bulwer Treaty] not to fight over this area. . . .

After that, Britain began losing interest in the Atlantic Coast of Nicaragua. Previously, Britain had claimed that the native tribes of the Atlantic Coast had a highly refined culture and were quite independent of Spain and then of Nicaragua. All of this time the British had fomented hatred of the Spaniards here on the Atlantic Coast. The British taught the native population to hate the Spaniards. And the Spaniards taught the people on the Pacific Coast to hate the people of this region. You had two European powers teaching the local populations to hate one another.

But after 1860 the British abandoned their protectorate, and in 1894 the Atlantic Coast was officially incorporated as part of Nicaragua with the help of U.S. troops. U.S. warships here at

Bluefields, off El Bluff, helped Nicaragua take over the Atlantic Coast. Before that time the Atlantic Coast was, to a certain extent, governed by its own customs and traditions. But after the Nicaraguans took over they systematically exterminated the natural resources of the Atlantic Coast. For example, the forestry resources were wiped out. If you go up north, near the border with Honduras, you'll find basically all of the pine forests exterminated. The mineral resources of the region were also systematically finished off.

This looting of the mines, for examples, was done in such a way that if you go to many Miskito villages now you'll find a number of families sick with tuberculosis, which they acquired working in the gold mines. In the old days there was a system in which all workers were required to take a medical exam every six months. The exam was basically an X-ray of the lungs. Now you would think that the X-ray examination was to identify the onset of tuberculosis or silicosis. And it was. But it wasn't meant to identify the initiation of the sickness to cure the patient. Once a shadow was detected on the lung, the miner was fired two weeks later and shipped back to his community without any compensation. This was the systematic policy of the U.S. and Canadian companies that were operating these mines in conjunction with the Nicaraguan regime that existed at that time. Until the 1970s, the miners were being paid about 1.25 cordobas per hour [the exchange rate then was 10 cordobas to the dollar].

The records show that during the 1940s and '50s Nicaragua was among the 10 greatest producers of gold in the world. Most of this gold was taken out of the Atlantic Coast. But what do you find if you visit these mining regions today? You don't find anything. That is, you'll find equipment that is obsolete. You'll find shanty towns and ghost towns. And you'll find a lot of people sick with tuberculosis, sick with silicosis. Since the Triumph, more than 1,000 miners who had lost their jobs, in some cases 20 years ago, have started receiving a monthly pension from the revolutionary government. It's not as much as they deserve, but it's as much as we can afford. We can't even afford it, but it's being done. In most cases they get between 1,200 and 1,500 cordobas a month; in some cases as much as 4,000 cordobas in monthly compensation, as a pension. [The cordoba is now pegged at 28 to the dollar.] These are people who became sick with tuberculosis and silicosis under the previous government. This government has no obligation to these people, but even so they're being taken care of.

Here on the Atlantic Coast the Somoza government controlled practically everything. The fishing companies were Somoza's companies or companies Somoza was in partnership with. The mining companies were foreign companies in which Somoza had a certain type of partnership. The lumber companies were basically foreign companies also. They exterminated our natural resources and then abandoned the country once the natural resources were exterminated. There were practically no schools, no roads and no hospitals. Contact with the outside world was extremely difficult.

Somoza kept the Atlantic Coast isolated from the Pacific Coast. He maintained a mutual isolation. His policy was one of "divide and conquer." He didn't interfere in the communal life of the people here. That is, he let them do whatever they wanted. "If you want to smoke marijuana, go ahead." "You smuggle drugs, go ahead." And the Atlantic Coast became a region in which different types of drugs were being pushed to different parts of the country, to the U.S. and other markets.

The fishing companies were established to export shrimp and lobster to the North American market. Notice where the fishing companies were established: two in Corn Island, one at El Bluff, one at Schooner Key and the smallest in Bluefields. If you wanted to improve the diet of the local population you'd select sites where communication and distribution were easier. But the idea was just to export lobster and shrimp to the North American market. So what happened? . . . With the establishment of these fishing industries what really happened was the systematic impoverishment of the diet of the people of the Atlantic Coast. That is, shrimp, lobster, turtle—the types of seafood that were a traditional part of the people—were not available anymore. When I was a kid growing up in this area you had people practically giving away shrimp, giving away turtle. Basically, no sale went on. For 5 or 10 cents you could get a pound of shrimp or a pound of lobster. Now the people can't get shrimp. They can't get lobster. They can't get turtle. They'd been fished out and exported to the U.S.

Z: What other kinds of problems did the Revolution face on the Atlantic Coast at the Triumph?

HOOKER: First, you found that people from the Pacific knew very little about the people from the Atlantic. And the people from the Atlantic knew very little about the people from the Pacific. They're two populations, two peoples who knew very little about each other's different cultures. On the Atlantic you have the Miskitos, Sumos, Ramas, Caribs and the English-speaking population. On the Pacific you basically have the Spanish-speaking population.

Now, when you have very little knowledge, that's when mistakes are made. If you're going to govern a region, you have to understand that region. If you're going to govern people belonging to a certain culture, you must understand that culture. And this lack of understanding, this lack of mutual knowledge, has created quite a number of problems which even today we are still trying to solve. It's not easy. You see, revolution is a very difficult thing. To change human beings, to really bring about a genuine change in human beings, is one of the most difficult tasks which any government, which any society, has ever attempted.

If you go back to the times of the Greeks and Plato and his Republic, you see they weren't successful. If you go back to the Moslems, you see that they achieved a certain amount of success. But it didn't last. If you go to the Russian Revolution, for example, in 1917, they still haven't been able to achieve the amount of change which is necessary to bring forth this new man. Revolution is a very difficult, very difficult thing because human nature is quite complicated. But we have to continue, and quite possibly in our country we might be able to achieve what some of the giants have not been able to achieve. But it's tremendously difficult.

If you go back to your own revolution, you saw huge numbers of people who had to leave the U.S. and went to Canada immediately after the new government took power. And most of their lands and properties were confiscated. To a certain extent, there was a population boom in Canada after the U.S. revolution. And you had a period of six years, from 1782 to 1788, before your first president, [George] Washington, was inaugurated. A revolution is a difficult thing and it requires a tremendous amount of understanding, a tremendous amount of patience, and volumes of conviction. Because in revolutions you are going to make mistakes. But when you have found you have made a mistake, you should be sufficiently honest to accept that and try to do better. But it's not an easy thing.

Z: How has the new government responded to the problems of the Atlantic Coast?

HOOKER: A kilometer of highway on the Atlantic Coast costs about three times what the same extension of highway would cost on the Pacific Coast. And there's another difficulty. You can work on road construction only about three or four months of the year here on the Atlantic Coast. On the Pacific Coast you can work road construction basically during the entire year. What I'm getting at is that construction costs here are about three times what they are on the Pacific. That is, for the money we need to build one hospital here, you can build three hospitals on the Pacific.

And there's another thing about the Atlantic Coast. The type of soil we have is soil that is very good for the growing of things such as coconuts, rubber, African palm—permanent crops. Our soil is very good for this. But it's not very good for the growing of beans, rice or corn—annual crops.

Now, coconut is a wonderful product. Once it begins to bear it will produce for 75 or 80 or more years consecutively. But the big problem is that once you plant a coconut it takes between five and six years for it to begin to produce. So the initial amount of investment which you need to get this crop into production is huge. The initial amount of investment you need to get, let's say, five acres of coconut into production is huge in comparison to the amount of money you would need to plant five acres of wheat, beans or rice. And you're not going to get any return on your investment until about five, six years afterward. Now once these things begin to produce, then you have it made. But to get them to begin to produce, that's where the difficulty lies. Because traditionally most of the people on the Atlantic Coast have been poor, they did not have this initial capital that is required to get these types of crops into production. What I'm trying to get at is that infrastructure on the Atlantic Coast is tremendously expensive. Maintenance of infrastructure is also tremendously expensive, much more expensive than it is on the Pacific. But even though it is damned expensive, what the Revolution has done in three years time is also really impressive.

For example, in the area of health and education the Atlantic Coast is where we have been most successful. For example, you have the hospital here in Bluefields. Before the Revolution the hospital here in Bluefields functioned for approximately four to five hours per day. After the Revolution an attempt was immediately made to get the hospital functioning 24 hours a day and to keep the hospital well staffed for 24 hours a day. What was the reaction of the doctors? Most of our local doctors were opposed to it. Basically, we were trying to get the hospital to offer its services 24 hours a day. If you were pregnant and you happened to have a baby on Saturday at 4 o'clock, or on Sunday, you were in trouble before the Revolution because most of the doctors would be drunk by then. You were definitely in trouble. And this is not bullshit, really. You can go and consult the records and check with the people that this is so. So when we tried to get the hospital to offer its services 24 hours per day we had lots of the doctors opposed to it. Three or four or five of the doctors who were here have left the country. But with the help of doctors from other countries the hospital is now functioning 24 hours per day, with resident doctors offering services during the entire 24 hours. This is not only in Bluefields, but if you go to the smallest communities you'll find health services where no doctors previously reached. The amount of consultations have increased by more than 400% since July 19, 1979. Things we've done in preventive medicine, for example, are really impressive. Preventive medicine is quite different from curative medicine. In preventive medicine you have to try to get people to change habits which have been acquired over a long period of time. You know, changing the habits of people—cleanliness, etc.—is very, very difficult. Curative medicine is easy, relatively easy. Your physician will operate; he'll give you some pills or other types of drugs. If your body responds well to this, you're cured. Fine. Now, preventive medicine means working with the population, working with the population in the different communities and getting them to acquire new habits, different habits, getting them to stop doing certain things they have been accustomed to doing over the years and years. So, initially, preventive medicine is very, very difficult. But even though it is quite difficult, I would say we've achieved quite a bit. I would pat ourselves on the back.

Z: How does government function on the Atlantic Coast?

HOOKER: Bluefields is different from many of the smaller communities. Here in Bluefields before the Revolution you had what was called an *alcalde* (mayor), who was overseen from Managua. That was the institution. The alcalde couldn't do anything without first getting approval from Managua. It was a government which was totally centralized. Now, in each of the smaller communities, especially the native communities, you would find someone who was named by the alcalde in Bluefields. People would go to that official with their problems. He would go to the alcalde. The alcalde would refer it to Managua. Practically nothing was done to solve the problems of the people. Before the Europeans came here, the type of structure you had was one in which you had a council of elders in each Indian village. They would come together to determine what was the best solution to the problem of their people. In times of war, a military chief was chosen, and during the conduct of the war the military chief was ruler, in effect. After the war, after the military conflict was over, things reverted to the hands of the council of elders.

When the British came here, they annointed someone as king. The Indians had no kings before. They had chiefs, but they had no kings before the British came. The British annointed someone as king in imitation of their own system. But it was, let's say, a kingdom that had no roots. When the British retired, the king had no popularity because it was a structure completely alien, a type of practice that was in complete contradiction to the type of relationships that existed in the different communities, which had a type of communal life in which members would get together to find solutions to their own problems.

Now, after the Revolution an attempt was made to establish neighborhood committees, CDSs as they are called. They're committees established to try to find solutions to the problems of specific communities. That is, to discover what are the main problems of the neighborhood. Supposedly, the people from a neighborhood should understand their neighborhood better than anyone else, because they have lived in that neighborhood over a long period of time. They are well acquainted with one another, so they should have more understanding of the situation existing in a neighborhood than, let's say, a judge; better than, let's say, a police officer. So they should try to solve their neighborhood problems right in their own communities. Now what we're finding is that some of the things that work on the Pacific Coast won't work on the Atlantic Coast. We're coming to the conclusion that we must identify the spontaneous situations in the different communities of interest to most members of the community and work with the people from those communities to try to find solutions to the problems. But if we go to the communities and we try to impose patterns which are alien to them, then we don't get any results.... We have, for example, problems here with foodstuffs. Not all foodstuffs, but there are scarcities of certain things here, such as flour. There's scarcity, for example, of toilet paper. There was a scarcity, for a while, of sugar. In December, there was some scarcity of rice. Now these are problems which practically all the members of a community are worried about. So we work with the members of a neighborhood to try to find solutions to them. Now the solution is not only getting Managua to send more rice or sugar, for example. But we'll work with a community to try to get the community to plant more rice, to plant more beans, to get the community to stop relying so much on refined sugar.

For example, when I was a kid during the Second World War and the years immediately following, there were tremendous scarcities then in all Nicaragua. There were scarcities of flour, of sugar. We had our people planting more rice, more beans, eating cassavas instead of depending on imported wheat for the making of bread. These are some of the things we're trying to get our people to begin to do again. Because, you see, with the type of semi-industrial development that was established, getting people to work in the fishing companies or to abandon the country, you have our people not producing what they used to produce. We used to produce all the rice we consumed on the Atlantic Coast. Now we have to redevelop our agriculture.

Z: What are the short-, medium-, and long-term goals for the region?

HOOKER: In the short term we're trying to satisfy the basic needs of the people. We're trying to make sure there's sufficient food. We're trying to make sure that adequate clothing is available. . . . We're trying to satisfy the housing needs of the people. We're trying to see that every individual has an educational opportunity here in the region. We're trying to meet people's health needs.

The other thing is to try to produce, for example, enough rice and beans in each region to satisfy the needs of that region. We're not getting into any big rice plantations. This area is not good for the planting of rice. But when you take into account transportation and other costs, it makes sense to produce a certain amount here for local consumption.

In terms of medium-range goals we're trying to get well-qualified people well trained. Most of our qualified people—a lot of them—have left the country. We're on a crash program to try to get new people trained. This isn't an easy thing. Because to train, let's say, a qualified economist, takes about five years of university training. And then after he gets out of the university he still doesn't know anything. He has to get the education of hard knocks of everyday living. You're talking, basically, a good eight years to train the experts we need.

Before the Revolution most educational opportunities were in the hands of people who were privileged or lucky. It was definitely in the hands of the minority. And these are the people who want to make money out of the skills which they acquire through education. Well, if you're working in revolutionary Nicaragua, you're definitely not going to get rich in terms of material benefits, salary-wise. In terms of conviction, yes. In terms of self-satisfaction, yes. Here there's lots of wealth to be acquired, but if you want greenbacks you're not going to get those things. If you want color television, fast cars, all this type of stuff, those kinds of things you're not going to get in our country. So, it's not an easy thing. It's a very difficult thing to go training these people.

In the long run we hope to improve our permanent crops.

We've already begun planting 5,000 manzanas of coconut. That's 8,000 acres of coconut. We've already brought some hybrid coconut seed from West Africa which we've just planted. We have the money already to plant this amount of coconut. This is going to take another five or six years. We've already begun planting about 27,000 manzanas of African palm for the first time here on the Atlantic Coast. But the African palm takes about six to eight years to come into production. So there is quite a bit of waiting ahead for us. We're trying to transform El Bluff in Bluefields into the most important port in Nicaragua. If we do this, then our products don't have to go through the Panama Canal. Most of our trading is done with countries in the Atlantic. So the goods could come directly to El Bluff. From El Bluff they could be distributed to different parts of the country. A port like this makes a tremendous amount of economic sense. In terms of transportation, for example, it takes a ship about seven additional days to go from El Bluff down to Panama and then up to Corinto [on the Pacific Coast]. So we've saving lots of money in terms of the cost of transportation.

A highway system is being built from Managua directly to Puerto Cabezas. Another is being built from Managua directly to Bluefields. But this is going to take some time. And then we're going to have Puerto Cabezas, Bluefields and Managua connected by highway. We're trying to modernize our fishing industry so that our fishing industry will not only bring us dollars from exports but also will contribute to a better diet for our people.

In terms of the forestry resources, it's a very tough job, but we're trying to get the campesinos not to cut down their trees. We're trying to preserve what is left of the forest because forestry products are becoming much more valuable.

We're trying to establish a scholarship system so the small towns where, for example, there's no secondary school, will be able to send the students to other towns where they'll be able to continue their education. These are some of the things which we're trying to do.

In terms of values, we are trying to get the present, the younger generation and the coming generation to value very dearly every other human being, to respect tremendously the rights and privileges of every other human being. We're trying to instill in them a pattern of behavior where if they have any more talents than their neighbor, they'll use that capacity in order to help others instead of themselves. If they're smarter than their neighbor, they'll use that intelligence to help those who are not as smart as they are or who are not as skilled as they are, instead of using that intelligence for their own enrichment. But again, it's not an easy thing. It's very difficult—very, very difficult.

Z: There was no insurrection on the Atlantic Coast and very little fighting against Somoza. How did the Revolution come to this area?

HOOKER: After the Triumph the representatives of the old government simply left the country. They were allowed to leave in most cases. After July 19, 1979, different revolutionaries came down, and have been trying ever since, to get a government to function effectively here. But again, it's not easy.

Z: How would you assess the success of the new government to incorporate the peoples of the Atlantic Coast into the revolutionary process?

HOOKER: Again, we have to look at history to understand the present. We had United Fruit operating on the Atlantic Coast. We had some affiliates of theirs, too, because United Fruit is not only a banana company. It was also involved in forestry. And while these companies were here they had native workers working cutting down the forest and loading the trucks to take the logs to the wharves or the sawmills. In many cases the salary which they were paid was higher than any salary they had ever gotten throughout their historical existence.

The type of contract which the companies had with the national government was one in which they were able to bring any amount of foreign beer, liquor or foreign goods into the country without paying any kind of taxes. Each of these companies made sure that they had well-stocked commissaries, the equivalent of supermarkets functioning in these areas. So what happened?

The salaries which the employees made went right back to the foreign company. They brought in things such as American yellow cheese and lots of canned goods which we're not accustomed to. They were quite tasty because your industry is very good at these type of things. Our people had Pabst Blue Ribbon Beer, Schlitz, Budweiser and things like this. They had all different types of whiskey. What did they leave for the people?

You go and look in the north and you'll find nothing. When the trees were cut down, the companies packed up and left. So now our people were left without their trees, their forest, which was their traditional source of food. Because, in many cases, they depended on hunting for a source of their livelihood. But when the trees were cut down, the animals also disappeared. But you'll find a number of the older generation speaking nostalgically, saying, "Oh, if another company would come into Nicaragua." The tragedy of the situation is that they have never really understood what was happening, what was being done to their livelihood, that the future generation was being endangered, that their children were being endangered, that every bottle of whiskey which they consumed meant less for their own children. They really never ever understood this. You'll hear them talking, "But these were beautiful times, wonderful times." In terms of the money circulating, the consumer goods, sure. There was lots of stuff like this. But in terms of Nicaragua, what did it leave us?

Part of our job is to try to help our people to understand their past and this is not an easy thing. People fall in love with their prejudices and their misconceptions. But we really have to try to get them to acquire a valid understanding, a correct understanding of exactly what went on, what is going on, and what will be going on in the future.

There's another situation. When you are a minority within a country, the leadership of a minority must be very mature, must not be impulsive. A majority can always stamp out a minority. So a minority must make a special effort to choose really mature leadership, intelligent leadership. And here, also, is where we had quite a few problems on the Atlantic Coast. For example, the leaders of the Miskitos were fellows who were just out of the University. You had Steadman Fagoth [Muller], for example, and Brooklyn Rivera. Steadman graduated from the university in 1978. Brooklyn more or less at the same time. You find these leaders promising "You're going to have good housing immediately. You're going to have everything you've never had in all your history immediately."

But on the Atlantic Coast, as we've seen, it's very, very difficult to bring about this type of change. You need time. . . . So when you go immediately after the Triumph promising your people all these things tomorrow, you're creating expectations that you cannot fulfill. And you not only create expectations you cannot fulfill, but you're laying the groundwork for future antagonisms. These have been some of the difficult situations through which this Revolution has gone.

I would say that we're not doing so badly, really. We're not systematically killing our people. We're definitely not doing this. We're not forcing people to remain in our country. If you want to leave, you can leave. When you go and you find that things are not paradise on the other side, and you want to come back, you can come back. This is basically what we're telling people. Now this is very costly to us.

Take, for example, the Moravian School here in Bluefields. For years this was the most important center of education on the Atlantic Coast. The first graduates from this high school were in 1951. From 1951 to 1981 we've had a total of about 730 graduates. Of these, you'll find approximately 300 in the U.S. Of the 300, about 250 left before the Triumph of the Revolution. Perhaps another 250 went abroad to other countries. We had a center of education train our people to abandon our region and, paradoxically, leave our poor area to enrich the U.S. Now if we had taught our people in this school to raise coconuts, they definitely wouldn't have gone to the United States. You can't grow coconuts in the United States. We were training our people to impoverish our region.

I would say we're not doing so terribly well, but we're chugging along. The more difficult the situation becomes, the more we are going to be forced to use our creative capacities. The more we use our creative capacities, the better human beings we are going to become. And we're going to develop a tremendous amount of self-confidence, self-reliance and pride in our country and in ourselves. And with this, we're going to be unstoppable.

Z: How are the labor unions functioning here?

HOOKER: The CST [Confederation of Sandinista Workers] works in the fishing industry. That's the major industry here. They've been able to do quite a bit of organizing. Before, you had practically no unions allowed in the area. When the miners tried to organize a union, the National Guard came in. It squashed all attempts at organization. Right now the attempts that have been made have been quite successful in the field of the organization. But the CST has difficult problems.

We're on a crash program to get every person in the country to reach more or less a sixth-grade level of education by 1986 or '87. Because many of our workers were uneducated, the amount of schooling they got is what they received during the alphabetization campaign. So one of the top priorities is adult education classes in all the different work centers. We're trying to push this as much as possible because to the degree we're able to provide our workers with the type of training which will enable them to develop their individual capacities and aspirations—to that degree we'll have a more productive work force.

Z: What has been the special role of religion and the churches on this coast?

HOOKER: The predominant church on the Atlantic Coast is the Moravian Church. The first missionaries to come here came in 1849—three Moravian missionaries—started things here in the region. For many years, the Moravians were the only institution that dedicated themselves to educational activities. They built schools and hospitals. If you are familiar with church activities, you know that a health program is one of the best ways to gain souls for Christ. When the Nicaraguan government was doing nothing in the area of health, the Moravians were the ones who had established the hospital here. When the Nicaraguan government was doing nothing in the area of education, the Moravians were the ones who operated the few existing high schools. Originally, they were, I would say, quite progressive. Their first headquarters was in Germany. They were under the supervision of the German Moravian Church up until the First World War. The supervision was then transferred to the North American Moravian Church.

The Moravian Church is, among the Miskitos, the predominant church—70% are Moravian. As I said, they did quite a bit for the people. They translated the Bible into Miskito. They translated certain hymnals into Miskito. They did quite a bit, I would say, of positive work during certain periods of our history.

Religion is a very difficult thing. I studied, for example, in a Moravian school—in the Moravian school here in Bluefields. During the time I was in the Moravian school, they never once mentioned the way the natural resources of the Atlantic Coast were being wiped out by the foreign companies. In no single instance was this ever condemned by the Moravians. In no instance was the behavior of the mining companies ever condemned by any of the different religious groups operating here on the Atlantic Coast. And they knew what was going on, because the X-ray examination was being done in some of their hospitals.

Now in the final summing up, has their influence been positive or negative? It depends on who's making the final summing up. Let's say you have a place that is traditionally Buddhist and you send a Roman Catholic preacher in there. Then you develop divisions among people who were once one. Is this good? Is this positive? In the goal in which we need to bring about a unified Nicaragua, has their role been positive? It's not an easy thing to say. If you were to speak with the Moravians they would say they've done a hell of a lot. And they have done quite a lot for the Atlantic [Coast] people. But in the final summing up, in planting

Ray Hooker, Photo by Deborah Beogle

a different type of culture in a people whose own cultural patterns are quite different than the ones that have been instilled, was this positive? This is what everyone has to answer for himself.

Z: How do the churches and government cooperate in the educational system here?

HOOKER: Here we have Baptist, Moravian, Anglican schools. In all these schools you'll find that the government is paying the salaries of most of the teachers. For example, the Moravian school—the government pays about 80% of its budget. And they name their own teachers, their own directors. They control their school. The same thing with the Baptists, the Anglicans. What the Revolution has found is that where these religious groups are genuinely interested in patterning their lives according to the basic teachings of Christ, you don't have too much incompatibility. When they pattern their behavior as love thy neighbor as thyself—darn hard thing to do—there's not too much incompatibility between the goals of the Revolution and the church. It's when the church is striving after political power and other types of temporal goals, that's where conflicts will emerge. In many cases the church and state have worked quite successfully together.

The religious schools are required to teach the official educational program of the government, but after they've taught the official program of the government they can teach their religion. For example, in the Moravian school you'll find a special class called Bible, where they teach about the Bible in all the different grades. For them, that's one of their most important subjects. They consider it much more important than chemistry or biology or social studies. . . . In the entire Atlantic Coast, practically all of the religious schools are financed more than 50% by the national government.

Z: The new government has mandated bilingual education for the children of this culturally diverse area. Has this worked?

HOOKER: That's the goal, but we haven't been able to put it into practice. It's a law, but we haven't been able to put it into effect.

The law says we're going to teach children in their first four years of elementary school in their native language and teach them Spanish as a second language. By the fifth grade they should be able to receive most of their education in Spanish and continue to receive their native language as you would study French or Spanish in American schools. But there are problems. The only books translated into Miskito are some of the books of the Bible. In Sumo, you have the New Testament. There are only 555 Ramas left. The whole group has been practically wiped out. Only 12 people can speak their original language. We want to preserve that language and culture. Making good teaching materials is very difficult. Our problem is to train people to speak Miskito, then train them to translate from Spanish to Miskito, and then train them to write textbooks in biology, social studies, etc. At this point we haven't had the manpower or resources for this. It's one of our major concerns, and we feel that to a certain extent we've failed in this respect. But, as I have said, revolution is a very difficult thing to make and we struggle each day to move forward.

* * *

PHILIP ZWERLING: You were born and grew up on the Atlantic Coast. How did the Moravian Church enter your life?

REVEREND NORMAN BENT: One of the outstanding features of the Moravian missionaries who came from Eastern Europe was their ability to play many roles. In addition to being preachers in many cases they were teachers and doctors. In every village they went to they established a church school to provide at least some basic education for the villages with the intention that they would be able to at least read a hymnal and take part in the worship of the church. They had provided a school in the village in which I grew up that took us up through elementary school. And then, if your parents could afford it or if they offered you a scholarship, you could go to the Moravian High School in Bluefields. That's how I got my education.

Z: The government didn't offer public schools?

BENT: Not until the last 25 years did the state begin to offer some public education. Then I went to a Bible school run by the Moravian Church to train their native pastors in Bilwaskarma. That used to be on the northern border, but it no longer exists, not for the last two years. During the evacuation it was destroyed. After that I went to the University of Costa Rica to earn a master's degree.

Z: Did you serve churches on the Atlantic Coast?

BENT: I have served three churches on the Atlantic Coast and now serve this church in Managua. I spent quite a bit of my ministry in social work as well.

Z: I was in your church in Managua on a Sunday morning and it seemed that most of the congregation was from the Atlantic Coast.

BENT: About 95%. The Moravian Church moved into Managua following the migration of eastern Nicaraguans. Because educational opportunities on the Atlantic Coast are so limited—beyond high school there is nothing—so 25 years ago young people began to move to Managua. In those days Nicaragua had a strong presence of foreign transnational companies. The technical skills of native Nicaraguans from the east coast who spoke English were in high demand and some of them who had only a high school education but spoke English were able to get very good jobs and wound up taking a Spanish-speaking wife or a Spanish-speaking husband and did not find themselves too welcome in the Spanish-speaking evangelic churches. They asked the Moravians to open a church, which they did 25 years ago. My church has 800 members, but the Moravian church community in Managua is just about 5,000 and we will be starting a second church here soon.

Z: To an outsider, how would you describe the impact of the Moravian Church on the Atlantic Coast?"

BENT: Nicaragua is basically a Roman Catholic country. [On the Pacific Coast] perhaps 80% are Catholic, and 20% Protestants of many different evangelical groups. But on the east coast these figures are reversed. It is probably 80% Protestant, and of those Protestants at least 90% would be Moravians. The Moravian church is *the* church on most of the Atlantic Coast. Since 1849 it has become the church of the indigenous community. To speak about the culture of the Atlantic Coast you cannot take away the Moravian Church from that culture. It is a church whose history and theology have to be based around indigenous culture. The impact of the Moravian Church has been very powerful. The pastors of the church in the villages continue, even though frightened by some of the political incidents, to play an important strategic role. Even the Council of Elders would still go to the pastor for final advice on any decision-making for community life in that village.

The Moravian Church successfully converted people in the black community, the Miskitos, the Sumos and the Ramas. The Garifunos, who came out of St. Lucia, Haiti and Dominica, speak not English but their own language and became Episcopalians and Catholics rather than Moravians.

Z: You grew up and went to school on the Atlantic Coast during the Somoza dictatorship. What was life like then?

BENT: Under the dictatorship life on the Atlantic Coast was peaceful, because of isolation. It is the most underpopulated and underdeveloped area of all of Nicaragua. It is the largest of all the 16 states. Somoza used the Atlantic Coast only as a vacation land. And, in May, for cultural activities around the May Pole festival. Or once every four years he would come around at election time. There weren't any real elections, but he would come around anyway and say there were elections. If there was a terrible flood, some of his top military people would come around and say, "We're sorry you have a terrible flood." So it was very peaceful and very quiet. But with a strong foreign presence.

The company stores of the timber, gold, banana, rubber and fishing companies were well-stocked with foreign goods. They were all U.S. and Canadian companies. So whatever signs of development one could see on the Atlantic Coast were the result of the dedicated missionary efforts of the Moravian, Episcopalian and Roman Catholic churches. Only *now* is the government building a new hospital. Only *now* have they brought a communications system to Bluefields and to Puerto Cabezas.

Z: Did Somoza leave the religious establishment alone on the Atlantic Coast to provide their own social and educational programs?

BENT: Oh, yes. He did not interfere with the church.

Z: And the Church didn't make waves in terms of the economic exploitation that was going on?

BENT: No. The missionaries were friends of the companies. The company owners went to church. So they could not speak out against the companies.

Z: And there was no history of struggle against the dictatorship as there was on the West Coast?

BENT: No. Whenever there was a problem with Somoza's military, the people would go to the church and the missionaries would go directly to Somoza, because the missionaries were good friends with Somoza. He would listen to the missionaries and try to satisfy them.

Z: So what did the people there think of the fighting that was going on on the west coast in '77, '78, and '79?

BENT: The youth began to listen to Radio Sandino, the clandestine radio station. They were in a fever. The youth started to become revolutionaries and to identify themselves with the struggle and to share the struggle. But they had no connection to get deeply involved. The Sandinistas themselves really didn't do anything to get the people of the east coast involved. There was no massive public support on the east coast for the Sandinistas.

Z: But the people of the Atlantic Coast welcomed the downfall of Somoza?

BENT: Oh, very much. They prayed for it. In our churches we prayed for it.

Z: How would you explain to an outsider the successes and failures of the Revolution on the Atlantic Coast since 1979?

BENT: I think to understand the success of the Revolution you need to describe the state of isolation that existed. You were meddling with a situation that hadn't been meddled with. And when you meddle with a problem, you bring about other problems. I would say there are three main reasons why it was necessary, and remains necessary, to make a revolution on the Atlantic Coast. A violent military revolution occurred on the Pacific Coast. But what was needed on the Atlantic Coast was a raising of consciousness and a genuine revolution, a transformation of society. Since violence was not necessary on the east coast, a well-planned revolution would have been successful. There are three reasons this is important.

One, the economic future of this country is on the east coast. All of the natural resources available in the country are over there. Minerals, gold, copper, iron ore, zinc—even though exploited for 70 years by the transnationals—are still available in large quantities. Timber is still available even though the foreign companies indiscriminately exploited our forests. Northeast Nicaragua is just one huge forest. Drive over the roads the lumber companies built and you will see the pine forests for maybe 200 miles across. Some of the best fishing spots in Nicaragua are on the east coast. All the rivers that open out and pour the waste from the mountains into the sea provide the best fishing banks in Central America. This represents a serious problem for the present Nicaraguan government because of not having a good air force or coast guard. The Honduran fishing fleet comes in and steals fish and gets away. Besides that, even the Nicaraguan fishing boats, if they are sent out to fish, run away and never come back. Other resources, like virgin land, constitute agricultural development for the entire country. If it's developed properly, by a socialist government, Nicaragua will not only grow its own food but also export food to Central America. So when you think of all of the natural resources still available, the economic future of this country is on the east coast.

Secondly, there is a need for revolution because the east coast of Nicaragua represents a very strategic geopolitical and military situation for the future of this Revolution against any possible invasion. Remember that in 1961 the Cuban invasion took place out of the east coast of Nicaragua [ending at the Bay of Pigs] from Puerto Cabezas. And along the coast around Puerto Cabezas all of the infrastructure prepared for that invasion is still there. CONDECA [Coordinated Defense Establishment of Central American Countries] was formed in Puerto Cabezas and their troops were first trained there. The people on the east coast do not have the same political education that the people on the west coast have. And so it is very important, that to protect itself, the Revolution must come to the east coast.

And finally, to bring to reality the old Indian treaties, the Revolution must come to the east coast. For example, a treaty that was signed in 1894 [when the Atlantic Coast was forcibly incorporated into Nicaragua by President José Santos Zelaya with the aid of U.S. troops] contains many things that were violated by all of the governments that followed. One thing the treaty says is that there should be a semiautonomous government. The treaty also says that revenue taken out of the resources of the Atlantic Coast should be reinvested on the east coast, with local government participating in those decisions. Another article exempts the people of the Atlantic Coast from military service. All of these things are violated today. The past government did not respect this treaty. The present government does not respect it.

To bring this treaty into reality—so that the political, economic and cultural benefits that the rest of the country has could be also enjoyed by the people of the east coast—the Revolution must come to the east coast. To do away not only with neocolonialism, but also with the internal colonialism that is still there—because very few of the government officials sent to serve on the Atlantic Coast are native *costeños*—the Revolution must come to the east coast. Bringing the Revolution into the east coast would make the

Reverend Norman Bent, Photo by Martin

treaty of 1894 a reality. The people of the east coast would then be given first-class citizenship in Nicaragua, the right to participate in the process of government, the right to participate in the decision-making process, the right to participate in the economy and culture of the country, and then Nicaragua would really become one great country.

But when you attempt to do those things, when you attempt to meddle with the problem, if you don't have all the techniques, you will make a lot of mistakes. And the Sandinistas made a lot of mistakes. One was transferring a revolution from one region of the country to another, with its structure and its slogans, when you did not have the same social situation there. Two, you did not have the best leadership early on to send over there. Three, there were cultural insensitivities by the people sent over there—linguistically, religiously, racially. The British and Spanish governments created an historical racial problem in Nicaragua. The people of the east coast describe a Spanish-speaking person with the word that means "the machete of a dog." A very nasty word. And the Spanish-speaking people on the west coast look at us and call us *los morenitos,* the little brownies. This historical hate created by these two powers, the British in the east and the Spanish on the west, is still very present today in Nicaragua and even, unconsciously, to our highest government leaders, who refer to us as *los morenitos.* It's not an institutionalized racism. It's not on the surface. But it's deep-rooted. How can we get away from that? It will take us quite some time. And this is why a revolution is important. . . . Third, the time frame for consolidating the revolution on the east coast was too rapid. No revolution there, no political consciousness, and you want people to be all Sandinistas overnight? Impossible. That was a problem. Fourth, undermining the authentic local leadership of the people, replacing them with other leaders who were also Indians but who had no connection to their people. They were in Managua to go to the university. They spoke Spanish. They shouted the slogans well. And they were trusted. But the authentic leaders were not trusted.

Z: We're talking about Steadman Fagoth and Brooklyn Rivera?

BENT: That's right. And you take them, and you place them over there and say, "You are going to be the new leaders of the people." Then you get in trouble with that. Fifth, and probably the biggest mistakes, were the cultural insensitivity and the military approach to the problem.

Z: When you say the military approach, do you mean the forced removal of the Miskitos from the north?

BENT: That plus arresting Steadman Fagoth when they discovered who he was.

Z: You don't think they should have done that? [Fagoth was discovered to have been a Somoza agent.]

BENT: They should have done it, but they should have consulted the people first.

Z: And then the people demanded his release.

BENT: And then you make another mistake. To satisfy the people, you release him. And you release him and say he must go to Honduras and bring back the people who have fled. Then he doesn't come back. Then you try a stronger military approach. When Steadman requests Indians to go to Honduras to build a liberation army, the Sandinistas say, "OK, we'll straighten out this problem. We'll show the Indians militarily who we are." And the Indians say, "No, we'll show you who *we* are!" So when Steadman sends back his men they are not looked upon as contras. They're only looked upon as Indians. And the Indian loyalty is not to Nicaragua but to their village, to "Mother Earth." Their rivers and lakes are more meaningful to them than all of Nicaragua. "Who are you who speak Spanish to us? You are the enemy. This guy who is coming from over the border is my brother, my son; he's one of mine. And I'll see that he eats and I'll see that he sleeps and I will see that he's not killed." And this was the situation.

The military approach that the government took was probably more destructive than anything else. That brought about much greater enmity between the people and the government. As a result there were even 700 people in prison up until December of 1983. They even accused the church of counterrevolution. And the church was not. But some of the leadership of the church had to take a stand and say, "We are not for bloodshed but we will speak out for the rights of our people." We took the role of being reconcilers. And the road of quiet diplomacy has worked. It took the government two years to listen to us. They realized their mistakes. It's not too late, but it's almost too late. Tomás Borge told us, "We went over there with too much revolutionary vision and too little understanding and too little love. We didn't listen to you earlier. Now we are trying to listen to you. We drove the people to become our enemies and we drove them into the hands of the CIA."

This is the reality. The government is struggling now to undo the mistakes they made. They have changed. They have repented. But the contras have not repented. And the United States government has not repented. So it is difficult to bring about total reconciliation. To describe the situation today, I would say 70% of my people are confused; they are neither with the contra nor with the Frente Sandinista. Fifteen percent, especially the youth, give limited support to the Revolution. Another 15% are on the fence and could fall on either side. This is the reality.

Z: You said it was "almost" too late. Is it too late?

BENT: No, it's not too late. We think that if the United States government would just pull out of this situation and permit the government to establish dialogue with the Indian leadership in exile then there's hope.

Z: But the government has said they won't enter into dialogue with the contras.

BENT: With the Indians they will, because they realize that they're responsible for the way the Indians acted. They accept that.

Z: Have people on the Atlantic Coast benefitted materially from the Revolution?

BENT: Oh, yes. There are a lot of achievements that can be seen. The people benefitted directly from the Literacy Crusade when it offered education in Spanish, English, Miskito, and Sumo. Health care is improved. Medical teams go through the villages every week. Whatever is available is totally free now. In Puerto Cabezas, the Moravian hospital, the only hospital, was donated to the government in 1980. Our missionary doctors used to see perhaps 60–100 patients there every day. Today, doctors are seeing up to 400 patients a day. And it's totally free. The church couldn't give it free. The church had to charge something.

Education, beyond the Literacy Crusade, has improved. There are more eastern Nicaraguans with scholarships for graduate work, more in universities today in Managua and in European countries, who never had scholarships before. People like Ray Hooker were privileged in the past because his father played a very important role in the Somoza government. He had a scholarship from the U.S. Embassy. Now there are many more scholarships available.

Many of the villages have electricity today for the first time. Puerto Cabezas never had running water. Now they have running water. This is a city of about 32,000 people. Food is subsidized now. So there are many good things that the people are conscious of and they appreciate that.

Z: Have you visited the relocation camps for the Miskitos?

BENT: Not the ones on the east coast. But the ones in Jinotega and Matagalpa, yes, because these are directly under my responsibility religiously.

Z: And you get reports from the other pastors who visit the Atlantic Coast?

BENT: Oh, yes.

Z: How do you respond to charges that these are concentration camps and that people are being mistreated?

BENT: I think that's totally false. People are free to leave the camps and to move around freely. They are producing and self-sufficient. They have nice little homes. Not the best. Not as big as the ones they had on the river. One cultural mistake the government made was in building these camps like a little Managua suburban community, which is totally wrong. We understand they did this to save on construction materials and land, but the Indian way of living is with a city block of land planted around each isolated and separate house. This is what they need so the wind can blow through freely. This doesn't make them happy in Tasba Pri [a large resettlement camp on the Atlantic Coast]. Beyond that, medical care is beautiful, there are good schools and bilingual education in Miskito and Spanish. In Tasba Pri the contras burned down the health clinic and kidnapped the doctor, who escaped and came back. The only ambulance was burned by the contras. The contras then took people to concentration camps. The camps in Honduras and Costa Rica are concentration camps.

I went to Costa Rica in December to explain the amnesty plan [of the Nicaraguan government] to the Miskitos and I found them there in concentration camps. The ones in Nicaragua are totally free. In Costa Rica they can't leave the camps even to go to the city. If they leave they are arrested and put into prison. It's even worse in Honduras. And they are recruited out of those camps for military service for the contras. In Costa Rica, I saw the recruiting office within the camp itself where Edén Pastora and Brooklyn Rivera recruit their men.

Z: How has the Moravian Church been affected by the Revolution? Has it, like the Catholic Church, been divided between a conservative hierarchy and a more progressive grass-roots?

BENT: We believe in the "priesthood of all believers." There is no hierarchy in the Moravian Church even though we have bishops and deacons and so forth. But there is a top leadership, beginning with the bishops, and a lower leadership. Because the indigenous community constitutes the Moravian Church and the conflict is with them, the church has definitely been affected. So what we have today is a church divided by two opinions. A part of the church supports the Revolution. A part of the church is very critical and mistrustful of the Revolution.

Z: Are those equal parts?

BENT: I would say yes, 50-50. Because of some of the recent changes of attitude of the Revolution, because of some of the better communication of the leadership of the church and the revolutionary leaders that is changing, and support for the Revolution is growing.

Z: Have these political differences intruded into the personal relations of leaders of the church?

BENT: No. That's one thing about the Moravian Church. It cannot be divided. It's sacred. It has not gotten to the point where people don't talk to each other. Some of us ministers are radical. Some are in the middle. Some are on the right. But we don't hate each other. We don't try to pressure each other. The Moravian motto is "In essentials, unity; in nonessentials, liberty; and in all things, love." Some of our pastors are strong on liberation theology, some are not; that's not essential.

Z: Have any of the pastors gone over to work with the contras?

BENT: We know of four who are discredited as pastors. Others are with their people in the refugee camps in Honduras to provide pastoral care.

Z: What do you mean by "discredited"?

BENT: That the church no longer calls them pastors of the Moravian Church. They have no right to claim they are pastors. The synod made this decision because of their military involvement with the contras. Because, historically, we are a "peace church," and if you get involved militarily you are no longer a man of peace.

The situation is very painful for me. Today it has reached the extent that the United States is arming the Indians on one side, and because of constant massive kidnapping of entire villages, Indians are asking the Sandinista government to arm them to defend themselves against the intruders. So the Sandinistas arm the Indians on one side and the U.S. government arms the Indians on the other side and watches the Indians kill each other. And this is very painful for us as church leaders. I have personally visited the U.S. State Department to talk. I told them their mistakes and abuses here. And that they should leave my people alone. And their response was, "No, they're in our hands and we have to make use of them."

The Sandinista government has made many mistakes. They're conscious of their mistakes. They've repented of their mistakes. They want to pay for their mistakes. But they're not permitted to pay for their mistakes. And that is so sad.

14. A Free Press or Censorship?

Xavier Chamorro
Pedro Joaquín Chamorro

Augustín Córdova
Nelba Blandon

In discussing the so-called "totalitarian" nature of the Sandinista government, foreign critics often point to the censorship under which the internationally known newspaper *La Prensa* must now function. However, few critics mention that Nicaragua is home to three nationally competitive news dailies—all edited by members of the same family—and all of which must obey the censorship provisions of the war-time Law of Emergency, in effect since the contra war heated up in December 1981.

The late PEDRO JOAQUÍN CHAMORRO became famous for his 30-year opposition to the Somoza dictatorship. The 53-year-old editor of *La Prensa* was shot to death by gunmen on a street corner in downtown Managua on January 10, 1978. Although never proved, most people believe Somoza was behind the assassination. Today his two sons and brother, editors of rival papers, claim the mantle of his heritage of democratic ideals.

We spoke with Pedro Joaquín's brother XAVIER CHAMORRO, 50, editor of *Nuevo Diario* (circ. 48,000); 32-year-old PEDRO JOAQUÍN CHAMORRO, the eldest son and editor of *La Prensa* (circ. 50,000); AUGUSTÍN CÓRDOVA, editorial page editor at *Barricada*, (circ. 80,000) led by the youngest son, 27-year-old CARLOS CHAMORRO; and with NELBA BLANDON, director of the Interior Ministry office charged with enforcing the censorship provisions of the Law of Emergency. Claiming increased censorship and harassment, P. J. Chamorro left *La Prensa* and Nicaragua in December 1984, following this interview. Traveling to Washington, D.C., he asked the U.S. Congress to increase covert aid to the contras.

* * *

PHILIP ZWERLING: What kind of work did you do during the Somoza dictatorship?

XAVIER CHAMORRO: I worked long and hard, under difficult circumstances, against the dictatorship, hand-in-hand with my brother Pedro Joaquín Chamorro. And when my brother was assassinated by Somoza's order on January 10, 1978, I took his place as editor of *La Prensa* to continue the struggle against the dictatorship. We fought with pens while others fought with arms until we had built a coalition which, in the end, was able to topple Somoza and all of the structures of the dictatorship. Just a week before Pedro Joaquín's murder, we met with the Frente Sandinista to solidify this broad coalition of all forces opposing the dictatorship. If anything, the murder of my brother raised the consciousness of the people and solidified opposition to the dictatorship, until people in every profession and walk of life were moved to opposition.

Xavier Chamorro, Photo by Philip Zwerling

Pedro Joaquín's 30 years of political struggle showed an evolution of political thought and philosophy. He came to understand the need for fundamental change in the system: in all of its political and economic structures. He saw that Nicaragua needed to become a new and distinct country after having been a colony of Spain and a dependency of the United States. *La Prensa* was an important tool in this struggle, a struggle which has been realized and won in Nicaragua today.

Z: And during this time, you worked as a journalist?

X. CHAMORRO: Yes. I worked with Pedro from 1958 when he was in jail following the assassination of Somoza García [Anastasio I]. At that time it seemed that everyone in Nicaragua was in jail. He was a political prisoner, so I came to help out at *La Prensa*. We worked very closely together. We were brothers, but we were also more. Sometimes he was a father to me and sometimes I was a father to him. We were brothers in struggle and in philosophy.

Z: Following the assassination of Pedro Joaquín, you became editor of *La Prensa*?

X. Chamorro: Yes, I had been subeditor and became editor after his murder. I remained as editor until May 1980, when 90% of the staff and workers of *La Prensa* decided to start a new newspaper where we could continue the kind of journalism we had previously known at *La Prensa*, and where we could follow the dictates of our conscience. So we began *Nuevo Diario* as a collective, and I became editor.

Z: Please say a little bit more about the family conflicts that led to this split at *La Prensa*.

X. Chamorro: The fundamental problem was a political disagreement. The other owners of *La Prensa* seemed to be looking for another change of government even after the Revolution, and looked to oppose the new government in every area. It was one thing to criticize to try to make things better, but it something else to simply move into a position of opposition to everything the new government was doing. It was not possible to be honest journalists in that ideological atmosphere. There was an internal struggle. I was removed as editor on April 20, 1980, and that was followed by a protest and strike by the workers. Finally, a formula was agreed to in which the workers, some of whom had worked at *La Prensa* for 30 years, received compensation from the owners, and I sold my interest in that enterprise. We used that money as capital to buy the paper and presses to begin *Nuevo Diario*. It was a new paper with a new name, but it was really *La Prensa* continuing, because 90% of the workers at *La Prensa* came to *Nuevo Diario*. *La Prensa* had been closed briefly by the earthquake in 1972. It was closed in June 1979 when Somoza bombed it, and it was closed in April 1980, but it reopened on May 19 under the name *Nuevo Diario*.

Z: It's not easy to start a new newspaper.

X. Chamorro: It's not easy, but we were experienced, and we certainly had experience after the earthquake and after the bombing of starting from scratch all over again. All we needed was a building, paper and press.

Z: What's the daily circulation of *Nuevo Diario* today?

X. Chamorro: We are the smallest of the three papers, but we are growing about 15% each year. We sell 45,000 copies daily.

Z: We enjoy *Nuevo Diario* most. It's more lively than *Barricada* and more truthful than *La Prensa*.

X. Chamorro: Well, we try to put out a paper that supports the

Revolution, but still remains critical. We are an independent newspaper: independent of the government, any political party or economic special interest. Our editorial pages are open to a wide range of diverse and conflicting ideological points of view. We believe that Nicaraguans have the right both to be informed and to react to information through our paper, which prints their letters and articles as well.

Z: What is the role of a free press in a revolutionary country?

X. CHAMORRO: I believe that the first thing is to be responsible to the truth and to the readers. It is also to be critical of mistakes and to offer alternatives to problems. It's very easy to simply criticize, but it's more difficult and more important to also point the direction to some solutions. It's a great responsibility in the political, cultural and economic development of the country. It's a great work and a great responsibility.

Z: And are you allowed to be critical?

X. CHAMORRO: Yes. I believe criticism is one of the great tasks of any journalist. We criticize problems that affect the public, like rising food costs or poor public sanitation. We criticize government policies with which we disagree. We have criticized the system of censorship under which three newspapers publish; however, we understand the need for censorship in the time of emergency. Censorship is not a revolutionary goal. For the first two years of the Revolution newspapers were not censored. The radio stations are not censored. The reports of foreign journalists in Nicaragua are not censored. The access Nicaraguans have to all sorts of information and to critical views is important and unhampered.

However, Reagan's policies, as outlined in the Santa Fe document (drawn up by Reagan's advisors), to try to destabilize the Nicaraguan government through a covert war led our government to try to defend itself concretely through the 1981 State of Emergency law that included media censorship. In Miami and California, the Reagan administration has allowed the public recruitment and training of ex-National Guardsmen, which has been reported on national television news in the U.S. Now these soldiers are in camps in Honduras and Costa Rica, from which they enter Nicaragua to murder people and destroy our crops. In addition, we face an international blockade of credit and aid. In the face of all this, the Nicaraguan government has the obligation to safeguard our people and our Revolution.

Censorship followed the start of this covert war, and if the U.S. would end this war, censorship would end as well. Every country in the world has invoked censorship in wartime, including the U.S. in the past. We hope the censorship will be lifted in Nicaragua in time for the elections in November 1984. [It wasn't.]

Z: How does the censor function in relation to *Nuevo Diario?*

X. CHAMORRO: Just as with the two other papers. We send our articles over to the censor, and they return them with notations as to what can or cannot be published.

Z: Is there a process to appeal a decision of the censor?

X. CHAMORRO: No, there's no real appeal process. If we disagree, we can pick up the phone and talk to them. Sometimes they change their minds; sometimes they don't. It's a very subjective business to interpret the rules and procedures.

Z: How is it possible to understand the process of change in the editorial line of *La Prensa* before and after the Triumph?

X. CHAMORRO: You have to understand the mind-set of the owners. Under the leadership of Pedro Joaquín *La Prensa* always opposed the dictatorship, and for this he paid with his life. Under my leadership, the paper supported the Revolution. Now a handful of other people make these decisions, and they are in opposition. But remember that the staff of *La Prensa* is here now. The only things that are the same at *La Prensa* now as in the past are the name, the color of the paper, and the color of the ink.

Z: Is *La Prensa* today an instrument of the counterrevolution?

X. CHAMORRO: Anyone who reads the paper can see the function it aims at.

Z: If Pedro Joaquín Chamorro were alive today, would he be working at *Nuevo Diario* or at *La Prensa?*

X. CHAMORRO: Look, if Pedro Joaquín lived, *Nuevo Diario* would not need to exist because we would all be at *La Prensa* with him. Pedro Joaquín always fought for what was best for Nicaraguans. He was always a revolutionary, and he would be with the Revolution today. This is what he had been working for and dreaming of.

Z: It's rare for us in the States to see a single family holding editorial positions in three competing daily newspapers. Do these differences cause hard feelings within the family?

X. CHAMORRO: In the first place, we live in the democratic atmosphere of this Revolution where there is space for all. And a family is not merely the sum of the political opinions of its members. It's more than that. It's made of blood and hearts tied together. We may disagree, but we remain family.

* * *

PHILIP ZWERLING: How is it possible to describe the state of freedom in general, and freedom of the press in particular in Nicaragua?

PEDRO JOAQUÍN CHAMORRO: Well, it's not possible to speak of freedom in a country where freedom of the press is lacking. Here there is only one public source of opposition to the Frente Sandinista, and that is *La Prensa*. And for two and a half years we have had to operate under government censorship. All other channels of communication are either under the control of the Frente Sandinista or simply parrot their line. I will show you a very thick folder, for example, of *La Prensa* articles censored by the government in the first 25 days of this month alone [May 1984]. The censor reads all of our articles and stories, and takes out or changes anything they don't like. Now, they've never ordered us to print anything we didn't want to print. If they did, that would be the end of *La Prensa*.

The clearest sign of the lack of liberty in Nicaragua is that a single political party, the Frente Sandinista, controls the government and all aspects of the government, including the office of the censor, without permitting opposition. They control the only two television stations [formerly both were controlled by Somoza], which gives them an absolute monopoly on television. There were four or five radio stations that I know of in opposition to the Sandinistas, and under the State of Emergency their editorials and news reports have been cancelled.

It's a basic necessity of political freedom to have a free, diverse and unrestricted press and other means of communication. This we do not have.

Z: Does the level of censorship change depending on political events?

P.J. CHAMORRO: It changes. Sometimes it's harsher than at other times. Certainly it was most difficult at the beginning when we weren't used to it. It lightened up at the end of last year and then became heavier again early this year. Issues change, and what they are sensitive about changes. They don't censor the sports pages. They don't usually censor political statements of opposition when they are released by political parties. But they censor information or particular words in news stories. For example, we cannot refer to the antigovernment fighters in the north or south

Pedro Joaquín Chamorro, Photo by Philip Zwerling

as "anti-Sandinistas" or "guerrillas." These words are censored and we have to call them "counterrevolutionaries."

Seventy percent of the time you can guess what they will censor; 30% we never know. They seize on the strangest things to react to. Right now they have a projected Press Law that would make censorship much more rigid and heavy. [This proposed law was later withdrawn from the Council of State by the Frente Sandinista].

Z: Do you have particular examples of how the censorship works now?

P. J. CHAMORRO: Look at this folder of censored stories for the month of May. See this story: "delete paragraphs 7, 8, 9, 10, 11, 12, 14." It's ridiculous. Hardly anything is left. It's simple repression of the press.

Z: And when you have many articles censored in a single daily edition, do you decide not to publish that day?

P. J. CHAMORRO: We're always prepared with filler material to stick into the white space left by stories that are removed or shortened by censorship. But when we're censored heavily, even that's not enough. We always plan to publish, but sometimes we are physically unable to fill out the paper and then we don't publish. That also happens when the censor returns material to us too late in the day to publish.

Z: And how many days in the five months of this year have you failed to publish?

P. J. CHAMORRO: About five days.

Z: Do you try to guess what will be censored and avoid that material in advance?

P. J. CHAMORRO: They usually censor national news, and 70% of the time we can guess their reaction. But we put our paper out for our subscribers and for the people who buy it in the street. We don't put this paper out for the censor, but for the people.

Z: How has the level of circulation been affected during this time?

P. J. CHAMORRO: Well, it drove circulation down quite a bit. Two years ago, we were at perhaps 70,000 copies a day. It kept going down to a low of about 40,000 and now slowly we've been going up again. Circulation today is about 50,000 copies daily. And this increase is in spite of the fact that *La Prensa* costs more than the others: 5 cordobas per copy as opposed to three cordobas for *Barricada* or *Nuevo Diario*.

Z: Is *La Prensa* always in opposition to the government and the Frente Sandinista?

P. J. CHAMORRO: In spirit we are an opposition newspaper, but in reality we're not. Because under censorship no real paper of opposition is allowed. We *are* in opposition to the Frente Sandinista. The nine "comandantes" made one revolution, but the Nicaraguan people wanted a different kind of revolution. They've betrayed the principles of the Revolution while we cling to that original vision of a Nicaraguan democracy.

Z: I've been in Nicaragua for four months now, and I've read many articles against the government in *La Prensa*.

P. J. CHAMORRO: Look, don't confuse informational articles and editorials. We are able to publish information in articles when these are the public statements of opposition parties.

Z: For example, there was an interview with a political party leader published two days ago that was very critical of the Frente Sandinista.

P. J. CHAMORRO: Correct. As I said, this is the technical difference. Criticism can be printed when it is contained in a public statement by a political leader. These are not censored. But news stories are censored. And our own editorials are not censored except when they are aimed at protesting the censorship. Some things are allowed, others not. But they decide. Look, we've got a Marxist-Leninist system here that will simply not allow a democracy to develop. As long as we don't follow a Marxist-Leninist line, we have trouble with this government.

Z: Government leaders have told me that *La Prensa* has chosen the role of *El Mercurio* in Chile or *The Daily Gleaner* in Jamaica in order to subvert the government.

P. J. CHAMORRO: Let me ask you a question. When Somoza was in power *La Prensa* was an opposition newspaper, and no one accused it of selling out to a foreign power then. Today we oppose this government in the same way and for the same reasons. We opposed Somoza, we oppose the Frente Sandinista in the same way. So, why now are we accused of treason? If they don't like your politics they call you names and make charges. We don't have foreigners working here. We don't receive money from foreigners. I've never read *El Mercurio*. I've never seen it in my life. Nor *The Daily Gleaner*. Look at who gets foreign help! Look at the Chileans and North Americans who work at *Barricada*. Look at the aid this government gets from the Soviet Union! This paper is put out by Nicaraguans for Nicaraguans. It's the Communists who have "internationalists" crawling around in every part of the government!

Z: How do Nicaraguans react to the point of view of *La Prensa*?

P. J. CHAMORRO: Look, ours is the most expensive paper, but people buy it. It comes out in the evening, while the others are morning papers, but people buy it. We sell more papers than *Nuevo Diario*. It's a phenomenon. Who buys the paper? We sell 50,000 copies. There aren't 50,000 bourgeois left in Nicaragua. The people buy our paper because they support what we're saying or want to read the only voice of opposition left in the country. Papers around the world, newspapers in the United States, attack the government, but no one calls them traitors to their country! No one compares them to *El Mercurio*. Papers in the U.S. attack Reagan every day. Only a handful of papers support Reagan. But no one questions the patriotism of these opposition papers. No one accuses them of taking money from the Soviet Union! Freedom of the press? Without freedom of the press there is no freedom. But this government in Nicaragua cannot tolerate a dissenting voice or an independent press.

Z: But as a paper of opposition, why doesn't *La Prensa* speak out against the counterrevolutionaries or Reagan's anti-Nicaraguan policies?

P. J. CHAMORRO: We were opponents of this regime before Reagan became president. We're not aligned with anyone outside Nicaragua. We are simply working day and night, against heavy odds, to protect the human rights and freedoms of Nicaraguans.

Z: You have all kinds of foreign visitors who call on you here, including European and North American political leaders.

P. J. CHAMORRO: Yes, they come here to check on the facts of what is really happening in Nicaragua.

Z: And when you meet with U.S. congresspeople, what kind of advice do you give them about U.S. policy vis-à-vis Nicaragua?

P. J. CHAMORRO: I have never advocated a policy of U.S. intervention in Nicaragua. I've never suggested they send Marines to change the government.

Z: Do you think there's any possibility of creating a free press under the Sandinista government?

P. J. CHAMORRO: No. I don't believe so, because the concept of a free press is alien to them. They believe in a press that is free to support them, like *Barricada*, but not in a press that is free to oppose them.

Z: What's your opinion of *Barricada* and *Nuevo Diario*?

P. J. CHAMORRO: *Barricada* is a paper that is exceptionally well done. It has a clearly stated point of view, a political line with which I disagree, but which is honest and open. It's well written and produced. But I can't say the same about *Nuevo Diario*. It sneaks around, pretending to be independent, while still never ever deviating from the Sandinistas. If *Barricada* is the open and public wife of the Revolution, *Nuevo Diario* is its back-street mistress.

Z: How then shall we understand the presence of members of your family in editorial positions at all three papers?

P. J. CHAMORRO: My younger brother Carlos is the editor at *Barricada*. Carlos, in one way or another, was always associated with the Frente Sandinista and the goals of the Revolution. I respect him very much for his commitment and integrity. He works and acts out of his ideals. I recognize this even though I disagree with him on almost everything.

My uncle, who is editor at *Nuevo Diario,* became a revolutionary on July 19, 1979 [date of the Triumph]. Before that he was always the biggest capitalist in the family. So I have no respect for someone like that who chooses his politics by expediency. Now that's only two members of my family. My mother [Violeta Chamorro, widow of Pedro Joaquín] was originally a member of the National Junta of Reconstruction, but she resigned in opposition to the Sandinistas, and is now president of *La Prensa.* Other aunts, uncles and my grandmother are all part owners in *La Prensa.* So, most of the family stands together.

Z: Your uncle Xavier told me that if your father were alive today he would be standing with the Revolution.

P. J. CHAMORRO: Neither *Barricada* nor *Nuevo Diario* have ever had the slightest interest in printing words from the political thought of my father. They prefer him as a dead monument rather than a political thinker. Often, when we've tried to print his words, we have been censored. My father could never agree to what is happening today: to censorship of his paper, attacks on his family, or attacks on the church. Everything he stood for and spoke for was opposed to what the Sandinistas are doing.

* * *

PHILIP ZWERLING: Could you give us a brief history of *Barricada?*

AUGUSTÍN CÓRDOBA: This newspaper formally began two days after the Triumph of the Revolution in July 1979. However, the revolutionary press of the Sandinista Front has had many predecessors. Those were diverse underground projects. One of the most outstanding of these underground papers, and perhaps the one most directly the predecessor of *Barricada,* was *The Trench.* It was mimeographed, but with very ingenious drawings. It was put out by a young militant of that time, Lenin Cerna [now head of state security]. It had a limited distribution, chiefly to students in the city.

Another paper of this era also published by students was *Rojo y Negro.* In the time of Sandino, red and black were the colors symbolizing Sandinismo. However, at the time *Rojo y Negro* was being published in the early sixties, the forces struggling against Somoza were known only as the National Liberation Front. Only later did it come to be called the Sandinista National Liberation Front. But obviously the use of the colors red and black in the name of a publication indicates there was already an element of Sandinismo present in the movement.

In the interior of the country there were other experiences.

Offices of Newspaper, Photo by Philip Zwerling

There were publications which presented facts and fundamental information about the Revolution and the Somoza government. These papers were all distributed in the same manner. Small groups went out and left the papers on doorsteps in the barrios. This might seem to be an activity of little import, but in Nicaragua in those times things were very different. Many times the youngsters would be caught and the consequence would not be a fine or a lecture, but torture and death.

In 1974, the FSLN began to develop international activities. After the armed takeover of the "Chemo" Castillo house [home of a Somoza supporter], the Front began publishing to other countries. This resulted in an international publication, *The Sandinista Gazette*.

Z: These international papers, were they published in Nicaragua or in Costa Rica?

CÓRDOBA: *The Gazette* was always published abroad. It was published in Cuba, Panama, Venezuela, Mexico and in California. It was the external organ of the Front. Through this experience the Frente Sandinista arrived at its present point of view. Another experience which also helped to shape Nicaraguan journalism is what we refer to as "Journalism of the Catacombs." In 1977, there was severe censorship of the press by Somoza. Journalists sought freedom of expression in the churches. Meetings were held in the churches and journalists read stories that were not allowed to be published under Somoza's laws. Many people would congregate in the churches to hear news and get information. There was always news of the Sandinistas. Sometimes, to punish people for this demonstration against censorship, Somoza's National Guard would come and surround the church and lie in wait for people to leave. Many times people did not want to leave the church after a session because they were afraid of the Guard.

These sessions resulted in whole churches being influenced by the effects of this oppression. Large numbers of Christians became involved in the revolutionary process through Christian base communities. These were some of the journalistic activities before the Triumph.

At the Triumph of the Revolution the FSLN took over Somoza's paper *Novedades*. The North American public was always surprised at the quality of this newspaper. It was very, very bad, and had a very small circulation. Somoza had no interest in creating a good paper. He did not encourage discussion nor allow distribution of information. The only function of *Novedades* was to aid the dictatorship. The paper was of poor quality and had no aspirations.

The press, which we here at *Barricada* inherited, was of poor quality and very old. The quality of our newspaper was much better, but we committed many errors. We used language that the people didn't understand. We wanted to inform them of everything that was happening in the whole world when our people were not even familiar with what was happening in the nearby countries of Mexico and the United States. We had no precise idea of what form the paper ought to have or ought to achieve.

The people were accustomed to another type of journalism and continued to look for sensationalism with reports of crimes, murders, nude women and so on. Our type of journalism, a responsible attempt to educate and communicate, was unfamiliar. The evolution and maturation of the newspaper of the FSLN was part of the development and maturation of the rest of the revolutionary process. It would have been impossible to achieve what we have without direct communication with the people.

We worked on our paper to meet the needs of our people and the party. In 1982, we began refining the framework and activities of *Barricada*. We changed the language we used with our people. 1982 and 1983 were two years of constant improvement in our newspaper. These were years that also saw the successful results of the massive literacy campaign. It doubled or tripled the potential number of readers of our paper. Also, the distribution of our paper changed; it expanded from being merely urban and close-by Managua to being distributed to the whole country.

In this process of growth and maturation, we also changed our format. We have a large section that is fundamentally national news, and page 2, which is a small section devoted to international news. It's probably a very bad section. We seldom talk of Israel or Uganda or Luanda or Tel Aviv, because our people don't know and don't want to know what are the differences between Africa, Asia and the Middle East. The presentations on the international page are limited by what the people want and can understand. At the same time, there is a requirement to inform and educate.

For example, should we explain to our brothers what is the difference between one faction and another in a war in Ethiopia? First, we have an obligation to explain what is happening in El Salvador because it's our neighbor and has a more direct relationship to our own developing revolutionary struggle. We have a priority to educate our people about the liberation movements of Central America and the Caribbean and Southern Cone. The other line that is necessary to include in the international news is the foreign policy of the Reagan administration and of North America in general. These are the fundamental elements we present in the international news, and then if space and time permit, we present other world news.

Page 3 is the editorial page, and presents the analysis of the Sandinista Front on various situations, and the national and international policies it needs to discuss and deepen.

There are friends from foreign countries who say our editorial style is very pedantic, that it's a political discourse. But it's done for a reason. There are many members of the party, and they don't have to come to a meeting to find out what the Front is thinking. They can read the paper and see what question the FSLN is considering.

Z: Are these editorials used in discussion groups?

CÓRDOBA: They are used in what we estimate to be the best possible way. Many military units and cooperatives and centers of production, and even groups in isolated areas, use the newspaper for discussion. When they receive the newspaper in the morning before they begin work, they read the editorial page out loud and then discuss it. When we hear of these activities it is very gratifying to us. It's an interesting phenomenon. The editorials are not ordinarily concerned with the recent events, but of a larger scope so that they would be of interest in remote rural areas some days later.

Initially, we received a lot of correspondence here at *Barricada* from many parts of the country, and we published it. Gradually, interest in this tapered off because it was a unilateral dialogue with the public. Then we created a section called "Popular Mailbox." We never knew what "Popular Mailbox" might become. It's the result of experience, and it came out of the expression of the people. It's set up like this:

Here we receive complaints, jokes and expressions of discontent with the state bureaucracy. Our revolutionary state, even though it might be revolutionary, is still a bureaucracy with faults.

We are the first to see this weakness and to combat it. Our people suffer due to inefficiencies in the bureaucracy and they complain about it here. But we don't consider it sufficiently satisfying only to publicly present the problem—only to say that in order to leave the country a person must have a ticket. When we receive a complaint of this type we test it out to see if it was an exception. If we find through experience that it was true, then we publish exactly what functionary said what and who did what.

Z: Are there changes in the process resulting from these stories?

CÓRDOBA: Yes, always, because it is not just us, but the people who are demanding change. This has caused us many problems. Here there are state ministries that have complained, who say they don't want to give information to *Barricada* anymore because we have the attitude of an enemy. But we aren't going to change our position and we have achieved changes.

Commandante Borge said one time that in this Revolution we have to be very discreet with our successes and very critical of our errors. And this is the line of *Barricada*. When the Revolution does something well, it is necessary to include it, but we should also put emphasis on our errors.

I know of only two ways to judge if a newspaper is doing well or badly: its economic situation and its circulation. *Barricada* occupies first place in the number of sales in our country. In 1983, our circulation was 100,000 daily, rising to 200,000 on special occasions. In 1984, our circulation has risen to 197,000 daily and on special occasions we have 500,000 readers. We have to calculate that one paper is read by four to six people. That's half a million people in a country of less than three million, a country that four years ago was practically illiterate. It's a phenomenon in communication, and for us it's an enormous commitment.

Our closest competition and adversary of the Revolution is *La Prensa*. *La Prensa* appeals to a section of the population which opposes the revolutionary process. It has the appeal that people are accustomed to reading in opposition journalism. And *La Prensa,* which for many reasons is not *the La Prensa* of before, is still the legitimate heir of this historic experience of opposition journalism.

The newspaper that is against the Revolution has greater possibilities of creating excitement and sensationalism by using manipulation and disinformation. In the beginning, after the Triumph, there were all manner of possibilities for using these, and *La Prensa* did.

One thing which we deeply respect in this country is the memory of Carlos Fonseca. He is an indisputable revolutionary figure. Even those who are not Sandinistas respect Carlos.

On the same day that we were paying tribute to Carlos Fonseca (we passed a law naming him Chief Comandante of the Revolution) Prince Charles of England was married to Princess Diana. *La Prensa* wrote articles about the wedding. One article detailed gifts the prince received, and another was presented in a very vulgar manner telling of the honeymoon and the lovemaking on the honeymoon. Between these articles on Prince Charles was a photo of Carlos Fonseca. It was a type of provocation. In this country these are moral and ethical principles which are distinctly Latino. There are things which are very clear to us, and *La Prensa* knows this.

La Prensa used these principles to make a political point. That's legitimate, but the form of presenting this type of thing is inexcusable even though the process permits it.

Let me give you another example. I believe in the value of the internationalists in our country. It's incredible. There are doctors here from every country, including the United States, and they are working for the health of all our people. *La Prensa* has tried to print that venereal diseases have increased because of the sexual activities of the internationalists. This would not be permitted in any country of the world. It is nothing more than misinformation, false and unpardonable.

Z: You don't believe freedom of the press means freedom to discuss anything whatsoever?

CÓRDOBA: Sometimes when we talk of freedom of the press it's as though we were talking of water or air. It's an abstract idea. However, freedom of the press doesn't exist in infinite space. It exists in a determined place with definite circumstances. We are familiar with the paths of many revolutionary processes and of many dictatorships, and we know how easily world opinion can be affected. One thing that is important in international opinion is freedom of the press.

If we consider the situation objectively it is easily agreed that the North American people have submitted to a censorship much greater than that of Nicaragua. The difference is that we instituted our censorship because of a state of emergency, and we instituted it publicly. We explained the reasons why. We did it in defense of our revolutionary process. The North American public experiences a censorship of omission. They are ignorant of thousands of things because of what is not spoken of. They are intoxicated by other types of information. It's a very subtle mechanism. That is why we wonder how the North American people can criticize us for our censorship of the press when they continue to censor theirs even when it's not necessary.

We have responsibilities which are concrete and which limit absolute freedom of the press. During the government of Allende in Chile, for example, Allende maintained a strict respect for the conservative bourgeoisie with an abstract freedom of the press. The press used this as more than a freedom and made itself into a weapon. It became a weapon that cost lives, that cost the process, that cost the life of its very president.

After the death of patriotic Chile a generation of sociologists—French, English and North American—have done excellent analytical work explaining the political errors that Allende committed, and one of these was his maintenance of abstract freedom of the press. We are not disposed to having our revolutionary process reversed, and we don't want another generation of sociologists saying we made the same mistakes as Allende.

So we have two things to weigh concerning censorship of the press: international public opinion and the experience of revolutions in the past. It's a political choice that we have analyzed. We decided to maintain the largest, widest degree of freedom in this area because we want our process to be distinctive, breaking with the myth that no revolution can exist without censorship of the press. During all of 1979, 1980 and 1981 everything was allowed to be published, from the sexual lives of the heads of the Socialist parties of the world to even making fun of our heroes. Any type of lies or calumnies was allowed to pass.

If you review the newspapers you will find a manual of disinformation. There was no censorship. Anything can be found: murders, monsters, supernatural phenomena, horrors, religious images having human qualities. This manual of disinformation we are familiar with, because it is produced by the CIA. However, after these first three years we arrived at a moment of political decision. This was pushed on us by the increased aggression of the Reagan administration. The mercenaries of the CIA began military incursions into the interior of our country. We had a war on both borders and *La Prensa* had become like a weapon.

I invite any sociologist to come here and to study the censored *La Prensa*, not *La Prensa* without censorship, but the censored version, and see what they find. Walesa of the opposition in Poland is a hero in *La Prensa*. The people here don't know who Walesa is or where Poland is, but *La Prensa* tells them. *La Prensa*, under censorship, reported that Fidel Castro has an anal illness. We don't believe that a Nicaraguan newspaper should speak of an alleged illness in the anus of the leader of another revolutionary country. To us it appears insipid. But this appears on the editorial page of *La Prensa* even under censorship. *La Prensa*, under censorship, has printed a story of a woman giving birth to a chicken, of a dog with two heads, and so on.

So what is censored? Military information and economic information are censored. We are a very tiny country—about half the size of California. We are small and everyone here knows everything. The woman who is in the war zone in the morning is in the market by midday and is telling everything of interest. And the people who were in the market at midday go home and tell what they heard. By nightfall everyone knows what will be in *Barricada* the next day. In a country like this, two hours is enough time for everyone to know what's important.

If people heard that tomorrow the price of gas will go up, in two hours there would be a panic. Everyone would run to the gas station. This would produce all kinds of incidents and accidents and would deplete the gasoline supply. This is only an example. The same rumor could be started with many products: milk, eggs, chicken, meat, fish, saying it's the last day they will be sold. This creates a chain reaction of hysteria and panic. It's collective, and it's very hard to control. In our society this is a very sensitive area and can have an incredible effect. So in this area censorship has a priority over abstract freedom of the press. This type of misinformation is part of the war. It's a weapon against the Revolution, and we have a right to protect the Revolution.

The other aspect of our censorship is military. We censor the news because we are in a war. We can't have a newspaper saying there are hundreds of casualties when there aren't, because there are hundreds of mothers who would run to the hospitals. We don't censor military news because we have military secrets. It's certain that the CIA knows what has happened before we do. We censor for the moral effect that the war has on the citizens, for the emotional impact. As Tomás Borge said, "The truth is the policy of the Revolution." Here our job is to inform the people in a national manner of the facts they already know. It's a very rare occasion when military actions are not known by our people. The problem is not military secrets, but the effects of military aggression on the people.

Z: Do you believe that the CIA uses *La Prensa* as it used *El Mercurio* in Chile?

CÓRDOBA: Yes, according to many North Americans who write about these things. They have shown us articles from *El Mercurio,* and from the Jamaican newspapers during the election of Michael Manley, and from the newspapers of Grenada, and have compared them to what *La Prensa* is doing here. The articles and the layout are the same—including the photographs. There are well-designed pages of *La Prensa* which are extraordinarily similar to the pages of *El Mercurio.* This is not an accident, but an action of the CIA.

In this century, this year, this moment, it is impossible to overestimate the importance of the media. That would be childish. We are in a war, but we don't underestimate the capacity of the enemy to use the communication media for psychological warfare.

We are not censoring freedom of expression; we are preventing the Reagan administration from using our framework of pluralism to put a gun at our back. We are controlling the weapons of the CIA. Hunger and panic can also kill. We have to defend ourselves, and that is why we have censorship and will continue to have it in spite of the enormous cost it has in international public opinion.

* * *

PHILIP ZWERLING: What is your official title?

NELBA BLANDON: I am director of the Office of Communications Media.

Z: Do you have other tasks in addition to that of censor?

BLANDON: We also are in charge of developing the art of cinematography and producing documentaries. We are concerned with popular education regarding cinema and the effects of cinema on society. We are also involved in the supervision of publicity—advertising in newspapers, television, and on radio. We have a law concerning the use of women in the media: women cannot be used as objects to sell things utilizing only the physical aspects of women. A woman must be presented as a whole human being. Part of the Revolution is the cultural transformation of values, and publicity (advertising) is an important aspect of this. In publicity, the role of a woman should reflect her rights in society.

Z: To promote these changes in society is it necessary to prohibit this type of advertising?

BLANDON: Prohibit advertising? We believe the ideal would occur when the means of communication wouldn't serve as vehicles to promote and commend consumerism, but instead our media would promote the popular health campaigns, adult education, the continuation of the literacy campaign, and right now to educate in preparation for the elections.

Nelba Blandon, Photo by Connie Martin

Z: For example, the newspapers now have ads selling consumer items. And there are movies that present women almost nude, as objects. There are also movies of horror and violence. All that exists now in Nicaragua.

BLANDON: The problem of advertising is a complex one. Here there is a sector of the population, the upper class, that is used to it and prefers it. Also, to prohibit advertising would throw people working in publicity and in advertising out of work. On the other hand, we have to guard against false advertising, illegal competition, and the image of women as consumer items.

Dealing with the cinema presents a somewhat more serious problem because films are introduced into this country through private enterprise. The quota of films these individuals can bring in is limited by the amount of dollars they receive from the central government. Because we need dollars to buy vaccines for the children, and agricultural machinery, the amount of hard currency allocated for buying films is small.

However, films, the cinema, is a major entertainment of our people. As in other countries in Central America it is a diversion par excellence. It is a major industry in Central America. The amount of dollars determines the amount and kinds of films which enter the country. The distributor for Fox or MGM does not worry about the quality of films all Nicaraguans will see. He worries only about making money. That is something he doesn't forget, and if Nicaragua is a market with little money he doesn't send us the best he has. If we were to prohibit all the films which exploit women and all the films with violence, bad quality or historical misinformation, then we would have no films in our country.

Z: Part of your work here is the censorship of the newspapers. Why is that censorship necessary?

BLANDON: That's a lot to tell. Before the Revolution all the means of communication were in private hands, or belonged to Somoza. This means they were used to remove people from information about their real problems: hunger, misery, privation and repression. This lack of information was itself a form of repression more sophisticated, subtler and often more dangerous than armed repression. The means of communication in the hands of Somoza played this repressive role.

Some of the communications media in private hands had another role. They were more humanistic and would timidly question the dominant system. Because of this questioning the Somoza dictatorship worried about the development of the private press. However, the owners of these communications media were not truly concerned about the rights of the poor and the working class. They were opposed to Somoza because he, through his excesses, was putting the system of the bourgeoisie at risk. They were defending the status quo, and in this way the established system. They wanted surface reforms and not the resolution of basic contradictions between those who ate well everyday and those who ate nothing.

After the Triumph, the communications media belonging to Somoza were confiscated. The media in private hands were not confiscated, but rather, their proprietors were guaranteed ownership. However, when the Revolution passed power to the working class, this created resentment in the dominant class.

Things were not as they had been before, because in spite of our limitations, we have guaranteed to the people what they need. Our programs include the Agrarian Reform, which resulted in a fundamental change in our economic structure, the Literacy

Crusade, popular health campaigns, the access of workers and campesinos to the universities. We have a project in which the children of workers and campesinos attend preparatory school and are provided with food, health care, housing and education. In four years they are ready to begin advanced education.

These are programs which affect the earnings of self-interest groups, such as those who interpret the title of doctor to mean a vendor of medicine, or the owners of enormous quantities of land. However, the problem is not the confiscation of land nor the nationalization of the foreign bank, nor the creation of a health system accessible to all. The problem is that the government has made it a goal for the working class to have access to everything—all services—and this is resented.

As a result, the former dominant class has used and is using all of its resources, including the media, to neutralize our gains and to capitalize on our errors. They berate us and call us communists, Marxist-Leninist repressors of religion. They say that the efforts of the government are something that is absolutely opposed to religious principles. This is very serious because we as a people are overwhelmingly Catholic. Their means for expressing their methods are excellent. They are means of communications in private hands, such as Radio Católica, Radio Cooperación, Radio Mundial and *La Prensa.*

Z: How do the limitations function?

BLANDON: Coincidental with the escalation of armed aggression and the economic war against us, there has been an increase in disinformation. Because of all this it was necessary to declare a state of emergency, and part of that was the institution of censorship. It is not an irresponsible act. That is not to say that any determined movement doesn't commit errors, either of excess or defect. These mistakes are products of inexperience. We have never before had to confront the dissemination of disinformation and the media of the powerful capitalists. They misuse the media whenever they can. For instance, when the Dutch journalists were so savagely killed in El Salvador, *La Prensa* reported that this killing was a crime provoked by the guerrillas. Other journalists were horrified at this lie. It capitalized on the free press of our Revolution.

Z: This morning when I spoke to Pedro Joaquín Chamorro he gave me a packet of stories for May which had been censored. Included among the censored items were the words "anti-Sandinista" or "rebels" in place of counterrevolutionaries. Why?

BLANDON: The terms "rebels" or "guerrillas" are terms which in Latin America indicate forces of the workers and campesinos. The middle class has never assumed the character of guerrillas and have never overthrown or destroyed a criminal dictatorship. From the Mexican border to Patagonia, to speak of rebels or guerrillas implies resistance to the exploiting class.

Their intention in using these words is to glorify the mercenaries of the CIA who are fighting on our borders. This would be like saying the war in Vietnam was made by North American rebels—not interventionists or invaders. Here these terms mean dignity and honesty. Now they are being used to try to sell the counterrevolutionaries. The *gringos* who are participating in maneuvers on our border with Honduras are not rebels or guerrillas on the side of our people. However, the belief of the opposition is that if you use a term constantly and systematically it can change public opinion.

Z: After the bishops presented the pastoral letter, *Barricada* printed articles personally insulting to Monsignor Obando. This wasn't prohibited.

BLANDON: It wasn't prohibited because we considered the pastors of the church who wrote the letter able to receive an opposing point of view. What we don't permit is the invention of defamatory campaigns of one person against another. What *Barricada* did was to present the history of Obando y Bravo. The upper class is trying to give us a different version of that history. This information is really the history of our people. The history exists and facts exist that our people will never forget. Our people have every right in the world to demand that this history be exposed to the light. The problem is that there are those who want to hide their history and are horrified that they may have to face people's outrage.

Z: Jokes about Obando y Bravo are permitted in the papers, but it's not permitted to make jokes about Carlos Fonseca or Augusto César Sandino.

BLANDON: This is very true. The law concerning the media sets definite limitations on the practice of humor. We believe that humor should not be an ideological weapon. We can't prohibit humor. We have weekly magazines dedicated solely to humor. However, we can't permit jokes about the fathers of our Revolution. The social base which reveres Fonseca and Sandino is the immense majority of the population. The upper class is a very small percentage of the population.

The people have an awareness, an instinctive political capacity, and by instinct they know who represents and who doesn't represent their interests. The students, peasants, workers, the people in the barrios would take offense if we allowed such jokes.

In this country there isn't a house in a barrio or peasant sector that doesn't remember a date on which a child or wife or husband or son-in-law or daughter-in-law or neighbor was killed, or a daughter was raped or a ranch burned. These are people who, when they read the pastoral letter, won't let themselves be represented in a dialogue with those same murderers who are still in arms against them. They see the counterrevolutionaries as *contra* [against] *their* Revolution.

There are many "anti-Sandinistas" in this country, but we would not say they are counterrevolutionaries. They are Communists, Socialists, Christian Democrats or members of the Popular Movement and Workers' Front who are not in agreement with Sandinista ideology, but they are not counterrevolutionary. Counterrevolutionary is a political direction.

Monsignor Obando represents a church that has world power. He doesn't represent the progressive position of many religious people in our country. There are priests and nuns who carry their Christianity to the people with a moral authority—not only their individual moral authority but also that of the church they represent. They assume their efforts not as personal missions but as a mission from the church. Monsignor Obando y Bravo represents a church that has world power. It is a monstrous machine and very well set up, and is now trying to isolate us internationally and divide us internally.

In the Santa Fe document they establish lines of action against the Revolution, and one of these is the use of religion. Since the Revolution there are more religious schools, more Catholic churches and more religious sects. And this occurred in spite of all our problems.

Z: There are faithful who believe the words of a bishop because he is a bishop. Can they be manipulated?

BLANDON: We find that the people observe what is happening in the Revolution and see that it contradicts what Obando y Bravo asserts. They can see that they have electricity and water, a little house, a telephone and a salary they can live on, a hospital system and free health care. All these are concrete actions which are evident. The people have faith in the Revolution.

Z: Could you describe how censorship works on a daily basis?

BLANDON: We censor economic information and military information. Our economy is under attack. We are living in conditions of war, and our production is not at the level of our demand. This means we have problems in supplying certain items: toilet paper, toothpaste, soap, school materials, transportation services, eggs, chickens, corn, beans. These shortages are sometimes the results of sabotage or aggression. Also, the policy of many private producers is to limit production and create shortages. Because this is a problem for the government, the government has guaranteed certain items to the people. But to supply corn and beans, the government has to rely on private production as well as state production. A campaign of yellow journalism of disinformation could create shortages, hoarding and price gouging. In this way, the channels of information could be used as a weapon against our economy.

In the field of military reporting we don't want our people to be victimized by false reports. We don't want to commit the same types of errors as we did before. In 1982, *La Prensa* lied and printed a story saying we had raised our quotas in order to aid the Salvadorans. It's true that we sympathize with the struggle of the Salvadoran people and we are in solidarity with them, but we couldn't possibly raise our production quota to help defend them.

On a daily basis the two newspapers which hit the streets in the morning, *Nuevo Diario* and *Barricada*, bring their copy to us the evening before. There is a team here which checks the copy for military news and economic news. Changes are made for the morning edition.

Z: Is there a way to appeal a decision by the censor?

BLANDON: It can be appealed to the Minister of the Interior Tomás Borge. We are not against this type of discussion. However, with *La Prensa*, for example, it is very difficult to establish a policy of dialogue in relation to the social damage an article might cause. Usually this type of talk occurs with the director of the newspaper. Without a doubt it's possible to remain cordial and have an open line of communication.

Z: Do you believe there is direct cooperation between the CIA and *La Prensa*?

BLANDON: I really couldn't say with certainty. A reporter from *La Prensa* has said that coordination exists between the American Embassy and *La Prensa*, but I'm not in their offices and I couldn't vouch for that.

Z: Please tell us something of your life and preparation for this work.

BLANDON: I studied law, but I have never practiced law. I studied at the University of León. My parents live in Matagalpa. I come from a middle-class family that was able to send me to school. That is something that was very unusual in our country. It was very expensive; the tuition, housing and food. I was studying at the university when I became involved with Christians who were concerned about the poor. We worked with the problems of health and literacy and nutrition. I saw close up the misery and problems of our people. It was obvious that a change was needed. I participated in the student movement and in working in the barrio. We worked clandestinely with the barrio committees and the mothers' committee to free prisoners, and with the hunger strikers. I was head of a student newspaper which we distributed secretly in León. We also had a loudspeaker, and when it was quiet in the city, at about 11 p.m., we would broadcast news of the struggle. And that's what I did until the Triumph.

15. The Comandante

Tomás Borge

If there is one person in Nicaragua who personifies the Sandinista struggle against the Somoza dictatorship—its tenacity, failures, suffering and eventual triumph—that person is, I believe, TOMÁS BORGE. Sole surviving founder of the Sandinista National Liberation Front in 1961, he is now the oldest member of the nine-person FSLN National Directorate and minister of the interior.

* * *

PHILIP ZWERLING: Would you speak a little bit about your personal history growing up under the Somoza dictatorship?

TOMÁS BORGE: I was born August 13, 1930, in the city of Matagalpa, 75 miles north of Managua with a population of 40,000. Carlos Fonseca was also born in Matagalpa and we were children of the same area. My parents were already quite old when I was born, in their forties. I was their only child.

My father was a pharmacist and my mother was a shopkeeper. My mother was very religious. She attended church often and worked with the bishop of Matagalpa. She was a devotee of St. Francis of Assisi. And I became a reader of the life and works of St. Francis, especially *The Little Flowers*.

I can see now that this close association with the Catholic Church and the Christianity of St. Francis were the main formative influences of my moral development. My mother wanted me to be a priest, but I chose the law instead.

In high school I worked with Carlos Fonseca [martyred founder of the FSLN and, with Sandino and Rigoberto López, one of the three most revered figures of the Sandinista struggle] to produce student newspapers that challenged the dictatorship.

In the early 1950s, in the University of León, we struggled to free the university from Somoza's control. Again, we published an opposition student newspaper and organized demonstrations against the CIA coup that overthrew the elected and progressive President Arbenz of Guatemala in 1954.

Anastasio Somoza [García] was executed by the patriot Rigoberto López [who died in the assassination] in 1956. In response, hundreds of opponents of the regime were rounded up, including myself. People were murdered or arrested, thrown into jail and tortured. I knew López, was accused of "harboring" him, tried by a military court, and sentenced to eight years in prison. I was 26.

Tomás Borge, Photo by Larry Boyd

By 1958, the university student movement had grown in numbers and militancy under the leadership of Carlos Fonseca. His research into the life and writings of General Sandino brought this history of struggle, which the dictatorship had tried to suppress, into the hands and minds of the students. Due to their demands, political prisoners, including myself, were released from the jails. When I was released, I left the country and dedicated my life and all of my efforts, from that time forward, to the revolutionary struggle.

Z: And how were your political ideas formed during this time of struggle?

BORGE: I was an early reader not only of all that had been written about Sandino and his ideas but also of the great writers and thinkers of the liberal tradition in Latin America like José Martí, Blanco Formona and Juan Montalmo. I was studying for my bachelor's degree and I was also reading Victor Hugo and other liberal Europeans. Other books that affected me greatly were the novels of a German writer by the name of Karl May. That's Karl May and not Karl Marx. Karl May wrote novels about the West of North America, even though he had never visited the United States. He related the adventures of heroes of the West characterized by their courage, nobility, loyalty and sense of justice. I wanted to be like these heroes. Since I couldn't live in the Old West of the U.S., I tried to apply these values to the injustices and hardships my own people faced here in Nicaragua. In law school I read the classics of revolutionary and liberal thought and dialectical materialism.

Z: During this time of your personal development, how did the reality of the dictatorship impact on your life?

BORGE: I grew up in the middle of the dictatorship. When I was only four years old, Sandino was assassinated, in 1934. In 1937, Somoza [García] consolidated his power and began the family dynasty. I began fighting the dictatorship when I was about 13 and a student in secondary school. I was always an anti-Somocista, and later I became an active revolutionary. I took part in all aspects of the struggle against the dictatorship. For this I was imprisoned several times, tortured and exiled.

Somoza repressed the students, the workers, political parties, everyone and anyone who challenged his power. There was cultural repression, economic repression and ideological repression. Somoza was an enemy of liberty, culture, democracy and justice. We fought for the possibility of liberty, culture, justice and development.

Z: What was your first personal contact with the dictatorship?

BORGE: When I was a high school student I was reading all of these books about liberty and democracy. One day Somoza came to Matagalpa to the school where I was studying. The administration had all the students line up to shake his hand, but when he came to me I refused to shake his hand. That was the beginning of my struggle against Somoza.

Later I was an eyewitness to the barbarities and crimes of Somoza. He had political prisoners killed in jail. He had people killed at every level of society. These crimes made revolutionaries of many people.

Z: And so, in 1961, you helped form the Sandinista National Liberation Front?

BORGE: In 1961 we were in exile. In Costa Rica we formed a revolutionary organization that included Carlos Fonseca, Silvio Mayorga, myself and others. Later that year, we met in Honduras and formed the Frente Sandinista and set to work to overthrow the dictatorship. We gathered combatants in the south of Honduras and infiltrated into Nicaragua across the Río Coco. In 1963, we fought in that area for six months. We had little training or equipment and our efforts led to one defeat after another. Most of the men who began that effort died in the struggle.

We reflected upon this failure and decided to work at political organizing with the workers' and students' movements. I did clandestine work in this effort in Nicaragua's cities. In 1966, after new fraudulent elections, we returned to the mountains again. Our best men were attacked and almost wiped out by the National Guard at Pancasán. This was a great military defeat, and Somoza announced that the FSLN had been destroyed.

But we regrouped and began again. From 1970 to 1972 we organized guerrilla bases in northern Nicaragua. The FSLN raid at the home of "Chemo" Castillo in 1974 resulted in the release of many political prisoners and brought international attention to the FSLN. I was in charge of operations in Managua then.

In 1976, I was captured by the National Guard. During the first nine months of imprisonment I was handcuffed, hooded and tortured. A military tribunal sentenced me to 180 years in prison, and I spent the next two and a half years in solitary confinement. In August 1978, Sandinista commandos captured the National Palace and took many congressmen and Somoza relatives prisoners. These hostages were exchanged for Sandinista political prisoners, including myself. The Triumph was finally won on July 19, 1979, 18 years after the founding of the FSLN. All of the other founders and most of the early fighters had died in that long struggle.

Z: Through all of those years, defeats and death, did you maintain a real expectation of victory?

BORGE: Yes, because we had deep convictions and confidence in the leadership of Carlos Fonseca. We were always sure of victory. We didn't know or believe we would survive ourselves. So many died. But we knew the movement would succeed and build a new society. We simply never knew if we would see this with our own eyes.

Z: Following the victory, what accomplishments of the Revolution can you point to?

BORGE: Little by little the dreams we had for all of those years are coming true. The first objective was for a popular victory, and this was the most important accomplishment for all that came after. That objective was realized, and from that moment we moved forward to build our country. We have done this in spite of great difficulties and all of the historical problems of underdevelopment.

If it were not for the war and the contras, we would have been able to accomplish much more. However, in the area of culture we have developed. We have begun to build a society that respects people and in which human rights are guaranteed. We had always dreamed of incorporating the Atlantic Coast into the full life of our country and, in spite of enormous problems and internal contradictions, I believe that we have made great progress.

We are creating a society of equality and beginning to overcome the problems in the way of that goal. Certainly our society is more egalitarian than it has ever been. We are developing the economy, but again there are tremendous problems. Not only the problems of underdevelopment but also the war the Somocistas conduct against Nicaragua and our errors and mistakes. Some of our dreams have been accomplished, but as soon as some are completed new goals arise.

Z: What other goals do you see?

BORGE: I think the most important goal is the construction of a new morality. For us, with all of our limitations, an economic crisis, the poverty of our country, and the intervention of the United States, it is very difficult. But the basis for the creation of a "new man" and a "new woman" exists.

For us the most important thing is to use these resources for the creation of a society of truly free people, of people capable of creativity, of people capable of nurturing in their minds and hearts a deep love for humanity in general. If we can reach this goal of creating a new morality, if we can rid people of selfishness, develop generosity for others, and respect for all, economic development will lack importance for those who have renounced a dependence on material things.

Z: What roles do the church and the Christian believers play in this Revolution?

BORGE: The ideals which the church maintains coincide fundamentally with the historic project of the Revolution. However, there exists a contradiction between the top hierarchical figures of the Nicaraguan Church and Nicaraguan Christians, and a contradiction between this hierarchy and the Revolution. Because the vast majority of Nicaraguans are Christians. And the vast majority of Nicaraguans are revolutionaries. Therefore, to say that there is a contradiction between the hierarchy and the grass-roots believers is to say that there is a contradiction between the hierarchy and the Revolution.

I believe that the moral principles of this Revolution coincide with the moral principles of Christianity. Of course, there are good Christians and good revolutionaries as well as bad Christians and bad revolutionaries. The struggle is between the bad and the good, not between Christians and revolutionaries. We are trying to create a society of good Christians *and* good revolutionaries. It may be that believers will have to choose between the hierarchy and Christianity. Jesus often said that you had to choose between your people and the Pharisees.

Z: How would you describe the level of aggression directed against Nicaragua today?

BORGE: The North American government has formed an army which is much bigger, better trained and better armed than Somoza's National Guard. The army we are facing today has more arms, more resources, more men, more sophistication, than the National Guard we fought for so many years. This army doesn't face us militarily on the field of battle, for this would be impossible, but attempts to create the conditions for direct intervention by the United States.

This army attacks and flees; it chooses civilian targets and kills teachers and doctors. Its goal is economic destabilization, and so it kills cattle and burns granaries. It is very hard for us to confront them directly because of these tactics. In creating this army the United States has set the stage for a war in all of Central America. Around us we see the militarization of countries like Honduras and Costa Rica and the internationalization of the conflict.

Z: And what will be the future of the military situation if President Reagan is reelected in 1984?

BORGE: The future will be a continuing aggression! The future will be a growing intervention! If Reagan is reelected, the possibility exists for general war in Central America. I believe there is a real possibility that the North American armies will try to intervene directly in Nicaragua. Reagan has no interest in the political desires of our people or in the lives of our soldiers. He is ideologically blinded so that he cannot see the reality of Nicaragua.

The United States has forces and resources to intervene. They have the power to come here and to kill everyone. The problem is that this is our country. North Americans will come and fight in a foreign land, but we will be defending our own country. If Reagan could sacrifice the lives of 1,000 soldiers here to gain his objectives here, I believe he would. The problem is that the cost of intervention in Nicaragua would be much greater than the invasion of Grenada, a tiny and insignificant island in the Caribbean. Not many soldiers died there when they invaded after that revolution had destroyed itself.

But here we have an armed people united in the Revolution, with experience in fighting to defend their land. A small intervention would quickly grow into a regional conflagration. The U.S. won't have to worry about the presence of the Soviet Union or Cuba here because they can't help us. We are responsible for our country and we are going to have to defend it with our own skins. It's not going to be the Russians or Cubans who are going to be the victims of the invaders but only we Nicaraguans. And there will be terrible deaths if there is an invasion.

Z: The Reagan administration denied you a visa to visit the United States. If you were allowed to go, what would you say to the North American people and their government?

BORGE: It is important for your government to realize that the hegemony of North America and the prestige of the United States and the authority of the United States does not depend on your aggressiveness or the quality of your military forces. It depends on the quality of your moral force. The Reagan administration is building up its military forces all over the world. But while its military force grows, its moral force diminishes. And your prestige and authority are diminished.

The poor and backward peoples of Latin America cannot respect a country which uses its power to support the corrupt and dictatorial regimes that keep them with their hands extended like beggars and dying of hunger.

Why doesn't the United States send doctors to the sick people of Latin America? Why don't you send teachers to the illiterate people of Latin America? Why don't you send technicians and engineers to help them develop their countries? But instead you send Marines to kill the people of Latin America. In this way, while Reagan seeks to make the U.S. stronger and more powerful than ever, the only road he knows to travel is the road of violence, force and crime. These are the historical consequences of the intervention the U.S. has chosen in Latin America. We don't want a war. We approach the United States with a desire for peace. But the United States is so much more powerful than Nicaragua that they will determine whether we will have war or peace.

While the Reagan administration has not allowed me to visit the United States, we invite any North Americans to come to

Nicaragua to see for themselves the reality of our Revolution. We welcome every visitor here with affection, including even functionaries of the U.S. State Department, congresspeople and even President Reagan himself.

We want friendship between the people of the U.S. and the people of Nicaragua. The North American people are our friends. They have not made war against us; their government has.

We know the people of the United States have struggled for world peace as we have, have struggled against imperialism and worked to end the Vietnam war by working against their own government. We have great affection for the people of the United States.

16. The Contras

Salvador Icaza
Rodrigo Gurdian

We traveled to Tegucigalpa, capital of neighboring Honduras, to speak with two of the leaders of the contras we had heard so much about. There are several counterrevolutionary groups. ARDE, the Revolutionary Democratic Alliance, led by former Sandinista Comandante Edén Pastora, and the MDN, Movement for a Democratic Nicaragua, led by Alfonso Robelo, a former member of the Revolutionary Junta formed after the Triumph, are both headquartered in Costa Rica. Rival groups of Miskito Indians have organized under the leadership of Steadman Fagoth in Honduras and Brooklyn Rivera in Costa Rica. The largest group of all, the FDN, the Nicaraguan Democratic Force [led by Adolfo Calero], has thousands of men on the Honduran border and openly maintains headquarters and public relations offices in Tegucigalpa. Bickering between these groups may have led to the wounding of Edén Pastora in an assassination attempt at his headquarters in Costa Rica in May 1984. It is charged that all of the groups receive varying amounts of funding from the CIA.

The two men we talked with represented the FDN and presented themselves as "training officers responsible for the political education of new recruits." The two, SALVADOR ICAZA, from a well-known family in León, and RODRIGO GURDIAN, younger brother of COSEP vice-president Ramiro Gurdian (see Chapter 5), and a large-scale cattle rancher in his own right, met us for the interview in the public coffee shop of the Honduran Maya, the most expensive hotel in Tegucigalpa. Clearly their operations in Honduras are hardly covert.

* * *

Salvador Icaza and Rodrigo Gurdian, Photo by Connie Martin

PHILIP ZWERLING: Who and what are the contras?

SALVADOR ICAZA: A counterrevolution does not exist. All that exists is the same revolution we Nicaraguans began to fight against Somoza forty years ago to overthrow a despotic regime. We were fighting for our liberty. We have yet to win that liberty and so we are still fighting. Only now we are fighting the Frente Sandinista.

Z: But didn't the Triumph of the Revolution on July 19, 1979 mark the end of Somoza and the beginning of liberty?

ICAZA: Yes, but liberty for whom? Now there is liberty in Nicaragua for the internationalists, for the Soviet Union, for the Cubans, all of whom are in Nicaragua today. But there is no freedom for the Nicaraguan people. The same people who fought against Somoza now fight against the Sandinistas because it is the same struggle. Now we fight against a new elite and new despots.

Z: But not only the Sandinistas. *La Prensa*, the organization of MIS-URA (Miskito Indians opposing the Nicaraguan government), and

Edén Pastora and his group have all said that there are former members and leaders of Somoza's National Guard fighting with the FDN today.

ICAZA: Look, I was never a Somocista. I was a government functionary with no political role. My family and I were very well known in León and throughout Nicaragua.

The National Guard of Somoza numbered perhaps 15,000. Of these, half died in the fighting or were murdered by the Sandinistas after the Triumph. There were forces in León, Matagalpa, Estelí and Chinandega out killing many members of the Guardia after the Triumph. Of the rest of the Guardia, many can be found in the prisons of Managua. A tiny minority of them went into exile and escaped, mainly to Miami.

The Nicaraguan Democratic Force doesn't consist of former Guardia. We have perhaps two or three with us. You could certainly count their number on the fingers of one hand. Ninety-five percent of our combatants are campesinos. You can speak with them yourself. Some of them have been fighting the dictatorship for 20 years. Many more of our fighters are in their late teens or early 20s. The Guardia was destroyed five years ago, when they were too young to have ever been part of it. Now the Sandinistas have much to gain by maintaining this image of the FDN as Somocistas or Guardia, but it just isn't so.

Z: But is there a place in the FDN for former Guardsmen?

ICAZA: The FDN keeps an open door to everyone. If there is a Guardia who comes to us with clean hands and a good name and without a criminal record then he can join our ranks.

Z: Today there are four organized groups fighting against the government in Nicaragua. Is there a possibility of an alliance among all four?

ICAZA: Yes, there are possibilities. There have been meetings to discuss it.

Z: Is there coordination between the groups in Honduras and Costa Rica to plan attacks?

ICAZA: Of course. This is possible because we have contact within Nicaragua between the troops of the different organizations and we work together. This is possible because the Nicaraguans don't support the Sandinistas. There are a lot of internationalists in Managua and plenty of Soviets and Cubans, but they are the only ones who keep the Sandinistas in power. The Nicaraguans understand that there is no liberty in Nicaragua today and no liberty of the press.

Z: Of course, the Sandinistas say it's impossible to have complete freedom of the press or to lift the Emergency Law during wartime. And you're the ones fighting this war against them.

RODRIGO GURDIAN: That's their problem.

ICAZA: Who's fighting the war? This is a war of the Nicaraguan people against the Sandinista government.

GURDIAN: Everyone is against the Sandinistas.

ICAZA: The Sandinistas raped my wife and killed my children. They have done things like this and everyone is against them. The reality is that with or without the help of the United States we are going to defeat and kill the Sandinistas and free Nicaragua.

Z: Well, the Sandinistas say that without the help of the United States there wouldn't be any contras.

ICAZA: Remember, we are revolutionaries, not contras. There is no counterrevolution, but simply the same people who fought against Somoza fighting against a new despotism. The FSLN would have you believe that we are the creation of the CIA and Ronald Reagan, but we are the creation of the Nicaraguan people themselves. There are two million Nicaraguans who support us today. If we didn't have the support of the Nicaraguan people all the gringo dollars in the world wouldn't be effective. But we can cross the border with impunity and operate within Nicaragua because we are in the hearts of the Nicaraguan people. One hundred percent of the civilian population of Nicaragua supports us.

We are successful because the people guide and shelter us and warn us of the approach of the Sandinista Army. These poor people, who are hungry themselves, feed us. They tell us where the Sandinista camps are and when their troops are mobilized. This is the same civilian population that opposed Somoza and now opposes the Sandinistas. In four years the Sandinistas have surpassed the cruelties and barbarities of the 40 years of the Somozas and now the people are against them.

Z: But in Nicaragua it's very easy to see the changes since Somoza's time, changes in health care, education, in literacy.

ICAZA: But look at this. Everyone knows that the Literacy Crusade was not designed to educate anyone; it was designed to disseminate Soviet communist propaganda. It was the same kind of Literacy Crusade they had in Cuba [in 1961] and in other communist countries. It was designed to spread Marxist-Leninist ideas and nothing else. We know it.

There have been minimal improvements in things like health care. But the Nicaraguan people didn't fight and die in the struggle against Somoza in order to receive a lousy malaria pill. We didn't fight for a shot of penicillin. We fought for much more, for our own liberty. And what is liberty? Not to be taken over by Cuba or the Soviet Union. We want our own liberty for our own people and that is what we are fighting for.

Stupid people in other countries may look at these little improvements and say, "These things never existed under Somoza." But does there exist freedom of the press in Nicaragua today? What about the genocidal murders of peasants in the combat zones by the Sandinista Army? These are the same kinds of things Somoza's National Guard used to do. They say we are the Guardia, but they commit the same atrocities the Guardia used to commit against the civilian population. Now they do it aided by internationalists, Soviets and Cubans.

We are Nicaraguans. The nine comandantes who rule in Nicaragua [referring to the National Directorate of the FSLN] aren't Nicaraguans. They've lost the right to call themselves Nicaraguans. They've sold their birthright to the leaders of other countries.

I have a son of 10 years of age. He and I have been in exile for five years now. He speaks English better than he speaks Spanish, and he has forgotten his homeland. He doesn't have roots in his fatherland. The nine comandantes, sitting atop a heap of bloody bodies, were trained overseas in communist ideas and have no idea how to speak to the Nicaraguan people in their own language and have lost the sense of what it means to be a Nicaraguan. That's why they have to be backed up and kept in power by Soviet and Cuban troops. That's the real foreign intervention in Nicaragua today.

Z: In Nicaragua, however, it's easy to see that your revolutionaries are not fighting the Sandinista Army or Cuban troops. Your targets seem to be civilian: health centers, granaries, teachers . . .

ICAZA: We fight the army, not civilians, and if the internationalists would get out of Nicaragua we could finish off the Sandinistas in no time at all. And if we have to fight an economic war to do this as well, we will.

Z: But an economic war hurts everyone, especially the poorest members of the civilian population.

GURDIAN: You've come from Managua. What's the ambiance there like now? Do people feel the war?

Z: No, it's very tranquil in Managua. It appears that the war is being fought only on the borders.

ICAZA: Oh, no. We've penetrated to within 90, 70 kilometers of Managua.

Z: Well, I can tell you that you don't feel it in Managua. And you don't feel it when you travel out of the capital. We've been north to Yalaguina, Ocotal and Jalapa, south to San Juan del Sur, and east to Bluefields without encountering fighting.

GURDIAN: Right now we are fighting around Ocotal. We can go anywhere. Because the people support us and because the people know that the Sandinistas are just like Somoza. They want liberty and free elections.

Z: What happens if the United States reaches an understanding with the Nicaraguan government?

GURDIAN: No way. Because the Sandinistas will never agree to free elections and a real democracy. With whom are they going to reach an understanding? The communists have taught the gringos how to reach understandings.

ICAZA: The gringos are unique in the world for having built a democracy and they can never reach understandings with the communist enemies of democracy.

Z: But today the U.S. lives in the same world with China and the Soviet Union without a war. Isn't it possible they could learn to live with the Sandinistas, too?

ICAZA: You can have agreements at the governmental level, but the struggle continues between the U.S. and the Soviet Union. The Soviet Union is always looking to conquer new territory. Their goal is still to take over the world.

GURDIAN: And that is the role of Nicaragua. It can be the first Soviet foothold on the mainland of Central America. And if they control Nicaragua they won't stop there. So you see here we are defending the interests of the United States. The democratic political system of the U.S. is beautiful for North America, but democracy doesn't work like that here. Here we are fighting against ruthless people who murder people on the streets with bombs. It happened right here in Honduras. Our democracy is completely different.

Z: It's difficult to label the Nicaraguan government a tool of international communism when Catholic priests serve in that government and church people support it.

ICAZA: Look, friends, the priests in the Sandinista government are terrorists and Marxists. And the Sandinistas are terrorists. All they understand is force.

Z: These Catholic priests are terrorists?

GURDIAN: Yes, they're assassins.

ICAZA: Look at the history of the Catholic Church. Look at the Inquisition.

GURDIAN: Remember what happened in El Salvador? Remember the assassination of Archbishop Romero? Who do you think did that to manipulate public opinion in the U.S.?

Z: Well, five National Guardsmen have been charged and convicted in that murder.

GURDIAN: No, the FMLN did it [Farabundo Martí National Liberation Front, the antigovernment coalition of guerrilla forces in El Salvador]. They try to turn public opinion against the government. And look what happens, they create a movement against the war and then you lose in places like Vietnam. The communists will do anything for their cause. Who do you think killed Pedro Joaquín Chamorro [*La Prensa* editor assassinated in January 1978]?"

Z: I thought Somoza ordered that murder of his political opponent.

GURDIAN: No, the Sandinistas killed him to turn public opinion against Somoza. The communists manipulate the press, news and all forms of communication to further their cause. But at least at this time Ronald Reagan is standing up to the communists and the U.S. has finally realized what's going on in the world and in our country. Central America is key to the national security of the United States and you know you cannot allow a communist base here near your southern border.

Z: Right now, Senator [Edward] Kennedy has Miskito Indians testifying before his subcommittee in Washington about the massacres committed by contra groups against the civilian population.

ICAZA: The communists can always find people to do their work for them.

Z: You're not suggesting that Senator Kennedy is a communist?

ICAZA: No, no.

GURDIAN: He's not a communist, but he likes to work with them. It's the same question of democracy again. In your democratic system people are free to work to overthrow that system. And that will be the end of your democracy.

Z: What happens if these efforts are successful and the U.S. withdraws its aid to your group?

ICAZA: We will keep fighting. We will get money for guns and supplies somewhere else and we will keep fighting until Nicaragua is free.

Z: Much has been written about the differences between the various anti-Sandinista groups. Someone has tried to assassinate Edén Pastora [in May 1984 in Costa Rica]. Was this the work of the Sandinistas or the CIA?

GURDIAN: I don't know, but I'm just sorry they failed.

Z: Why?

GURDIAN: Because he's a Sandinista, too, and he doesn't stand for the same things we do.

Z: I've been in Nicaragua for five months now and I have seen obvious signs of support for the government there, including revolutionary demonstrations by large crowds of Nicaraguans. Why do you think you have support within the country?

GURDIAN: Look, those people turn out in the streets because they're told that if they don't demonstrate they won't eat. The government has the power to manipulate them, threaten them and intimidate them. Believe me, our cause is supported by 100% of the Nicaraguan people.

ICAZA: Those people who are demonstrating, shouting, raising their fists, are the same people who used to turn out to support Somoza. They just go whichever way the wind blows.

Z: You've both been in exile for nearly five years. It must be a difficult life for you.

GURDIAN: In Nicaragua I was a cattle rancher. I had one of the largest ranches. I know how to run a business and how to make money. I can use these skills here and I can survive here. But it's not the same. No matter how long I am in Honduras, still I am a Nicaraguan and I want to return to Nicaragua. The life of an exile, of a person without a country, is very hard and very sad.

17. The Wounded Fighters

Noel Ricardo Laguna   Gregorio Contarejo Zamora
Santo Domingo López   Martín Martínez Sánchez
Alguiles Flores   Delu Pineda

One of the most moving and hardest interviews we had was with wounded soldiers in the Convalescent Center in Las Colinas. Here, in a wealthy suburb of Managua, in a mansion abandoned by a Somoza supporter at the Triumph of the Revolution, young soldiers come to recuperate from their wounds and rehabilitate their bodies.

We sat in a room with perhaps 20 of these men, some able to sit in chairs, but with many in wheelchairs or flat on their backs in hospital cots. Although they seemed to welcome the attention of visiting North Americans, some clearly had a message they wanted to communicate, while others were quite reticent to discuss their war experiences.

Their ages ranged from 14 to 27. All had enlisted voluntarily. They sat in a circle and listened as six of their number spoke to us. They were NOEL RICARDO LAGUNA, 20; SANTO DOMINGO LÓPEZ, 15; ALGUILES FLORES, 27; GREGORIO CANTAREJO ZAMORA, 23; MARTÍN MARTÍNEZ SÁNCHEZ, 18; and DELU PINEDA, 14.

* * *

PHILIP ZWERLING: How long have you been in the Army?

NOEL LAGUNA: Since it was founded five years ago.

Z: Where did you serve?

LAGUNA: I was deployed at the border near Jalapa.

Z: How were you wounded?

LAGUNA: I was wounded in combat when our company responded to an attack across the border by the mercenaries hired by the CIA. They came from Honduras and penetrated deep into our territory. The contras would cross the border and when they finished firing they would withdraw to a tactical position back in Honduras.

This day we had a compañero located in a position facing the border, some hundreds of meters from the border. Our lookout advised us that the contras were taking a place. We engaged them and the combat lasted three hours. We took the site, overrunning it. We routed them and they withdrew to Honduran territory.

Z: What was your wound?

LAGUNA: I was wounded in the chest. A bullet from a sniper entered my chest. This wound damaged some nerves. I have had several operations to try and regain use of my hand. I've been here 20 days, more or less, but they operated on me three times in the hospital. I was wounded a year ago, on July 4, 1983. When I was first wounded I was taken immediately to the hospital in Jalapa to save my life because an artery had been opened and I was dying. After five days I was transported to the military hospital here in Managua. I hope to regain use of my hand here. We would say that it's the hope of each one of us who is in a wheelchair to walk one day; to be able to recuperate and to continue the struggle for our Revolution, for our country, and for our people.

Really, the military situation that we are facing at this moment is not the most difficult situation. The power of the people at the border never wavers but rather increases. We have completely defeated the counterrevolutionaries in the military field. In spite of all the attacks the consciousness of the people grows daily. This means that the counterrevolution is not a danger to the Revolution.

Each moment, every day, we cause them constant defeats. They are defeated by our combatants, who enter patriotic service voluntarily, by the reserve troops and by the heroic Popular Sandinista Militia. These armed forces together have beaten the counterrevolution, which at this moment can be found broken up, which at this moment can be found disbanded because they have not had success.

But the most difficult situation facing our country at this time is the economic situation. The Reagan administration is not only trying to overthrow us militarily but it also wants to suck our blood in the economic situation. It has mined our ports in a criminal attempt against our Revolution. So the most difficult situations we face are economic, but not in the spirit of our Revolution.

[We don't blame anyone here for that situation. We blame the imperialists, the assassins who kill our campesinos in the mountains. We blame the counterrevolution and Reagan. If the contras were not armed, financed and directed by the CIA it wouldn't have the capacity to mobilize and conduct this war. The CIA personally directs actions against our people. It was the CIA who personally mined our ports with very sophisticated mines and used special speedboats, which aren't manufactured anywhere in Central America. The CIA is intervening directly in our country.]

Noel Ricardo Laguna, Photo by Peter Kelly

[Z: During your service at the border did you find concrete evidence of U.S. involvement with the contras?

LAGUNA: Yes, many of the military supplies that the counterrevolutionaries use are made in the U.S. This is part of the proof that the CIA is meddling with us. The FALs aren't made in Central America, the webbed belts aren't made in Central America, the mines that we have spoken of aren't made in Central America. None of the arms that the contras are using, including their technical equipment, is made in Central America—it's all made in the U.S.]

* * *

Z: Where are you from and where were you stationed?

SANTO LÓPEZ: I'm from Quinjo. I was a combatant in the southern zone against ARDE, the counterrevolutionaries directed and guided by the traitor Edén Pastora [former Sandinista Comandante Zero] and the CIA. They are assassins. Every day they kidnap and kill peasants and destroy cooperatives. They are the ones who leave families orphaned. It's them that always create the provocations. It's because of them that there's a conflict between Nicaragua and Honduras and between Nicaragua and

Costa Rica. They are trying to promote a direct invasion by the army of the United States.

Right now in Honduras there are maneuvers like Big Pine I, Big Pine II and Granadero I, that involve thousands of U.S., Honduran and Salvadoran troops, that have the objective of helping these soldiers become familiar with the terrain and to prepare them for a possible invasion of Nicaragua.

We've been experiencing an escalation by Reagan since 1981. It began with "Red Christmas" that year. It began by putting plastic explosives in children's toys. They tried to provoke a war in this manner. They gave them to us because they are trying to destroy our people. The toys were to be sent to all Nicaraguan children. They didn't achieve their objective because the Ministry of the Interior and State Security detected the plan before it could be effected.

Z: How long were you in the army?

LÓPEZ: Almost four years. I started when I was small, just 12. But as a Nicaraguan, as a revolutionary and as a citizen I have to defend this Revolution, which is a just Revolution. We can't have imposed on us again that which was imposed on us in the past. This is a just Revolution and that is why we defend it.

Z: How were you wounded?

LÓPEZ: I was wounded in combat in the southern zone. We were advancing, routing the counterrevolutionaries, when I was wounded. It's certain that we are of flesh, too. But the conviction of us revolutionary combatants is not the same as theirs, because they fight for dollars. They don't have a just cause for which to fight. They fight for dollars because they are paid by the imperialists. So many millions of dollars are paid for this by the imperialists. I was wounded in a place called Agua Caliente in the southern zone. My wound is not very grave. A bullet entered my leg and fractured the bone. But it's nothing. I'm going to get better. I'm going to get out of the hospital and continue fighting. If I die it doesn't matter because others will follow us.

*   *   *

Z: How much time do you have in the army?

ALGUILES FLORES: Six years.

Z: You started before the Triumph?

FLORES: Yes, I had a year in before '79.

Z: Where did you serve?

FLORES: Many different places. Many in the north.

Z: How were you wounded?

FLORES: We were searching in the forest. We were following the mercenaries, who had invaded some 30 kilometers into Nicaraguan territory from Honduras. We tried to drive them out. They don't have any moral force to help them. They have no reason except the money they get to be contras. But what we have to think and support us is something else. My wound was a fracture. Friends were wounded also. This happened seven months ago.

Z: Do you believe it is possible for Nicaragua to defend itself against these attacks by the contras?

FLORES: Yes, because there is no Nicaraguan who is disposed to kneel and submit himself to a dictatorship again. This resistance has cost us much blood and will continue to cost us blood.

Z: It's an especially high cost for the youth of this country.

FLORES: We are among the first to take up arms. After us, our children may have to defend the Revolution to continue to defend the Triumph, because the Triumph has made us free. We achieved this.

* * *

Gregorio Cantarejo Zamora was lying flat on his back on a cot, unable to move more than his upper body.

Z: How long have you been in the army?

GREGORIO ZAMORA: Since the Triumph of the Revolution.

Z: Where were you wounded?

ZAMORA: In the northern zone, in Segovia.

Z: What happened?

ZAMORA: We were walking, on guard, in the frontier zone and we had a confrontation.

Z: What is your wound?

ZAMORA: A bullet. I got a bullet in the back. We were in a half-circle, fighting. I didn't see anyone behind me. It must have been a sniper who felled me. This happened last month, on May 21. I was the only one wounded.

Gregorio Cantarejo Zamora, Photo by Peter Kelly

Z: Is there much danger in the frontier zone?

ZAMORA: The border area with Honduras is the zone in which the contras penetrate the most. After the Triumph, when the Guard fled, they came to this zone and from the beginning they have raided us from this area. In this zone there are many casualties because here the *compañeros* experience much combat. The contras have also caused many civilian casualties, often poor campesinos who are working the soil or who are in their houses and open their doors. If they aren't willing to join the contras, they are shot. It's a very unjust thing.

We don't mistrust any *compañeros*, and all of our combatants are volunteers. Many have joined the contras out of fear, and often they die in combat. There are places in northern Segovia where the women are alone in the houses because the contras have taken the working men. The only men who are left are those too old to fight and the kids. Such unjust things.

We are fighting on behalf of everyone. We are men of conscience; that is why we are working in the Revolution. We are struggling so that our country can survive and solve its problems. We fight for a just cause and not for other interests. We want peace, and because of that we will struggle to the last drop of blood to obtain peace for our country.

*   *   *

PHILIP ZWERLING: What part of Nicaragua are you from?

MARTÍN SÁNCHEZ: I'm from Boaco in Chontales.

Z: How long have you been in the army?

SÁNCHEZ: Three years. I served on the northern border in Ocotal. The counterrevolutionaries enter our country and we have to remove them. They try to cross the border into Nicaragua and then we chase them back. We can't follow them across the border. But if they come further inside we would destroy them all. We have recovered Northern American backpacks because they have American names. All war supplies are from the U.S. through the CIA. Everything is American—their rations are American, the rifles are American.

When they leave Honduras and enter Nicaragua their main objective, above all, is to create terror in the border area, to assassinate campesinos, to kidnap and recruit campesinos. Many campesinos have gone because they were forced. The women are raped at the border and killed—including a child of six months that they grabbed away from the mother and beat because she didn't want to go to Honduras. Near the border we met the cousin who was burying the child. The woman was not to blame. We met him when we were looking for contras who had crossed the border. It's an injustice. We are fighting for the peace. We don't want war.

For my part, I would be studying. I wouldn't be at the border fighting. In normal times I wouldn't be fighting in the military. But, above all, we are fighting for the peace. We don't want more war because the war is sad. Here there is, for example, a child. He is only 14, and because of his revolutionary consciousness he enrolled in the army.

Z: When were you wounded?

SÁNCHEZ: The twenty-fifth of October in the area near Jinotega.

Z: What happened?

SÁNCHEZ: The counterrevolutionaries had burned the town of Pantasma. We climbed the hill on which they were stationed and began combat. There were some 500 Guardia and we killed 60 of them. Then they took advantage of their refuge in Honduras. I was wounded in the head and a bullet entered my right leg. They go back to Honduras to recuperate and prepare for their next attack. Planes from Honduras fly over our country to give them information.

* * *

While speaking, Sánchez had indicated the plight of the child seated next to him. This soldier, Delu Pineda, is 14 years old. At this young age, he had been wounded, necessitating the amputation of his left leg below the knee. Because of his age, his comrades paid special attention to him. He didn't want to talk but the others urged him on. He was very shy, his answers brief, and I guessed he had not yet come to terms with the life-changing wound he had received. Crutches made him mobile, but artificial limbs are not now available in Nicaragua.

* * *

PHILIP ZWERLING: How long have you been in the army?

DELU PINEDA: Two years.

Z: Where were you wounded?

DELU PINEDA: In Jinotega.

Z: What happened?

PINEDA: We were on search and I received two bullets, one in the chest and one in the leg.

Z: Are there other young volunteers like you in the army?

PINEDA: Yes.

Z: Why?

PINEDA: Because we are fighting in the mountains. Because the contras come to the mountains and frighten the people and kill them.

* * *

Noel Ricardo Laguna, the first to speak, offered some closing thoughts.

LAGUNA: We are called revolutionaries but here in Nicaragua we don't want war. We are lovers of peace. We fight. We struggle in

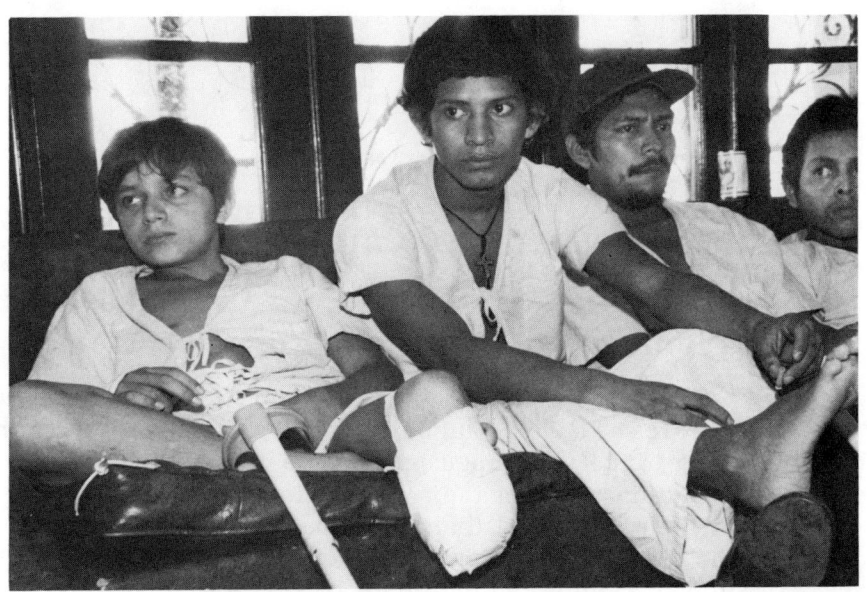

Delu Pineda on left and Martín Martínez Sánchez with other wounded, Photo by Peter Kelly

international forums for peace, at the United Nations and in the Conference of Nonaligned Countries, where we are members. We struggle also in the Congress of the United States with Reagan to find a political solution to end the intervention and the insurgency. Take this message to the people of the U.S.

Also we are against imperialism and against the Reagan administration. We are not against the people, not at any time. Because it is clear that among the people in the U.S. are *compañeros* who are in the streets demonstrating against the North American interventions not only in Nicaragua but also around the world. These are *compañeros* who take to the streets with slogans and placards saying enough to the covert invasions in El Salvador, enough to the missiles the U.S. is putting in European countries. It's proof that people in the U.S. don't want a war here either, because a war in Central America would be harder than the war in Vietnam.

We are Christians and we don't want to kill, but what is being done to us is unjust. We don't want the war but we are bound to resist. The people and the army will defend the country energetically.

It is important that you take this message home with you, that we Nicaraguans love our Revolution. We want this Revolution and we will live and struggle as revolutionary Sandinistas until the last man falls.

18. Life in the Barrio: Ciudad Sandino

Juana Romero Maura Otero
Nubia Romero Sister Peggy Healy

One way to see the Revolution in Nicaragua is to see it through the eyes of ordinary Nicaraguans who live in the neighborhoods. The Revolution many of them helped to make has profoundly changed their lives, and their continued participation helps to shape the revolutionary cause of the country.

In Ciudad Sandino, an enormous barrio (pop. 45,000) on the edge of Managua, we spent an afternoon with three women residents and talked privately in their homes. We spoke with them about the changes they had seen, their work in the CDSs (Sandinista Defense Committees), in walking vigilence (nighttime patrols to protect the neighborhood) and in the health and literacy crusades.

These three women of Ciudad Sandino are JUANA ROMERO, a 38-year-old resident and worker at the health center; NUBIA ROMERO (no relation to Juana), a 16-year-old health brigadista, and MAURA OTERO, an activist in the CDS.

* * *

CONNIE MARTIN: How long have you lived in Ciudad Sandino?

JUANA ROMERO: Twenty-two years. It wasn't Ciudad Sandino then. It was called Bella Cruz. That was before OPEN 3. OPEN 3 was born after the earthquake of 1972. It had been raining very hard and there was flooding. Many people were living near the lake, and Somoza didn't want those people there because they were poor and living in box houses. They were using the services that Managua had to offer. The majority were people who didn't have a place to live. The Christian community was noticing them and that's what worried the government. There was a Christian community of Jesuit priests and Maryknoll sisters that wanted these people to have better housing conditions.

It happened that Don Blandon had invested in the land which is now Ciudad Sandino—all this land. He sold it and then later resold it. All the people who lived by the lake were moved here.

M: Why after the earthquake were people moved so far from the city?

J. ROMERO: Because Somoza was not interested in having any poor people live around the houses he was building. The farther away they were the better for him. The poor people were "cleaned out" of the area.

M: At the time the people were brought out here, what was here?

Juana Romero, Photo by Philip Zwerling

J. ROMERO: Nothing. We suffered for lack of water. We had to buy it from vendors, and it was very expensive. There was no electricity.

M: How did the people begin to organize?

J. ROMERO: We began organizing with the consciousness we had at that time. That is, we saw each day how we were more oppressed, left with less and less each day. We were hurt as much by the system of society as by the economy, because the same society that had abandoned us would not give us a way to earn money. By means of the Christian base communities we realized that as human beings a different life ought to be ours. We were human beings, not animals. Each one of us began to realize that we were not alone. We formed a circle and it grew and became larger. We saw ourselves united as one person, and human in all aspects. Because of our united strength we began to protest for water, for transportation, for electricity and for sanitation—for all the necessities we didn't have. At this time we were paying more for water than the rich people in Las Colinas.

M: How did you protest?

J. ROMERO: When we had a good group of people with awareness of the situation, we would protest in the barrio. But we were afraid. The Guardia would restrain us, would throw bombs, would treat us very badly. There were usually many casualties. Many women who were with us were raped in their homes. The Guardia would do that.

M: During this time what did you do?

J. ROMERO: We had a first aid station. Getting to the hospital was almost impossible because no one had a vehicle.

M: How many people were in OPEN 3 in the beginning?

J. ROMERO: It began with few people, but kept growing until now—there are 45,000.

M: It's a true city.

J. ROMERO: Yes, but we don't have the conditions for a city. We have the population, but we don't have the conditions.

M: What was the role of people here in the Insurrection?

J. ROMERO: In the armed Insurrection the participation of women was very strong. That is to say, our role in the revolutionary process was a continuation of what we had already been doing—building moral, protesting, sharing the little we had, and also maintaining safe houses, carrying messages, working with AMPRONAC and giving first aid in emergencies. At this time we had formed a collective to share necessities. During the Revolution we worked days and nights.

M: Five years after the Revolution, how is Ciudad Sandino organized?

J. ROMERO: In five years we have seen great progress. We have gotten streets, a market which we never had before and a health center, which was begun by the people with the help of the Ministry of Health. We also have three other health posts here in Ciudad Sandino. We were able to achieve this in spite of the fact that we are in a war and constantly defending against aggression. It's proof that all the people organized can make a difference. It's possible to work with the little we have and to accomplish much. With the millions that Somoza had, nothing was done for us.

M: How was this health center formed?

J. ROMERO: This house belonged to a Somocista. During the Insurrection he informed on a group of [six] young people living at Laguna Xiloa. He told the Guardia, and then they were assassinated. So one of the health posts is named "The Heroes and Martyrs of Xiloa."

Because of our work in the Insurrection we learned how to organize ourselves. We decided one of our primary needs was health care and we asked the Ministry of Health to help us. We are part of a larger organization, the Consejo Popular de Salud (Popular Health Council). In each zone there is a Popular Health Council and in each zone there is one health representative in each CDS. Information and education are passed on via this organization.

Health is not only the concern of doctors but also the work of the people. The people are in charge of their own health, and with all of us involved in this struggle we will eradicate completely many illnesses. We people of Nicaragua need to continue onward with the same spirit with which we have achieved so much, and we can arrive at our goal—to be a healthy and free people.

M: How many people work here everyday?

J. ROMERO: About 60 here in the health center. If we include the other three posts, about 140 in all.

M: How many people receive services here?

J. ROMERO: Around 250 each day—that's medical attention only. There are other programs for mothers and for children concerning pregnancy and child development.

M: What is your work here?

J. ROMERO: I help cleaning up, packing bandages, mimeographing health manuals. I help anyway I can. I really am in love with the work. I like the gains we are making. We have planted many things. Now knowledge is for everyone, and that is why we have made such advances.

M: What do you think will be the future of Nicaragua?

J. ROMERO: There will be changes; a society in which we will not have sick children or children wandering the streets. We will have better housing and better living conditions for all.

M: Do you have children?

J. ROMERO: I have six sons. The youngest is nine and the oldest 21. They were all well raised on rice, corn and beans.

* * *

Nubia Romero, Photo by Philip Zwerling

CONNIE MARTIN: How long have you worked as a brigadista?

N. ROMERO: Three years.

M: When did you begin?

N. ROMERO: In 1980. I began with the first health campaign.

M: Why are you interested in health?

N. ROMERO: I wanted to help the children. Before, under Somoza, we had little health care. Twenty-five percent of the children in the barrios had serious problems and we didn't have a clinic or a health center. There were no health campaigns as we have now every month to ensure that no one has missed a vaccination.

M: How are the brigadistas trained?

N. ROMERO: We take courses. New brigadistas enter a training program given at a college. The training touches on all the skills a brigadista needs to know, such as first aid and how to give vaccinations.

M: How many brothers and sisters do you have?

N. ROMERO: Nine. One of my brothers is in Cuba studying to be a medical technician. He will be there for six years.

M: Do you also want a career in health?

N. ROMERO: Yes, I want to study medicine.

M: How many hours each week do you work as a brigadista?

N. ROMERO: We usually vaccinate on Saturdays and Sundays.

M: What do you do besides being a student and a health brigadista?

N. ROMERO: I am in the militia, in the Sandinista Youth. I participate in all these things. I also do neighborhood guard duty.

M: Why do you participate in so many things?

N. ROMERO: Because I see, as do other young people, that we have to work to make a new society and a new world.

M: Do you have memories of the time before the Triumph?

N. ROMERO: My brothers were involved with the Sandinista Front. They handed out leaflets and information. One day near the end of the Insurrection, close to the time of Triumph, a man came to warn us that the Guardia was coming. We had no arms here, only a tiny pistol. My brothers fled the house. One of my brothers went south to San Juan and across the border into Costa Rica. He had been denounced and it was said we were running a house for the Sandinista Front. Other brothers went to the mountains. Only one of my brothers stayed here.

M: Are you also involved in the church?

N. ROMERO: Yes, we have a church here and a base community. I work as a catechist.

M: What does a catechist do?

N. ROMERO: I meet with the children and prepare them for their first communion. The work of a catechist is not only to read the Bible, but to practice our religion, to show the children how to love and to struggle for them.

M: You see no contradiction between your Christian faith and the Revolution?

N. ROMERO: Clearly, there isn't any.

M: Why not?

N. ROMERO: Because as Christians we care for humanity, and as revolutionaries we care for humanity. So for me there is no contradiction.

M: In terms of the age of its population, Nicaragua is a very young country. What are the young people building here? What type of country?

N. ROMERO: We young people want to build a country where poverty doesn't exist and we are all equal.

M: What do you think about the bishops' pastoral letter [of Easter 1984]?

N. ROMERO: I don't believe there is any good in this letter. It wrongs the young people—our flesh and blood who are defending us—if we would do as Monsignor Obando suggests and pardon the former Somoza guards. As for me, I can't forget everything. It was the Guardia who killed my brother. I don't agree that as a Christian I should forget what they did and have a dialogue with them because they continue to kill us. They want to establish imperialism and dominate us. I don't want imperialism. I want a developed country. I don't agree with the pastoral letter.

M: Did one of your brothers or sisters participate in the literacy campaign?

N. ROMERO: My sister did. I was too young.

M: Tell us something about your cultural work.

N. ROMERO: We have a theater group. Right now my sister is in Matagalpa. She is in charge of a film. This film will be shown in the U.S. I belong to this group, but they didn't permit me to go along because it was in the war zone. They are going in to those areas where our young people guarding the border need some recreation. They will present cultural events and they will film the movie. Part of the film will be a dialogue with the youth there. When they return home, we will present works of theater here.

* * *

CONNIE MARTIN: Could you tell us a little about yourself?

MAURA OTERO: I have lived 11 years in Ciudad Sandino. We came here after the earthquake because we had no house. The house in which we were living was damaged. When we came here there was nothing, absolutely nothing. My children were small and they grew up here. When the struggle came, all of my sons participated. The youngest was 16 the day of the Triumph and the oldest was 19. I have three sons and they all participated in different ways. One was involved in a college organization. He studied during the day, and at night went to clandestine meetings. Another son made and distributed flyers and leaflets, put up posters at night, sometimes until 2 in the morning. My third son was a combatant. He was at great risk of the Guardia. In a large barrio like this one, the Guardia entered at all hours. If they had picked him up, they would have killed him. This was the worst danger. I wasn't doing anything. I stayed in my house. I was afraid. Later, after the Triumph, I became involved in the health center and with organizing.

During the Insurrection the Sandinista Front was in the mountains fighting. Here the people were more hidden in their struggle. At times there was contact almost from house to house. Many participated and we got rid of the dictatorship rapidly. But many of us were afraid. We didn't know what a literacy campaign was or what a vaccination campaign was. We began to know more with the Triumph.

There was much change and much struggle and difficulty. I thought I was going to die of hunger because there was nothing left here. We have done much more here in four years than was done in the forty years before. With the strength of all the people we have organized and struggled and advanced. And we won't quit. In spite of everything we won't turn back. We will continue going forward.

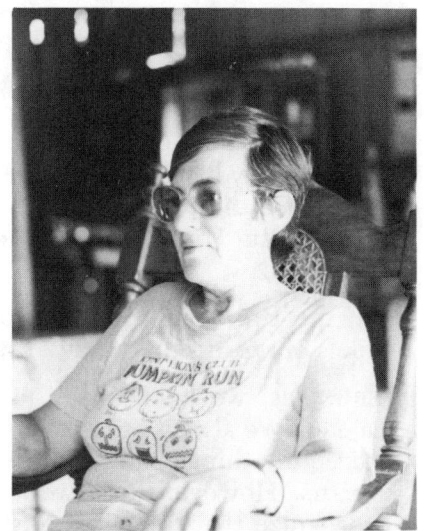
Maura Otera, Photo by Philip Zwerling

M: Do you have examples of achievements?

OTERO: Before, we never thought we would have a paved street or a market. We have a health center we never had before and three health posts.

M: Is everyone in the barrio a member of the CDS? How does the CDS function?

OTERO: Every zone (barrio) has a committee of six members; a coordinator and secretaries of defense, social events, organization, economics, policy and information. The CDS functions block by block. Every block committee also has six members. There are also state CDS organizations and a national CDS organization.

M: What happens in a typical block meeting?

OTERO: For example, today is Wednesday. There is a zonal assembly and it is held in the plaza of the barrio. The six members of each zone meet there and they discuss all the work that has to be done. Then each zone committee meets with its block coordinators. At the block level, program implementation begins. In a block meeting the people might say, "Look, in the local store we don't have milk for the children." Then the coordinator has to respond—to explain why there isn't any milk and to find out what to do. These things have to be explained so the people will understand them.

Not all the people are in the CDS and not all the people are aware of our situation. Sometimes they're confused, so it's necessary to explain to them. We tell them why things are lacking. We tell them we are in a war. Here in Managua it isn't evident, but there are people dying daily. Right now, at this moment, there are *compañeros* in combat at the border. They are fighting day and night. . . . There is also an economic blockade. But we are not going to die of hunger.

On every block, in every barrio, in every zone, at every corner, there is the CDS, AMNLAE and the Juventud Sandinista [Sandinista Youth] to help the people and to try to resolve each problem.

M: In the U.S., the opponents of Nicaragua say that the CDSs are tools of repression, a way to spy on the people.

OTERO: Yes, we know that this is being said, but what does this mean? We always have to hear that we are acting badly or we are directing things badly. It's because they don't want a revolution for us. However, here we are proud of the Revolution and we recognize that there are mistakes because we are human. It's a part of our development. But we are going to continue correcting our errors.

We do not use the CDS to coerce anyone. For example, if I were director and I asked you why you didn't do guard duty last night and said I was not going to give you your food supply card—this doesn't happen at any time in any way. The card for supplies is given to all whether they do guard duty or attend meetings or participate in the process or do nothing. Everyone is given a card. We don't do anything to anyone.

About work cards. If I am applying for a job in the government ministries, I need a card from my block committee because people on my block know me. They know if I'm a good person or a bad person and they know I'm not an infiltrator.

We can't send our enemies to work in the ministries. Some ministries are very sensitive and not just any person should work there. People need to be well recommended because here we have to protect our government leaders. We fear for their lives. Some think that if they kill the leaders of our government they will terminate the Revolution. This isn't true. They would have to kill *all* of us. *We* are the Revolution.

* * *

One North American nun who has lived and worked for years among the people of Ciudad Sandino is 35-year-old Maryknoll sister, PEGGY HEALY. I interviewed her in the offices of the Central American Historical Institute, with which she is also associated.

* * *

PHILIP ZWERLING: Would you tell us about your early life in the U.S. and how you wound up in Nicaragua.

SISTER PEGGY HEALY: I was born in White Plains, New York, in 1948 and I grew up mostly on Long Island. My family was a large Irish Catholic family. I think that my upbringing was not only a happy one but a very substantive one in terms of faith and in terms of— not politics certainly—but in terms of service to others. So it seemed natural that I joined Maryknoll in 1968 and with them earned a master's degree in nursing and did my nurse-practitioner training in pediatrics at Columbia University.

In January 1975 I came to Nicaragua. The first place I worked was Ciudad Sandino, until 1978, when I returned to the U.S. for what we call a "year of reflection," a Maryknoll and theological study. I stayed in the U.S. after that and worked for a church-sponsored project at the Washington Office on Latin America until 1980. In March of 1980 I returned to Nicaragua. I'm now the regional coordinator for Maryknoll sisters of Nicaragua and Panama. I live in Ciudad Sandino today, but no longer work there.

Z: What was life like in Ciudad Sandino under the dictatorship and what is it like today?

HEALY: Ciudad Sandino used to be known as Operación Permanente Emergencia Nacional 3 or OPEN 3 (Permanent National Emergency Operation 3). In 1969, Lake Managua flooded and people who were in Santo Domingo parish had their homes wiped out, and so for several months they moved away from the water and they lived in tents provided by the Red Cross. When it became clear that they could not stay there and the lake had not receded, they were shuttled out to three different areas in the city. In early 1970 people first went out to OPEN 3, which was really just an open field then. About 200 people began life out there. It was a cotton field owned by the Blandons, a large family of landowners.

Blandon basically decided not to grow cotton because he could make more money having people out there. People paid rent every month to the landowner but were never able to get title to their land because this was what they called at the time a "clan-

241

destine" barrio, an illegal barrio. The government knew they were there, of course, but by never legalizing them landowners could make money without giving up title even when they paid all the money the land was worth.

OPEN 3 was 13 kilometers outside the city. People who had gone out there had no transportation, no water, no anything. It was literally a barren, treeless place where people could simply set up what little they had rescued from the flood.

During that time our Maryknoll sisters built a place out there so that they could be with the people. That's how the barrio began. When I went out there, there were about 25,000 people living there. It now has about 45,000 people. So this was begun prior to the earthquake in 1972 and it continued to grow through the years because people needed a place to live.

Sister Peggy Healy, Photo by Philip Zwerling

It was always a very marginal area. People had to walk all those miles to Managua to find work. As time went on, the parish brought in water by pump so that people would have water. There was no running water in the homes. Before that, trucks had come into the area to sell the people water at inflated prices. Bus transportation came much later, too.

So these people, who were really quite poor to begin with, were really pioneers in the sense of going out there in such need that they simply had to set up house wherever they could. The barrio grew in the first years, but grew tremendously after the earthquake because so many people were then left with nothing. When I arrived in 1975 there was a well-established barrio that had actual streets, lots and houses. There was a parish house, public water faucets and six established zones, four of which had electricity. No one had running water and you still had to buy your water in barrels or stand in line at the public tap.

The people who lived there came from many different backgrounds, but many came from peasant backgrounds. The women worked in the market or as domestics in Managua. The men worked in factories or as artisans. There was a high level of child employment; children selling Chiclets, candy, newspapers or shining shoes. The kids couldn't go to school because the margin of survival for their families dictated that they work. The number of children who went to school was very low. Illiteracy was very high and health conditions were extremely limited. With no running water there was high water contamination and a very high rate of infant mortality in the barrio. We were constantly assisting people to go to the hospital or giving actual medical care to babies who would die in 24 hours. They would get diarrhea in the morning and be dead the next day because of malnutrition. People were not vaccinated. The health centers that Somoza had never reached out to the barrio.

In a place of 30,000 people, they had one clinic when I arrived there. There was no emergency care. For health workers to be out there was like being sent to Siberia. I can remember working there as a nurse in the beginning, trying to work with the women in preventive medicine for their children. I also worked in the parish with Christian base communities.

It's very different now, but I remember back then when measles broke out in the barrio—measles just wiped out kids who were malnourished. When you saw measles coming, it was just like the plague. When we saw that outbreak in 1976 I went everywhere, to every department of the Health Ministry to try to find vaccine. Finally I got 40 doses for a barrio of 30,000 people. Now to think that between 80 and 90% of the kids in that barrio are vaccinated is just a miracle for people who saw that history.

The Christian communities in Ciudad Sandino began as the basis of parish work in Santo Domingo. People there were already involved in the work of Christian communities before the earthquake. The idea was to read and to study the Word of God and bring the Word of God as a light to their lives, to use it as a way to better understand their own reality and to respond to it in a Christian way. When they came out to Ciudad Sandino, they continued this work. These communities grew in our parish until there were two or three in every sector of the barrio. The basic pattern of the Christian community was to come together twice a week. Every week a different group would come together and try to plan what the celebration of the Word would be around a certain theme. They would put out readings and songs that people could use for that. And whatever night of the week your Christian community came together as a whole, they would spend that time really very prayerfully looking at scripture and what it meant to them. The point of having a Christian community is so that the Word of God speaks to each one of us. It doesn't come in all of its truth out of anyone, but in fact together, when we really reflect on the Word of God and how it touches our heart, our life and our reality, then somehow we're enriched by that Spirit that allows us to come to some deeper knowledge of what this Word means in our life.

In the beginning, when I didn't understand Spanish, the meeting seemed very long to me, and I couldn't grasp it, but as time went on it was the one thing I never ever failed to go to in the barrio because for me it was so life-giving. In the people there you could see the tremendous strengthening role it had in their lives. It had a role in their looking at their reality and seeing what they had to do as Christians. And that referred to very simple things in the barrio, like service to those members of the larger community who were in particular need. It led them to try to form their own resources through fairs and bazaars, and that sort of thing, to try to build up their own Christian community or to try to build a place to meet in. When I first went out there they were still meeting in each other's houses. As time went on, they built a small, tiny house that was their church. Later, they looked at needs in the barrio and how the Christian community could respond to those needs as a group motivated by faith. Naturally, their action began to be more politically involved as the situation of repression grew worse and worse.

The situation was just cutting back on poor people. One example of that was the struggle the people had there for water in 1976. The water company had come in finally and put meters in front of every house and put in water tubing for everyone. Everyone was just thrilled; they thought, "Wow, we're finally going to have a spout in front of our house." But when the first bills came they were charging people about four times as much as they were charging rich people in Managua. And that just really touched people.

They had never organized before, they had never really come together over any issue. But water was so central to their lives that it really touched a depth in them. They just couldn't afford the bills. So the barrio, in June 1976, organized for the first time in a very incredible way . . . people really began to work together. They wouldn't pay their water bills. They had massive demonstrations which, given the repression of the government, were really amazing. But this was so unjust it mobilized them for the first time.

For three months they persevered in this struggle over the price of water. They got the price reduced. More important than that, people had learned to work together and that if they worked together they could do something together. So the barrio moved right on from there to get a cemetery for the barrio. There was not even a place for them to bury their children anymore because the only place they had was filling up over in the next barrio. They went and took over a piece of land which under Blandon's contract was supposed to be the cemetery and had never been used for that because he wanted to use it for housing to get more money. The people cleared the cemetery and began to bury their children there because it was theirs. The National Guard came in and unburied their children, which was to them the most horrendous thing that could have been done. And again, no matter how just their cause was or what they tried to do or what kind of peaceful means they tried to use, they just kept getting more and more repression.

Soon the barrio came to be known as a barrio that was subversive. In some ways that's correct, because Ciudad Sandino is not a barrio that was heavily politicized at all in terms of people being members of opposition political parties or people that were really involved in the Frente Sandinista. They were people who had their lives deeply touched by this regime and who were organizing out of that to get what they needed.

When they went on from the cemetery, which they finally won, they went on to the buses, because the buses were insufficient. There was only one bus route and it didn't go to the places they needed to go, so they started again on that.

By that time we were into 1978, and when Pedro Joaquín Chamorro was killed, almost all of the barrios began to get more involved in the national reality of the Insurrection rather than keeping with their own needs and demands.

The barrio worked hard together and suffered a great deal of repression, which was very hard for them. The National Guard often came in by force and took people out of their homes. People disappeared. People were shot on the street. Just a tremendous amount of repression. As the Insurrection came up, Ciudad Sandino was not central to the fighting because of its location. The barrio was bombed from the air and when the National Guard came in, the men would go to the hills behind the barrio and the women would go to the Red Cross Center to face whatever had to be faced. A number of young people went off to fight, including some members of the Christian community as well. So the Christian communities' involvement evolved through their own faith experience as the struggle deepened. They did these things as part of their faith commitment to their brothers and sisters.

These are small communities of 20 to 40 people and their main concern is to come together and share their faith and understand the Word of God in the light of their reality. But part of that light is to act on that history and to do something about it. So these people would tend to be leaders within the barrio and people who assumed leadership in these struggles. But there was also other leadership that emerged from the barrio outside of the Christian communities, from the youth organizations or the workers' organization. None of them was big. Nicaragua was not an organized country before the Insurrection. So you had members of other groups who were not from the Christian base communities and they came together and pulled together a directorate of the barrio that was really a mixture of people from the base communities and other different organizations. So the Christian communities certainly played a very important role.

For the Christian communities this participation also had to it a deep angle of conversion. In their own lives, coming together and meeting together, all of us still brought our own weaknesses of gossip and what have you. What was amazing about the Christian base communities is that you could still see all of our weaknesses and yet within the community people were energized to make sacrifices for others and that gave them the strength to be really heroic in their struggle and to really risk themselves for others. It was a tremendous source of strength for the people.

When these Christian communities were formed, we joined as members. We also had pastoral responsibilities within the parish; for example, preparation for the sacraments, parish council and all of the tasks that go on within a parish. So these Christian community members were the real core of the parish. They were usually on the council and prepared the sacrament. Our role was to enable them to be the people who were doing the basic work of the parish. It was their church and their reality. Our role as enablers involved our helping them with things like group dynamics. It also developed that the leadership was involved in theological and biblical preparation, and they needed all kinds of other input on a faith level. So we also took on a lot of that responsibility. When the time came for the struggles that took place in the barrio, the church building was the only place big enough for the people to meet and the church immediately became a center for that. So the parish team accompanied the people in this whole process. For many of us this was our first experience.

I'm not a community organizer. I wasn't out there showing people how to do it because I didn't know how to do it any better than they did. We were learning together—both how to confront this evil and to do it in a way which was consistent with people's faith. We learned, as time went on, how best we could be enablers to empower people to face these situations.

But it must also be said that we ourselves [nuns and priests] were deeply converted and deeply changed by these people in our own understanding of the Gospel and in our own understanding of what our mission was. We had to learn from them. It really affected my life more than any other experience I've had in Nicaragua, to understand from the poor what the Gospel means to them, which is very different from what my understanding of the Gospel means. It was a mutual process of evangelization that was going on at that time. It was a mutual process of learning from each other, of learning from these struggles, and what to do in them. None of us were experts. We mushed through it together.

It was a very exciting time in the barrio because, as I say, it was the first time people came together, and because you began to see the values of the Gospel and human values made real. When one person had their water cut off, another person gave them water; when one was put in jail, people really dug deep into their pockets to get them out; when there was a fast for the political prisoners, people came out of their houses and really risked being out there. You saw people come out of themselves, get to know each other, and to take risks for each other. That was hard in some ways because, of course, there were differences and difficulties and divisions. But, in fact, it was a remarkable period of time where people laid the base for all kinds of activities that are able to go on in the barrios today.

Since the Triumph of the Revolution you see that in Ciudad Sandino some of the things that began in those times have really taken root and the people are moving together. For example, last week a house on our block burned down. I guess one of the kids who was left alone knocked over a vigil candle and the whole house went down. Within two days the CDS, the block committee, collected 17,000 cordobas [$600] from the neighbors. That's an enormous amount of money from poor people. It indicates the level at which people are willing to dig into their own pockets. And it indicates the level of organization where people feel comfortable in giving to an organization that they know will help them too, if they have problems. It's a level of decisionmaking that has developed, which is not terribly advanced, but which, considering where the people started—not even being able to make an agenda—and where they're at now in being able to move ahead on many decisions about their lives, is an incredible movement.

All of Ciudad Sandino is not that tightly organized even after the Revolution. Not everyone in the barrio is a Sandinista. There are a lot of people in the barrios, like a lot of people in Nicaragua, who still spend their lives trying to make ends meet; life is still hard. It's very hard to break out of patterns of individual survival to communitarian projects, to working together for things.

The block committee usually handles things that are as concrete as how many pigs there are on the block and where they're leaving their waste and what kind of a health problem that is. And vaccinations and things like that.

Z: And do the Christian base communities continue to function?

HEALY: Yes. There are new ones, and the one I began with still meets. It was difficult during the war. The government was very suspicious of the base communities. People were watched, people were followed, people were arrested. There was that kind of repression. And then, at the end, when people were out in the streets doing anything they could to overthrow the Somoza dictatorship, it became harder and harder to meet. At the end, in July 1979, when it remained to reconstruct a whole country, people joined other organizations to do that kind of work. The first year the base communities were not an immediate priority.

But then, over these last years, people realized the importance of people continuing on in these Christian communities. And this has been a priority within the parishes. Now again, the Christian base communities in Nicaragua are not the majority of the church and they may never be. But the reality is that they feel very serious about following the church-inspired documents of Medellín and Puebla. That's central to their mission as they respond to divisions in the church. These people want very deeply to be a part of the church; they don't at all feel that they're apart from it, because they're moving in the directions the bishops of Latin America have given them. It's important to realize that these are not some heretic crazies out there, but people who are very much in line with what the bishops put forth at Medellín and Puebla and they feel a strong call of faith in their lives to follow that line.

Z: How has life changed in the barrio?

HEALY: I think in the barrio you can see the physical changes that have resulted. You see it when you drive into the barrio. The first thing you do is drive in on a paved road. We never had anything paved in the barrio at all, which was a real problem for bus transportation because it ruined the buses. There's a new bus route that's been added to the barrio where before there was only one. Now we have new buses. It's still not enough, because now people have new possibilities to go out to work. And you see the buses jammed here on Sundays because now people have the chance to go out with their families to a park, to celebrate and enjoy, and to be with family. So you almost always see the buses filled here because the level of consumption has gone up so enormously.

And that's true in every case. When you get to grains and cheese and basic foodstuffs, people's abilities to consume are much higher than before. That's why there are shortages, because the country can't keep up with that level of consumption.

In the barrio there's a brand-new market. For the first time people have a market quite close to them that they can go to, and which also provides employment in the barrio.

In the area of health, as I said, 80 to 90% of the kids are vaccinated—people vaccinating themselves, rather than professionals. People from your block trained to do this sort of thing. There's an emergency service now. There's a brand-new clinic that has laboratory services now. There's a daycare center and a day hospital for psychiatric patients. There are social services here that were never before offered. In terms of education, the schools are packed now. The evening sessions are filled with adults. The level of illiteracy has dropped enormously. Infant mortality is down tremendously. People generally eat better and look better. There's not the number of funerals for children that we had before. And, if they do get diarrhea, which is still a problem here, you don't see the kind of death and mortality that came out of that before.

People now have received title to their land in perpetuity—which means that it belongs to their family. They cannot sell the land to anyone else, and some people don't like that because they think it's limiting. But this was done because speculators were looking Ciudad Sandino over in the last year of the war because there was water and electricity there by then. Banks were being built all over the place. We were thinking, "What does this mean?" People were buying up the land out there and selling it at much higher prices. So what the government is trying to avoid is having poor people in need take their land and sell it to a speculator for no money at all, or for very little money, and then the speculators are able to take over this barrio again and people never get to keep their land. It's a real problem. But at least people know that when they say they have title to their land for their family in perpetuity, that's theirs. So that's a change in the barrio also. There are a number of things that still need to be accomplished. People's lives are still hard. And, of course, this war makes things difficult as well.

Z: When I was out in Ciudad Sandino I saw streets and buildings named for Maura Clarke and children named for her as well. What was her impact on the barrio? [Maryknoll sister Maura Clarke, who had worked in Nicaragua for many years, was killed along with two other nuns and a lay missioner in San Salvador in December 1980. Five National Guardsmen were convicted of the crime in 1984.]

HEALY: Maura came out to the barrio after the earthquake. Maura was in a Santo Domingo parish in Managua when the earthquake hit in 1972. Their house was affected and they had to lower themselves on sheets out a second-floor window to get out. They spent many months out in the streets helping people, and then in a tent city that they had set up for the victims of the earthquake.

Then she came out to live in Ciudad Sandino and became a part of the parish team out there. She was there until 1976, when she returned for service in the States. During her years in the barrio Maura became a deep sign of faith, hope and love for these people in her person, in her generosity and in her service. She became a real deep friend of many people in the barrio.

Sometimes we [Maryknoll sisters] were targeted by the National Guard because they saw us living there, because they saw us accompanying the people and so on. We were under great suspicion and pressure. We were watched and threatened. State Security would arrive at the house or stop our car on the street and try to take away our loudspeakers. People were very supportive of us, and deep friendships formed in the mutual support that was necessary in this struggle.

Maura is remembered for her participation in the struggle and for her willingness to be present to whatever needs there were, whether there were problems in the home life, or people being kicked off their land, or whatever. Many times she would go to a landlord to argue for a family, or make sure they had legal help. Whatever the needs were, she displayed a tremendous generosity and willingness to help.

Within the barrio there are several things named for her, not only a monument with her picture, but also there's a child-care center and a park and block committees that have all been named after her. But she really lives in people's hearts and minds. In some ways, it was very hard for her to offer to go to El Salvador and leave the people here. When she was killed, people felt she had become a part of them and their lives in this Nicaragua. And all of us feel the same way. I was supposed to be assigned to El Salvador and I was with them just two weeks before they were killed. When they were killed, I came back to Nicaragua.

Z: What's the future of barrios like Ciudad Sandino?

HEALY: What's important now is their reality, their vision of what's necessary. This government has taken active steps to try to solve some of the problems. But when there are problems or difficulties, it's important for us to be a force that continues through the Gospel—the basis of our faith—and through the perspective of these poor people to continue to be the people who accompany them. If one can then support the things of the kingdom of God, which is central to our mission, those things that really move toward the kingdom—like people helping when that house burned down or people being vaccinated—those are things that need to be supported and encouraged out of our faith. Woe to us if we don't.

On the other hand, when there are things that need to be criticized, that don't go directly to the needs of the poor, that are problems for them, then also we have the responsibility to be a critical force within this process. That's the role of the poor also in this Revolution: to be a critical force and at the same time a participant force because this is their Revolution.

In a way it's the same kind of thing we were doing before, but it's also a constant new process. Before, we talked about Exodus and how people had to get out from under the Pharaoh, and when they finally do that they've got 40 years of walking in the desert. And Nicaragua today is like that. There's stumbling. There's a revolution with clay feet in some ways, and with difficulties and pain. Those things have to be recognized and worked on with some kind of hope. The reality is that many of the steps that have been taken are deeply human and consistent with what we know from Jesus and are important elements of the kingdom that have to be promoted.

/972.85053Z98N>C1/